Dirk Buchta / Marcus Eul / Helmut Schulte-Croonenberg

Strategic IT Management

Dirk Buchta / Marcus Eul
Helmut Schulte-Croonenberg

Strategic IT Management

Increase value, control performance,
reduce costs

3rd edition

GABLER

Bibliographic information published by the Deutsche Nationalbibliothek
The Deutsche Nationalbibliothek lists this publication in the Deutsche Nationalbibliografie;
detailed bibliographic data are available in the Internet at http://dnb.d-nb.de.

3rd Edition 2010

Editorial Office: Stefanie A. Winter

Gabler is part of the specialist publishing group Springer Science+Business Media.
www.gabler.de

Cover design: KünkelLopka Medienentwicklung, Heidelberg

Printed on acid-free paper

ISBN 978-3-8349-1825-3

Preface third edition

Each company must create value, also and especially by means of IT - in this respect, since the first edition of this book has appeared, nothing has changed in recent years. New is that companies understand the relationships between IT-use and its effect on the actual business in a better way. An A.T. Kearney's study has brought up new findings from this time forward. Thereafter, the companies are indeed aware that their IT should also cover strategic aspects, but on the contrary they see themselves often more hampered than helped by IT when it comes to strategic planning. A topic, which has gained significance over the past years, is sustainability.

In the discussion about IT, the expression "Green IT" is often used. While the focus here is placed solely on hardware and equipment, this book follows a broader approach: it deals not just with the perspective of system providers, but in particular with the perspective of manufacturing companies. Thus, "Green IT" can even become "Green Business."

Düsseldorf, January 2009

Dirk Buchta, Marcus Eul, Helmut Schulte-Croonenberg

Preface:
What is Strategic IT Management?

This book is based on many years of experience at A.T. Kearney in the consulting sector for strategic information technology. We see 'strategic IT consulting' as strategy consulting geared towards the senior executives responsible for IT; generally, the CEO or a board member responsible for IT, possibly the CIO, and sometimes a head of unit or the director of a subsidiary. 'Strategic' as opposed to 'operative' means not implementing IT but focusing completely on the issue of how added value can be created for the company by using information technology.

Strategic IT management means stabilizing and increasing the sales of the company through new IT-assisted processes and IT systems. IT also means improving the margin protection of products and services, and enhancing customer attraction and bonding.

To achieve this aim, strategic IT management requires a combination of strategic know-how and a thorough knowledge of the company and relevant sector. From the cost angle for the company, key considerations are finding the right vertical scope and issues such as IT sourcing, IT outsourcing and IT insourcing. Companies giving appropriate consideration to both the sales and cost angles of IT are able to achieve significant added value.

This strategic IT guide incorporates the lessons learned from hundreds of strategic IT projects carried out over the past ten years: it covers virtually every field in which in-formation technology is currently employed from major international conglomerates to successful, sectoral SMEs, from the manufacturing industry (e.g. automobile, processsing, engineering, consumer goods, high tech, aerospace and the construction industry) through service providers (e.g. the power industry, logistics/transport, airlines/tourism, retail, telecoms) to the financial services sector, pharmaceuticals/healthcare and the public sector.

This strategic guide provides IT managers with tried and tested solutions for their specific questions and business situations combined with clear practical advice. We also hope that students of computer science, business administration or information management will find it a useful complement to the existing literature and of benefit when entering their chosen careers.

Düsseldorf, October 2003

Dirk Buchta, Marcus Eul, Helmut Schulte-Croonenberg

Table of Contents

Introduction

The Value of IT – New Perspectives for Utilizing IT

What value does IT provide for the company? This has been the key question for IT managers and decision-makers at board level since technologization began. From the introduction of the first automated data processing systems to integrating value chains across enterprises, the potential of IT to generate benefit and, in the final analysis, generate value for companies has grown in leaps and bounds.

In the 1970s, the value of an IT investment for automating individual operations consisted of faster and cheaper handling of paper-based activities, and therefore, for example, shorter time-to-invoice and collection cycles for faster inpayments. In the 1980s, the triumphal march of the PC and the first integrated applications not only reduced business process costs, but also accelerated and optimized entire business process chains. For example, in the mid-1980s, systems such as SAP R/2 were already offering integrated processes for everything from procurement, inventory management and distribution to accounting and controlling. Processes ran more smoothly, interfaces were optimized or eliminated, in short: huge potential for reducing business process spending was created. In the 1990s, Enterprise Resource Planning (ERP), Customer Relationship Management (CRM) and Supply Chain Management (SCM) then made it possible to integrate business processes across the value chain.

Since most enterprises began using the Internet at the end of the 1990s, there has been a shift in focus from simply utilizing IT to utilizing it to create and add value. The driving force behind investments has not only been the cost-cutting potential of IT, but also its potential for adding value: IT enables new markets to be discovered and allows companies to overcome the challenges of globalization. Through IT new products are created and IT becomes a sales-relevant part of existing products. Since IT has also started directly impacting operations, it has become a value driver for enterprises.

However, the paradox of IT remains: The real value of IT is not produced where the costs are incurred. The effects of cost cutting and improving the quality of internal processes is recorded by the controller, the increase in sales is registered by the head of marketing. It is the IT manager however who remains responsible for the costs. But what is the relationship between the cost and the benefit of IT?

Strategic IT management enables enterprises to generate value from the use of IT: i.e. measurable and controllable sales boosts and cost savings. Strategic IT management has three crucial imperatives that create new perspectives for using IT:

■ **Drive value!** IT justifies its existence through its support of corporate strategy. Deriving IT strategy from corporate strategy and/or shaping corporate strategy via IT strategy increases IT's potential to reduce business process costs and benefit operations, and ultimately enhance revenues, and create value. Case studies from a number of sectors show how IT can be used as an enabler for business. The more IT alters business operations, the more the company itself will be transformed. Carrying out this transformation in such a way that the user is able to reap the value of IT is the task of enterprise transformation. Successful external growth and streamed portfolios demand comprehensive adjustments to both IT and business processes as part of IT merger integration and IT carve out.

■ **Control output!** The value of IT can be measured and thus controlled, but only if the organizational framework of IT governance is a given. IT governance provides a blueprint for IT within the company – a kind of IT 'highway code'. IT planning that is an integral part of corporate planning identifies cost saving potentials and ensures that the IT budget no longer restricts value enhancement. IT performance management is a universal IT management and control instrument that quantifies and controls the value of IT in direct alignment with corporate strategy.

■ **Reduce costs!** Cutting costs in IT also means increased performance, yet not by making sweeping cuts across the board. IT optimization involves providing the best possible support for business processes at the lowest possible cost. Furthermore, setting up internal IT service providers and sourcing IT externally as part of IT out-sourcing and IT offshoring will also further enhance the cost-cutting potential of the IT.

Based on numerous international consulting projects and worldwide studies, we are convinced that IT generates more value through its benefits for operations than is generated by reducing spending in the IT department itself. In fact, far from spending too much on IT, most enterprises spend too little: In many enterprises less than five percent of the IT budget is allocated to strategic IT projects. In sectors with fierce competitive pressure and a high level of innovation, this is not enough to compete successfully in the long term. Certainly it is essential to reduce IT spending – not least in order to release some funds from the IT budget for strategic projects. However, in strategic terms, it is not reducing IT spending that is most crucial, but rather increasing the impact of IT on operations.

In order to develop IT value, many enterprises must first fundamentally alter their mind-set: IT should not only be employed to realize planned increases in company value. As a value driver, IT has the task of identifying and proactively fostering the value enhancement potential of the company. The IT department is more than a glorified technical maintenance team and troubleshooter, rather the CIO is one of the architects of the company along with senior management, and it is his job to contribute to increasing the value of the company – top and bottom line.

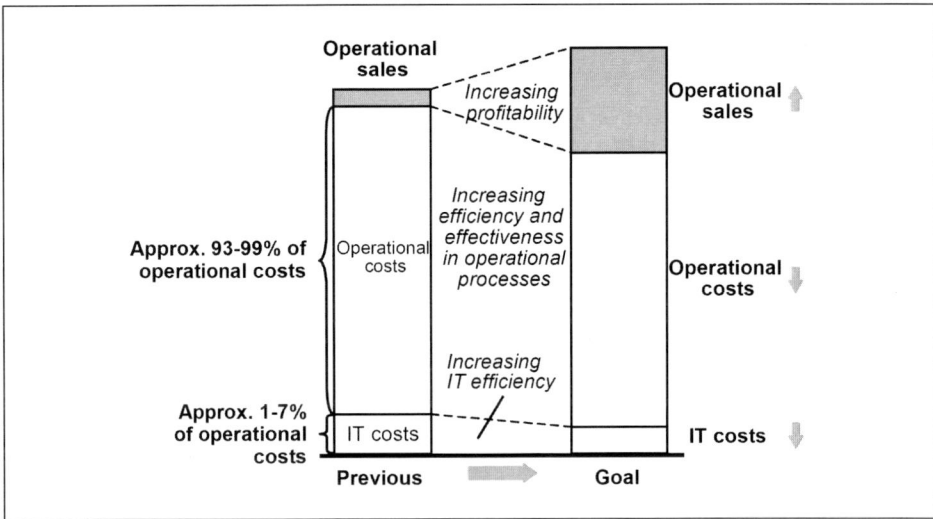

Figure 1:   *The value contribution of IT;*
              Source: A.T. Kearney

IT investments must be just as measurable as any other investment in terms of the impact on sales and costs (figure 1) – and also in terms of its contribution to increasing the value of the company. Compared with IT's potential to increase the profitability of business processes, assure revenues and increase sales, the cost savings achievable within IT have relatively little impact. Generally speaking, depending on the sector, enterprises reckon on IT costs of around 1 – 7% of sales (see figure 2). Saving 20 percent of these costs could mean reductions representing 0.2 to 1.4% of sales. If the IT budget is large enough, this could well mean considerable cost savings.

In contrast to this, again depending on the sector, total business costs amount to an average of around 90 percent of sales. Using IT to specifically increase value in the area can have a positive effect, for example through faster order-to-dispatch times, higher quality, stronger customer bonding and 'more intelligent' product design. Rather than focusing on lowering IT costs, enterprises should make efforts to implement their IT so effectively – and at the same time of course so efficiently – that they achieve the greatest possible effect on their operations – by reducing business process costs, assuring revenues and increasing sales.

Leading enterprises are already using IT with immense success to create value. And these are not only enterprises in IT-oriented sectors such as the automotive industry, telecommunications, power industry, banks and insurance or manufacturing companies that have traditionally based a high proportion of their business processes on value creation through IT. A number of leading enterprises from sectors that appear to be less IT-oriented, such as manufacturers of agricultural machinery or office furniture are also enjoying a competitive edge thanks to the sales-boosting use of IT. Furthermore, rapid technological progress and market developments will make it hard for the competitors of these companies to catch up.

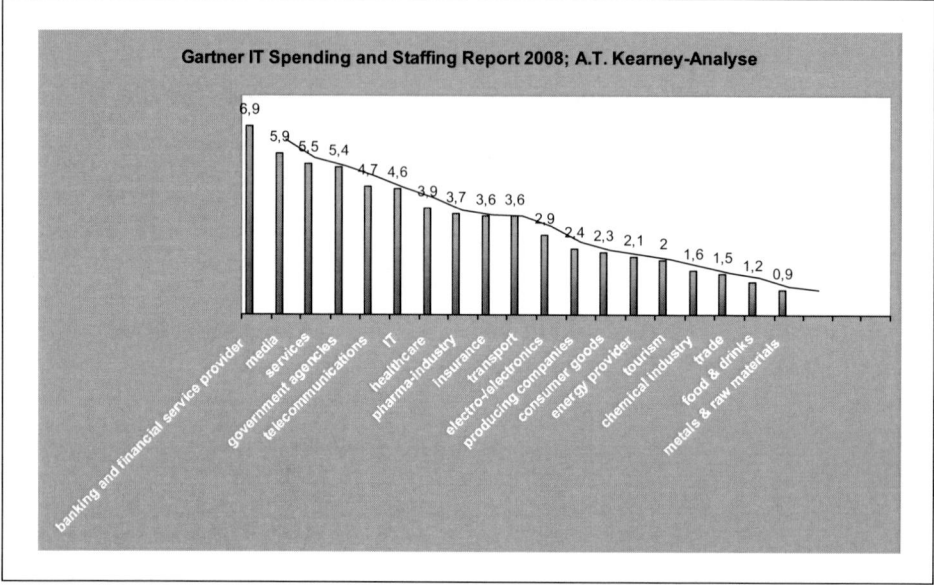

Figure 2:   *IT expenses/IT budget as a percentage of sales in 2002;*
                Source: Meta Group, 2002

This book presents strategies used by enterprises that efficiently utilize the value potential of IT for their organization. It offers IT executives – be it at group, unit or senior management level – concrete assistance with implementing strategic IT management in their respective organizations.

Part A: Enhancing Value – IT as a Value Driver for the Company

CRM, CAD, ERP[1] – the world of IT is teeming with acronyms that promise considerable benefits for business operations. Yet managers themselves are usually only sure of one thing: these terms all involve huge costs. How can they find out which IT investments are worth the expense? This is one of the most widely-debated issues at congresses and in the IT press and also between IT managers and senior executives. And the answer is seductively simple: those IT investments that make the greatest contribution towards implementing the goals of the company at the lowest possible cost are the ones that make most economic sense. But which investments are we talking about?

Future-oriented IT investments must be closely aligned to the goals of corporate strategy. Therefore the job of *IT strategy* is to identify innovative projects that will sustain the competitiveness of the company and increase its value down the line. Using IT in this sense as an *enabler for business* means:

- *Reducing costs for the company* (but not only IT costs) – e.g. by reducing inventories thanks to optimized production planning (for example in the automotive industry), greater transparency and better logistics planning –

- *Strengthening revenues* – e.g. by enhancing customer bonding through CRM thanks to more information about the customer and closer contact with them or through better supply chain management through marketplaces – or even

- *Increasing sales* – e.g. through new business fields such as information services or higher customer benefits through additional product features and supplementary services to the product and 'intelligent products', which bond the product user more closely and permanently to the company and reinforce the customer's inhibitions to switch to other suppliers.

Today most enterprises are well equipped to use IT as an enabler for their operations. Motivated by fears of all DOS-based computers and other systems threatening to crash if not properly prepared for the Y2K crisis at the turn of the millennium, enterprises made enormous investments in IT systems, which in many cases meant replacing legacy applications with ERP systems. The investments made to keep operations up and running were successful – either because the real danger was overestimated or because equipping oneself with new,

---

[1] IT terms are explained in the glossary.

higher capacity EDP systems (or modifying existing IT systems) prevented the 'year 2000' disaster from happening: no major shutdowns were reported in the new year (but indeed some smaller ones were). But what counts more is that most enterprises entered the new millennium with high-powered, future-oriented IT systems – perfect conditions for innovative projects. Even the collapse of the Internet hype did not quell the enthusiasm of most enterprises for considering future-compliant IT applications to support operations, including web-based services.

A worldwide study carried out by A.T. Kearney and Harris Interactive substantiates the growing significance that leading enterprises attach to IT for the success of their business. 144 senior executives from European and American enterprises with over 500 million US dollar revenues from the five key industries: automotive, telecommunications & high-tech, consumer goods & retail, finance & insurance, and the processing industries were interviewed about their IT priorities for the year 2003. More than 90 percent had invested in IT as an enabler for their business operations. 65 percent of the enterprises that had grown considerably faster than their competitors in the past five years had made investments in IT that are effective and in clear orientation to their corporate goals. These enterprises have consistently implemented IT not only to improve business processes, but also to specifically enhance the effectiveness and efficiency of their relations with both customers and suppliers. Even more astonishing: over 75 percent of these enterprises are striving to use IT to specifically ensure or increase revenues, for example, by implementing CRM tools to improve customer relationships.

Yet not all companies have the premises for utilizing the potential of IT, although most leading companies have created the right conditions over the past few years. In an annual study carried out in association with US magazine Line56, A.T. Kearney ascertained that the number of enterprises developing their IT strategy with a direct reference to corporate strategy rose from 55 percent to 62 percent between 2002 and 2003. These sector-best companies already introduced new technologies in the start-up phase (63 percent) or at an early stage of maturity (55 percent). But there are still a high percentage of enterprises not yet using IT to realize value for the company.

Between focusing on cutting IT costs and focusing on using IT as a value driver, a company can find itself in one of four stages:

■ *IT as a cost driver*: In the first stage, IT is regarded as an overhead factor and thus caught in the classical 'overhead trap': reducing costs is of prime importance. The only measures taken are those that can contribute to a reduction of IT spending. In order to lower IT operation and maintenance costs, for example, the applications are harmonized and the infrastructure is standardized and slimmed down (*cf.* Part C, Chapter 1, 'IT Optimization'). Although this kind of optimizing the existing IT system holds some potential benefit within the IT department, it does not support the long-term strategic goals of the company. IT is restricted to the basic minimum and projects for new or improved IT solutions are radically cut back. Sooner or later the IT budget is spent almost exclusively on operating and maintaining IT, which at some point will have to be reduced as well.

■ *Optimize business processes with IT:* Enterprises that use IT to improve their business processes, reduce business process costs and improve process quality are an essential step further. In this stage, IT indirectly supports corporate strategy, but the value enhancing potential of IT is not being used to full capacity. However, in order to exploit the potential of IT on business process level, the organizational structures and processes in the company are changed. Furthermore, IT can be used to realize rapid synergies in business processes during merger integration.

■ *Ensure and increase sales with IT:* Added value is captured by enterprises that weigh IT costs against the direct IT benefits that can be expected for business. In this stage, IT directly enhances customer orientation, the effectiveness of the revenue side and the integration of the company across the added value chain in direct alignment with corporate strategy. In merger integration, IT not only helps realize business process synergies, but also opens up market-side synergies.

■ *Develop new business fields with IT:* In the highest stage of development, IT itself becomes a business carrier, either through 'IT intelligence' in existing products, which creates new or improved product features (e.g. the self-diagnosis and remote-control maintenance of technically complex capital goods with rotating work locations), or as IT-driven services, which supplement the use of the existing product by the user (e.g. computing up-to-the-minute information about traffic jams in the navigation system of a car). This can lead to new business fields for existing products. Suitable innovative IT projects are identified in the scope of the systematic development of an IT strategy. The introduction of new IT systems is anchored in the company with innovative concepts such as BOT (see Part A, Chapter 3, 'Enterprise Transformation') to realize the greatest possible IT benefit. An IT integration platform enables new business fields from mergers and takeovers to be exploited.

These phases fit together like building blocks: The well-directed use of IT in line with corporate strategy delivers added value for the company through low-cost IT, optimized business processes and increased sales, by opening up new business fields, and creating value for the customer through improved services or innovative product features, as well as value for the shareholders and stakeholders through increased stock prices thanks to higher sales or better cost management.

However, realizing added value with IT will always be restricted to the extent to which users exploit IT functionalities, i.e. there is more to it than just integrating IT strategy into corporate strategy. Leading enterprises not only modify their IT, they also align the entire company structure (including all the interfaces) to their customers and suppliers as part of a comprehensive *enterprise transformation* process, so that IT can achieve its positive impact on the business processes.

A special role is also played by IT in supporting the external growth strategies of enterprises. When properly implemented, IT has a lot of influence on the short- and medium-term success of mergers in the form of well-directed *IT merger integration,* as well as on the success of disinvestments with *IT disintegration.*

1.   IT Strategy – Using IT for Value Creation

Today the business operations of enterprises in many sectors would be unthinkable without IT. Dynamic competition, increasing cost pressures and growing customer requirements force enterprises to make constant adjustments – to their IT as well. The technical possibilities here are infinite – however, which IT investments make sense when depends on the specific market and competitive environment and the strategic goals of the company.

The new perspectives offered by today's IT solutions make IT a propeller for change: In many sectors nowadays the question is no longer 'Which IT modifications are necessary to react to current external changes?' but rather 'Which IT prerequisites are necessary to support our corporate strategy long term?' Some examples:

- *External growth through mergers and takeovers* – Prerequisites of IT are, for example, multilingual systems and open architectures that enable fast connections to newly-acquired business units (see also Part A, Chapter 4, 'IT Merger Integration and IT Carve-Out').

- *Internal growth through 'virtual' customer bonding* – Prerequisites of IT are, for example, the support of integrated call centers and e-business as well as B2C applications.

- *Internal growth through innovation* – Prerequisites of IT are, for example, customer relationship management and flexible production and billing systems.

Thus, how a particular corporate strategy is formulated provides valuable information on how IT is organized. As part of a value-oriented IT strategy, the business units and the IT department systematically identify the future-oriented and competition-critical IT components that promise the greatest value enhancement for the enterprise. A company-wide IT roadmap points the way to implementation ('IT blueprint'). On the basis of this, depending on their specific situation, enterprises can use innovative IT applications for optimizing business processes, assuring revenues and increasing sales as well as for developing new business potential. At the same time they can learn from enterprises already experienced in the use of IT as an enabler for business.

Deriving IT strategy from corporate strategy

Just what specific value potential a company can achieve by using IT depends – like the corporate strategy itself – on many internal and external corporate factors. In practice, most enterprises have a tendency to derive IT modifications from the requirements of the business units. This type of procedure is an essential cause of the general dissatisfaction with IT that is prevalent in many enterprises – not only in senior management and the business units, but in the IT department as well. The business units regard their expectations of IT as being insufficiently fulfilled, while the IT department sees itself confronted with the challenge of meeting unrealistic demands, or is unable to fully exploit the actual potential benefit of IT. The senior executives see the IT investments, but are unsure about the (mostly also time-delayed) benefit.

The solution to this dilemma lies in a systematic strategy development process: In the first step, value enhancing IT projects are established under consideration of internal and external influential factors in close alignment with corporate strategy. In a second step, they are evaluated using a business case and in a third step they are integrated into a prioritized implementation plan (figure 3).

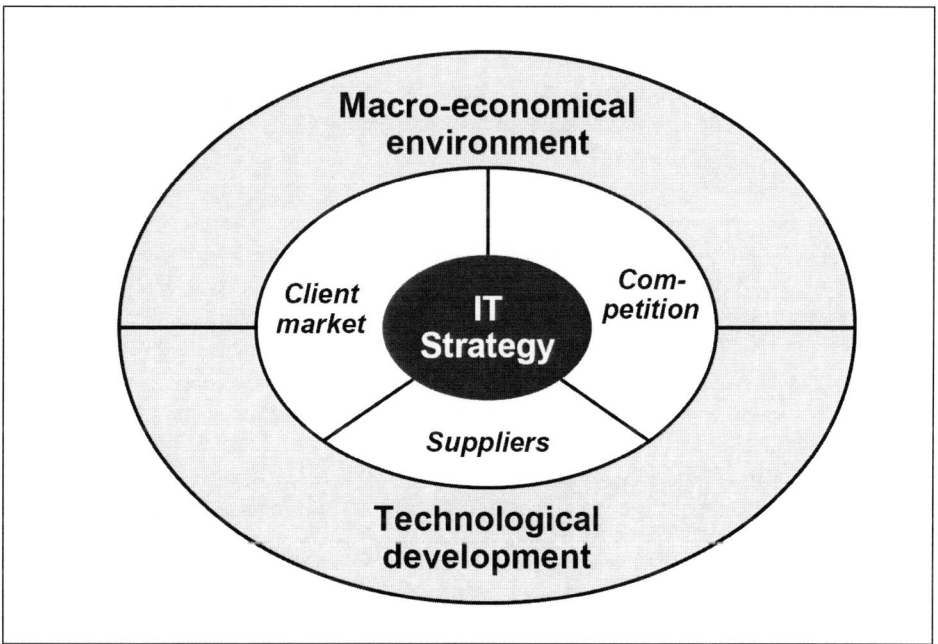

Figure 3:   Influence factors on IT strategy development

Once the corporate strategy has been developed, a value-oriented IT strategy with a broad perspective must be initiated, which takes not only company specific aspects with customers, suppliers and competitors into consideration but also macro-economic influences and innovative technological trends (figure 3). When developing a corporate strategy it is a matter of course to include macroeconomic trends such as changes in age structure, user behavior patterns, customer demands, and global developments, in order to analyze the future market and cost-cutting chances of the company. As a rule, these are diverted directly into the requirement of IT strategy, which puts the company in a position to make use of this value creation potential.

Tips for IT strategy development:

▪ Involve the business units in every phase of strategy development: At the beginning the users must be involved in order to develop the long-term strategic IT requirements together with the IT department. If the IT department then makes a proposal for implementation in IT strategy, the business units must again be involved in the financial evaluation with the business case.

▪ Be open to change: When the future IT system is being developed, company-specific solutions must be tried and tested. Applications that are no longer in line with company goals must be unconditionally eliminated and migration and replacement strategies must be developed.

When developing IT strategy it initially appears unusual to be dealing with the same questions that also arise in the development of corporate strategy, for example: 'How old are our customers today, how will this age structure develop over the next ten years?' or 'What needs do your customers have today, and how do these needs and the buying behavior grow in line with a changing age structure?' However, such questions are immediately plausible if we take a closer look at the effects of macroeconomic changes on target group marketing: Younger people have a wider range of needs, but less money and time than older people; older people like to be approached in a more specific way. These factors have consequences for Customer Relationship Management (CRM) in terms of customer segmentation as well as whether customer segments should be approached using anonymous mass marketing or cross-selling offers on the one hand, or with exclusive, individualized offers from a small but high-quality product range on the other. Thus, IT strategy does not simply estimate the results of corporate strategy, but rather evaluates for its part the influential factors that are already taken into account in the development of the corporate strategy, with regard to its implications for IT.

In addition to the IT requirements that result from the company-specific market and cost chances and macroeconomic trends, we also have the technological innovations of IT and sector-specific IT developments. Consumer goods manufacturers, for example, should include applications such as vendor managed inventory, universal Collaborative Planning and Forecasting Replenishment (CPFR), in collaboration with the retail trade or Radio Frequency Identification (RFID) in their IT and process portfolios. When developing general technological innovations like CRM or SCM, the best practices of other sectors should also be kept in mind.

In addition to these strategic IT requirements, which result from market developments and changes in the competitive environment as well as technological changes, it is important to take into consideration the in-house requirements of the various value creation phases of the enterprise – from the business units and affiliated companies – and the requirements of suppliers and customers.

Developing an IT strategy for a consumer goods manufacturer

A consumer goods manufacturer, when formulating its long-term corporate strategy for a period of ten years, devoted itself mainly to the topics of international expansion and the consequential restructuring of its logistics. When developing IT strategy, it became clear that it needed to include additional environmental factors. The company initiated a joint project involving the business units and the IT department to set down a long-term IT strategy. To this end, the company environment, i.e. the macroeconomic environment, which is particularly important for consumer goods manufacturers, and the long-term technological trends were first analyzed and their relevance evaluated.

Parallel to the macroeconomic environment, an analysis of the foreseeable long-term technological changes in the field of consumer goods was carried out. Changes in manufacturing technology, for example, will result in changes to the supply chain. One technological development that is especially important to the company is RFID (Radio Frequency Identification). RFID makes it possible to equip each individual piece of merchandise with a non-contact electronic transponder, which records information about the item from a distance of several meters and reports it to a receiving device. The widespread use of RFID will have an enormous impact on logistics and on inventory planning and control. Additionally, RFID makes it possible to electronically record which goods are bought by a certain customer. All of these consequences will greatly alter internal business processes and open up a high level of potential benefit for the companies that use it – and at the same time make considerable demands on IT.

Companies now know which IT components are strategically most important for the future orientation of the enterprise. However, purely qualitative utility estimates of abstract 'improvements in quality' are not sufficient reason for the innovation offensive that this would necessitate. Only a business case that compares the costs for the necessary investment with the results that can be expected, and which also evaluates the time scale for this investment (see figure 4), is able to quantify the impact of IT, illustrate its contribution as a value-enhancing enabler for business, and control its redemption in the organization.

The preparation of the business case necessitates close collaboration between the IT managers and the users in the business units. As a rule, it is possible to determine the cost side, i.e. one-off investments in IT (e.g. licensing costs) as well as the running costs (e.g. annual maintenance costs) quickly and clearly. The potential cost reductions resulting from the increased efficiency of operations (e.g. cost savings in logistics through lower inventories due to faster order-to-dispatch times) as well as the sales potential with marketing-oriented technologies (CRM and others) can only be determined in collaboration with the business units, as they are responsible either for the specific process costs in a certain area or for the marketing results.

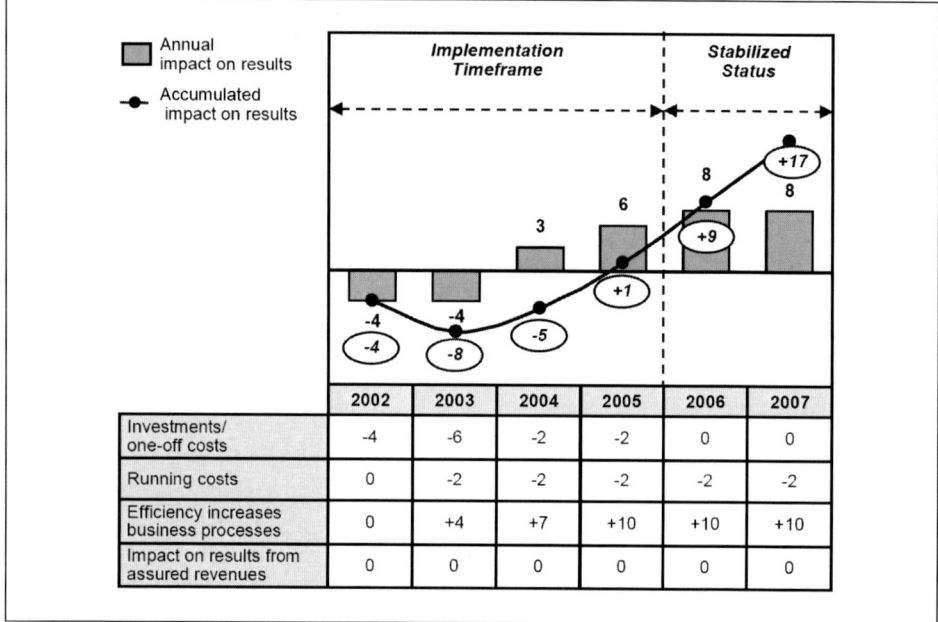

	2002	2003	2004	2005	2006	2007
Investments/ one-off costs	-4	-6	-2	-2	0	0
Running costs	0	-2	-2	-2	-2	-2
Efficiency increases business processes	0	+4	+7	+10	+10	+10
Impact on results from assured revenues	0	0	0	0	0	0

Figure 4:   Calculations of business cases

In a third step, the set strategic IT requirements must be evaluated consistently in terms of their contribution to revenues – optimizing the business process costs as well as revenue increase and assurance, from which the running IT costs for maintenance and customer care have been deducted. This systematic prioritization is portrayed in an IT innovation portfolio. For a manufacturing company the portfolio, which evaluates and prioritizes the established IT requirements consistently in terms of their contribution towards optimizing business process costs and revenue assurance, could look something like figure 5.

Most enterprises are in a position to considerably improve company revenues by using a strategically planned IT strategy. To achieve fast results, the most profitable investments should be implemented as pilot projects. While initial results are already made at this point, a binding and quantified implementation plan safeguards the realization of the overall productivity increases that are being targeted. An important factor in the implementation plan is to consider, in addition to strategy guidelines, the individual background situation of each area, as even the best IT will not have any impact if it is not accepted by its users (*cf.* Part A, Chapter 3, 'Enterprise Transformation').

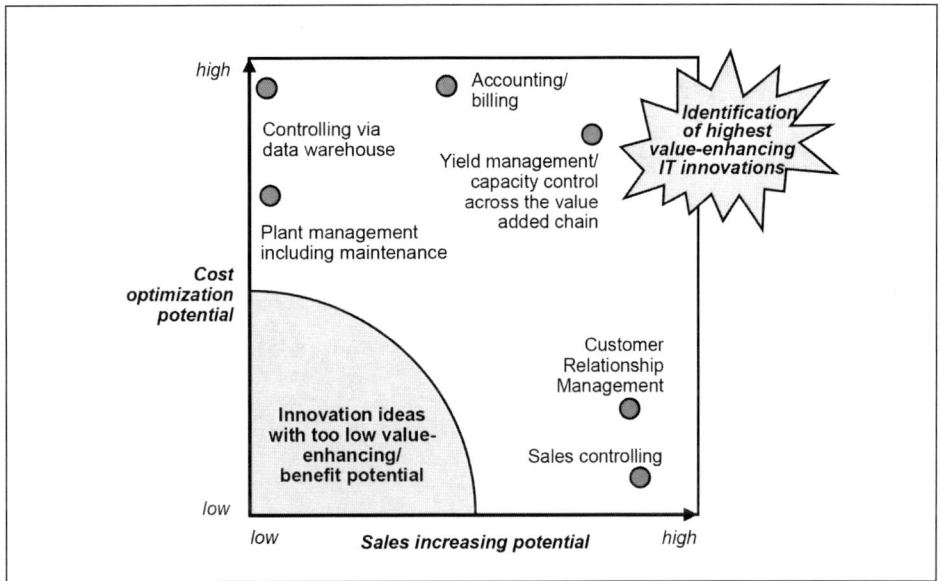

Figure 5:   *IT innovation portfolio of a manufacturing company*

2.   Using IT as an Enabler for Business

The value of IT is measured by the results that enterprises can achieve by using IT in primary business. Many enterprises have already had extensive experience with innovative technologies. It is remarkable that the pioneers in the use of new technologies include not only IT-oriented sectors, such as banks or the automotive industry, but also sectors in which the concept of value creation with IT is not evident at first glance, for example container logistics enterprises or manufacturers of agricultural machinery.

However, not every IT application has the same impact on every company. The possible effects of IT are influenced by a number of internal and external factors. The potential benefit of using data warehousing, for example, depends among others on the degree of standardization of IT in the company. In many cases, the customers and suppliers must also be persuaded to align their own interfaces to the new IT systems of the enterprise, for example when supply chain management systems are used.

When today's enterprises think about the value enhancing use of IT for their business operations, they are in no sense entering unknown territory. They can learn from enterprises in other sectors who have already successfully implemented IT to optimize their business processes, to directly assure or increase their sales or to use IT as an integral part of their end product to trigger new customer demand, thus directly developing new sales potential through the use of IT:

The following examples show one of the many possibilities for enhancing the value of IT.

▪ *Optimizing business processes by:*

- cutting costs in business processes by introducing and optimizing ERP
- boosting efficiency and improving customer service with IT solutions and mobile communication technologies
- reducing and improving supply chain output with integrated supply chain planning systems (SAP APO)
- reducing costs with IT-assisted maintenance in machinery-oriented business lines
- sinking procurement costs through comprehensive system support

▪ *Assuring and increasing sales by:*

- diversified potential benefit with data warehousing
- faster product development with Product Lifecycle Management (PLM) in engineering-oriented industries
- increased sales with CRM technologies
- faster turnover by shortening clinical phases until registration with IT-assisted document management in the pharmaceutical industry
- higher level of customer bonding through better information exchange in global container logistics

▪ *IT as a component of the end product through:*

- independent IT-assisted services
- intelligent products

In practice, the potential effects of IT function like building blocks. For instance, it is nearly impossible for a company to develop new, IT-assisted business fields if the company has not intensively studied the use of IT for increasing efficiency and assuring revenues, thus gaining an understanding of the IT learning curve.

2.1   Optimizing Business Processes

Through well-aimed IT investments in optimizing business processes, an enterprise can not only lower costs, but also as a rule increase benefits. For example, the order-to-dispatch time is shortened, flexibility is increased and transparency created, resulting in higher customer satisfaction. New working methods help reduce the error rate, thus cutting warranty costs as well.

Examples of cost and potential benefit by optimizing business processes with IT can be found in almost every sector. The following examples demonstrate how enterprises in all sectors are well advised to assess the potential as quickly as possible, as the results of their competitors are high and it will not be easy to catch up with the resulting competitive advantage.

2.1.1 Reduced costs in business processes through introduction and optimization of ERP

In many cases, the IT landscape of enterprises has grown over time, and includes numerous solutions of their own and isolated projects. With the introduction of an ERP system, for example SAP, between 20 and 40 percent of business process costs can be cut – provided that these structures and the processes of the company are changed, in addition to introducing the ERP system (*cf.* Part A, Chapter 3, 'Enterprise Transformation'). But even after extensive business process optimization through the introduction of an ERP system, more efficient use of the systems will generally achieve significantly better results (see figure 6).

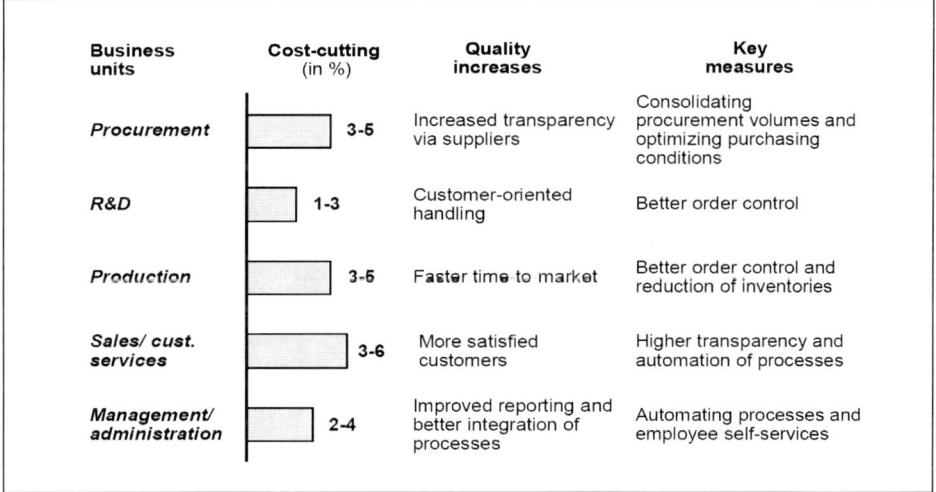

Figure 6:   *Optimization potential of installed ERP/SAP systems;*
                 Source: A.T. Kearney

A manufacturing company, for example, had already installed SAP R/3, but despite several improvements was still dissatisfied with the overall effect on operations, and was looking for further possibilities for optimization. In the final analysis, it became clear that when the SAP R/3 system was installed, a consistent alignment with the best practices of other enterprises had been neglected. Together with the business units, additional cost-cutting potential in the existing SAP R/3 landscape was identified in the essential operational process areas.

This situation is not untypical. Many enterprises have invested a lot of time, effort and money in the introduction of ERP systems, but without achieving the anticipated impact on operations. This will remain one of the most important projects in many major enterprises over the next few years. The problem can only be solved through close collaboration between the IT department and business units.

2.1.2   Increased efficiency and improved customer service with IT solutions and mobile communication technologies

Currently of special interest – particularly in enterprises with geographically farflung operations, for example construction companies, services/maintenance enterprises or organizations with widely-distributed capital goods – is the use of mobile communications technology for optimizing internal operations processes. Such 'mobility offensives' combine the IT support of vital business processes with data-oriented communication. Contrary to conventional business processes, the data communication is mobile, in other words 'wireless', and high-speed, for example via the GPRS and UMTS telecommunication services.

The use of such communication and IT solutions is especially interesting for controlling and billing maintenance work and for the service technicians or maintenance teams in charge of doing the work. For example, orders can be taken 'online' by the sales force and compared directly with current inventory stock. This has a positive impact on delivery reliability for the customer on the one hand, and accelerates processing on the other. Additionally, direct input of the order at the customer's company prevents errors that could lead to complaints, as well as extra data processing work, for example for data typists.

In the case of a manufacturing company under a very high level of competitive pressure, whose 400 service employees were responsible for 12,500 technical sales devices, the introduction of mobile handhelds in combination with a central service dispatching system reduced annual costs by 1 million euros net, while customer satisfaction was increased and the existing number of employees used to better capacity. These benefits resulted from a one-off investment of 1.1 million euros.

2.1.3   Cost reductions and improved supply chain performance through integrated supply chain management systems (SAP APO)

Supply chain management holds great significance for the value creation of enterprises in many sectors. In the chemical industry, for example, management of the entire supply chain from customer orders to the delivery of goods, through marketing, logistics and production represents a significant cost portion, amounting to up to 10 percent of revenues. This includes the costs of the physical stock flow in the warehouse, shipping and transport, and equally important are the costs of planning and handling, in particular inventory costs, equipment costs and handling costs.

However, the benefit of supply chain management is not limited to cost management, but rather lies primarily in the impact on operations. For example, in the chemical industry, particularly in the purely price-controlled commodities sector, the logistics service performance of a company is of great importance for competition. A high level of delivery reliability, short delivery times and immediate delivery options are important selection criteria for suppliers. A company must be in a position to give exact and immediate information about dates and availability, react flexibly to changes of orders, and offer innovative logistics service concepts with e-commerce or Vendor Managed Inventory (VMI) systems.

Supply chain management systems, such as Advanced Planning and Optimizing (APO) from SAP or supply chain management solutions from i2, JDEdwards or Manugistics, can considerably improve supply chain performance. Many enterprises in the chemical industry, especially in European countries, use SAP APO to improve competitiveness and lower costs:

- Delivery reliability is systematically stabilized through the planning feature anchored in the system.

- Thanks to better system-aided optimization of delivery services, equipment costs and inventory costs, the delivery time can be drastically shortened and delivery performance significantly improved.

- The ability of customer service staff to provide information as well as the response time – the time period up to order and delivery date confirmation – are considerably improved through system-aided availability checks.

- Inventory and equipment costs are considerably improved through the integrated, company-wide availability of key data, order data as well as mathematical optimization parameters.

However, supply chain management solutions are often introduced on a purely system-oriented basis, which then causes an even higher level of complexity. Only with a supply chain concept that aims at simple structures and which focuses on the essential features of the supply chain management system will a company be in a position to realize the entire benefit of IT.

2.1.4   Reducing costs with IT-based maintenance in machinery-intensive businesses

In enterprises with large, high-maintenance and perhaps also geographically widespread inventories, maintenance of the equipment is a high cost factor and, at the same time, key to competitiveness. Ideal for such enterprises are IT-driven production methods for planning, monitoring, managing and controlling maintenance jobs – with clear cost optimization potential.

A good example is power management network operators on all voltage levels. At present, network operators are feeling enormous cost pressures, particularly due to the political environment, and also pressure to yield good profits for their shareholders, which they can only achieve by substantial optimization. The strategic challenge now lies in realizing cost improvements, whilst maintaining the availability and quality of the energy supply and the necessary power transmission equipment, including electricity networks and transformer stations, at an availability level that is satisfactory for the customer, thus ensuring that such widespread blackouts as have occurred in the USA or the UK are not repeated in Germany.

An effective IT-assisted maintenance strategy begins with the maintenance systems, the network and all that is necessary for operations, as well as geographical information systems. Intelligent maintenance systems for process cost optimization consist of three simple components (figure 7):

- a back-end system in the central office, for example SAP PM

- local, easy-to-handle devices, for example palms, which can be used anywhere by the service technicians, and whose software is linked to the backend system via an interface and which have two essential features: receiving controlling and organization data for the service technician ('What needs to be done today and where?') and sending back status updates to the backend system ('What maintenance work was done on which components?')

- a high-performance, flexible communications technology

The implementation of such an IT-assisted maintenance strategy necessitates an IT structure that is streamlined to the maintenance systems. Besides workflow support, for example in recording and carrying out maintenance activities or their documentation, efficient coordination between the field office and the field staff via a suitable communications technology plays a key role. It supports planning and executing work schedules, and the execution of analyses and evaluations using a consistent and integrated database. This makes new, more efficient types of work, like for example 'starting on the spot', possible for the first time: service technicians no longer have to go to a central control depot where jobs are distributed and prepared, but rather can call up the information right at the location and start working right away. Our experience with network operating utility companies has shown that the productive work portion of service technicians – i.e. the portion of the time in which actual maintenance work is done, can be increased by up to 35 percent.

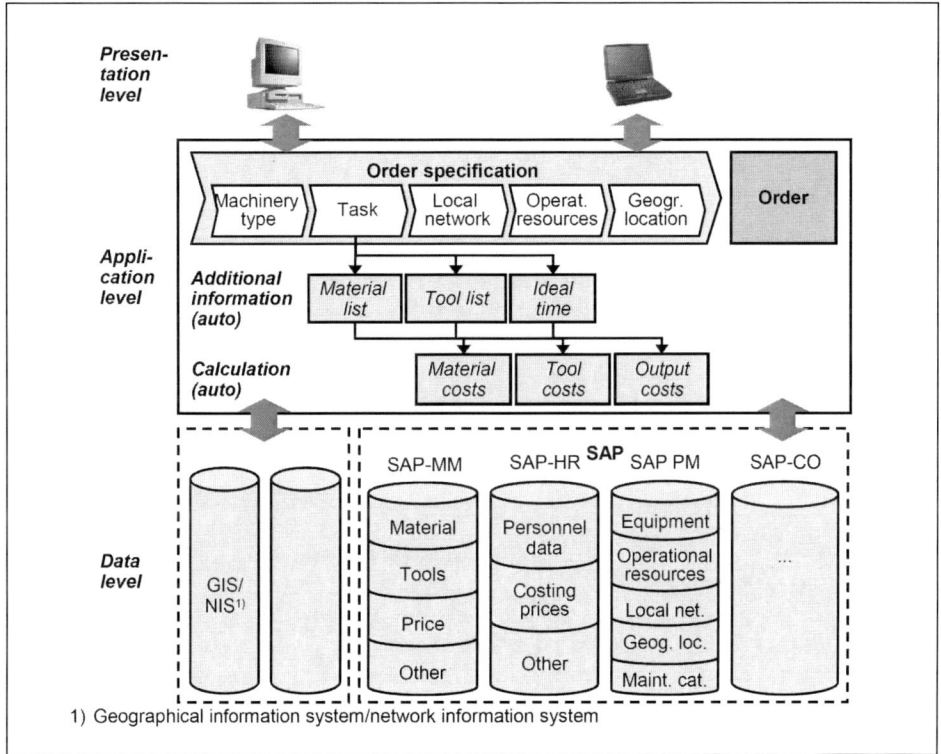

Figure 7:   *IT architecture for maintenance systems; Source: A.T. Kearney*

2.1.5 Reducing procurement costs through comprehensive system support (data warehouse)

The necessity for cost optimization is currently causing companies across all sectors to search for cost reducing potential in procurement. However, a lack of data transparency often prevents the benefit of procurement optimization from being fully realized. Particularly in heterogeneous and international corporations, the fundamental question of which business unit should provide which products and services in what quantity from what supplier represents an unsolvable problem. But if they do succeed in consolidating the group-wide demand in framework agreements with selected suppliers, the hoped – for optimization potential still has no impact on revenues. In order to realize the savings, the actual procurement must be carried out by the user in accordance with the negotiated framework agreement. And documenting the use of framework agreements and determining and preventing purchasing being done outside of existing contracts will also require transparent group-wide purchasing data.

The group-wide procurement volume of an internationally operating conglomerate with over 120 operative companies was not transparent enough. The system landscape in operative purchasing, with 15 SAP systems and more than 75 companies with legacy applications, was greatly differentiated and the relevant purchasing data were very heterogeneous:

■ The purchasing systems were individually configured and had varying data formats

■ There were over 300,000 supplier files, most of which were redundant

■ There were more than 12 different systems for the classification of materials

For various reasons, the purchasing system was difficult to harmonize, both in terms of the technology and also policy. For this reason an IT-assisted solution was chosen, which was able to function without such harmonization. Based on the data warehouse technology from SAP a new infrastructure was implemented, which enabled a direct link to the relevant systems for deducting purchasing data. The required data harmonization was achieved with the help of a mechanism that automatically allocated deducted purchase documentation, for example invoices and orders, to different merchandise categories in a uniform classification system. This automated processing is done on the basis of rules and heuristics, which, with the help of all available information e.g. supplier, material classification or order text, carry out the probability-based allocation of the individual purchasing documents.

The harmonized database that has now been created enables the evaluations necessary for successful purchasing to be done. In addition to transparent purchasing volumes across the conglomerate, the use of framework agreements can be consistently documented and the payment behavior of individual business units can be analyzed (see figure 8).

To improve the quality of the purchasing data for the medium term, parallel to the implementation of the system, various initiatives were introduced that aimed at optimizing the operative purchasing processes and systems. This way, for example, category-specific, web-based processes were implemented for purchasing services and a group-wide uniform classification system was further implemented. With the improvement of the data quality on the level of operative purchasing, which then offers an improved basis for achieving the necessary data transparency, the cycle is complete. A further advantage for the company: the necessary investments could be directly amortized due to the potential benefit. Altogether, the system support leads to savings in the procurement processes amounting to 11 percent of a procurement volume in the order of a single-digit billion figure.

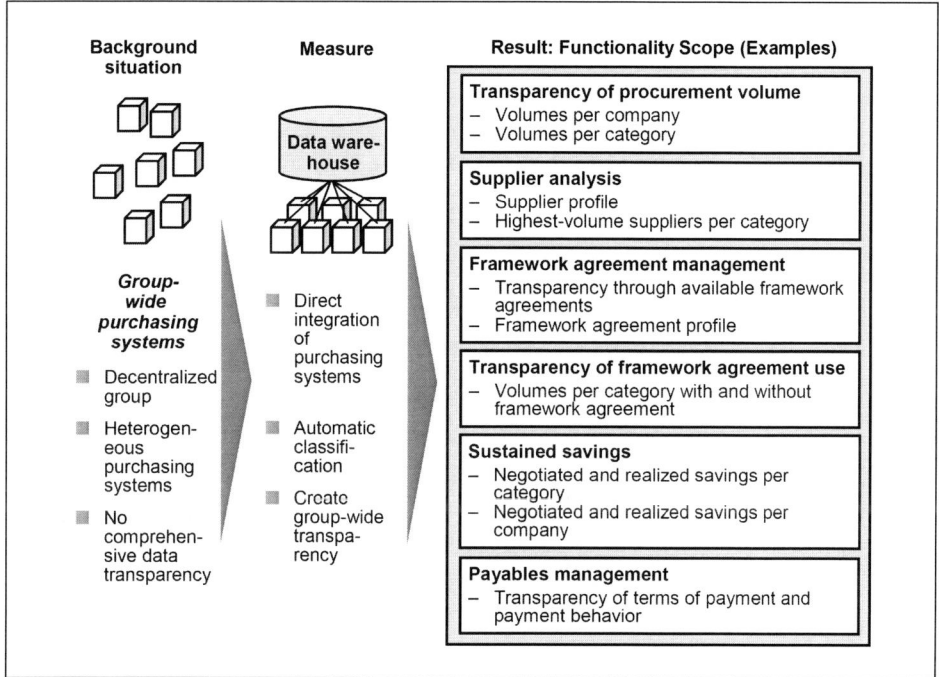

Figure 8:   *IT structure for procurement optimization in decentralized corporation;*
              Source: A.T. Kearney

2.2   Assuring Revenues and Increasing Sales with IT

Leading enterprises use IT specifically for assuring revenues and increasing sales. To this end, IT investments in distribution-related applications, for example order processing and customer management, are particularly relevant. An effective CRM concept with the appropriate CRM IT application helps the company, among others, to achieve additional sales, for example through cross-selling or by building up specific customer bonding and reclamation programs.

On average, five percent of additional growth in sales can be realised in German and Austrian companies (following an A.T. Kearney from 2007), if IT would be used appropriately. The interviewed top managers complained about lacking assistance of IT considering growth-relevant corporate functions such as Business Intelligence and Customer Relationship Management (CRM). Consistent data, short response time of IT in terms of responding to requests as well as transparency considering the concrete use of IT, is what the interviewees described as important for a company's success in the first place. The interviewees indicated that lacking IT support put back growth initiatives mainly in the sector of Business Intelligence, followed by initiatives in CRM, Pricing and Sales, and Product Lifecycle Management.

The reasons for that are not only rooted in the IT sections alone. In most cases the demands from IT in terms of strategic business objectives are not sufficiently formulated. Every fourth company evaluates the actual corporate value added of its IT projects only, and more than one third of the top managers indicated that the lacking transparency considering the surplus of an IT project constitutes a growth barrier. In doing so benefits can hardly be retraced, because the parameters of project success are mostly geared to cost reduction and not to growth. In this process, sales growth of three to eight percent in companies of all industries – from Financial Services, across Automotive to Pharmaceutical industries – can be achieved by applying the right IT strategy. For example lead times can be reduced and critical business processes can be automatized and therefore accelerated significantly.

One of the most important reasons for the lacking benefits from IT is still founded in the "classical" perception of IT as being a pure cost factor. In many cases companies do not understand IT as a growth lever. Only 19 percent of the interviewed companies involve IT in the strategy phase of growth projects. In general, ITpersons are nit asked before strategic planning is completed (33 percent) or not even before it gets implemented (19 percent).

There are evident shortfalls in determining the responsibility for the design of business processes. Basically, the business side is defining its processes but withdraws in the course of specification and leaves the detailed planning to the IT. For analysing the benefit contribution, the necessary specifications for a common business case of business and IT are often missing.

Considering future IT investments in terms of growth capability of a company the interviewed top managers assume, that the relevance of data warehouses and ERP systems is about to decline in the future. Gains are expected mainly in new distribution channels and in IT as a part of a product and service offers.

To realize the highlighted growth potential, four main levers have been identified: IT has to make its benefit contribution transparent to the company. Based on this, a common vision should be developed, how IT can assist in achieving the company's goals in an optimal way. A goal oriented IT business model should constitute the basis for that. Therefore IT-Infrastructure, IT-Governance and IT-Sourcing must be realigned or rather altered. In some industry sectors the use of IT for revenue assurance and sales growth has already become a must for companies not willing to accept a competitive disadvantage. Customer demands increase with more customer oriented offers, for example in the after sales service with regard to faster new product introduction or more suitable logistics services.

2.2.1   Diversified potential benefit through data warehouse technology

The use of data warehouse technology is suitable not only for optimizing procurement, but also for improving company-wide controlling, not only from the financial point of view but also in terms of logistics. The cause of the increasingly widespread use of data warehouse technology lies in the historically growing complexity, diversity and incompatibility of many existing IT landscapes in enterprises of every sector. In such a situation, a data warehouse is often introduced as a 'super' system or a 'super' data pool. Like a vacuum cleaner, the data warehouse 'sucks up' all relevant financial and logistics data from the various previous systems, harmonizes them during this 'sucking' process through entry filters, which create comparability, and stores the data. On the output side, through a more-or-less flexible evaluation logic ('data mining/data marts'), the desired reports are made, usually linked to Key Performance Indicators (KPI) (see figure 9). This gives senior management and board members – often for the first time – a comprehensive and complete picture of the processes in their organization and with it the basis for improved decision-making and control.

The benefit for the enterprise arises from the well-aimed application of this information in the day-to-day work of the organization. In addition to the already-mentioned example of procurement optimization, this includes a wide variety of practice-oriented types of applications and potential benefits:

- A mobile communications company with around 5,000 employees implemented a data warehouse for financial Key Performance Indicators to be able to optimally control performance and costs in a stagnating market and better align investments in the further expansion of the telecommunication networks to actual demand.

- A consumer goods manufacturer with turnover of over 30 billion Euros introduced a data warehouse to better align product development and marketing processes to the individual life cycle phase of the products in its comprehensive product portfolio and to react to declining sales through product diversification, product innovation or product marketing. The effective product development time from the identification of a 'dying' product to the introduction of the replacement product could thus be cut in half, while sales in individual regions increased by up to 30 percent. Additionally, the marketing budget could be cut by more than 500 million euros   and all that with a higher level of marketing effectiveness.

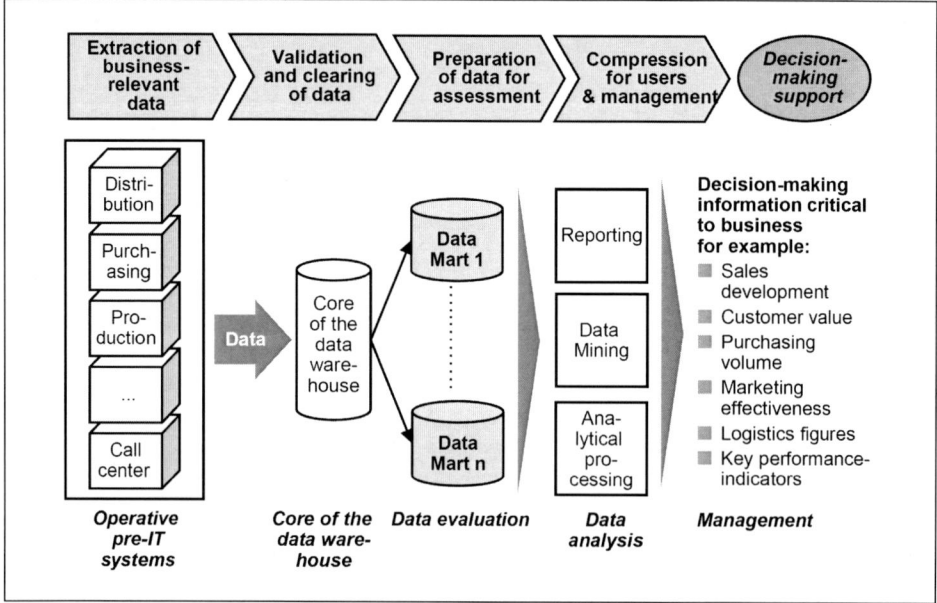

Figure 9:   *Typical architecture of a data warehouse; Source: A.T. Kearney*

■ A major media company introduced a data warehouse to better coordinate developing the market with the product catalog and for a more direct customer approach. In this way, many internal processes were clearly slimmed down. Thanks to the improved fine-tuning between production and demand in the individual market regions, the returns rate was lowered by almost ten percent. Also, the system was attributed with having delivered the essential know-how for turning a regional music hit into a gold LP/CD.

■ A major bank and a major mobile communications company both used a data warehouse for better control of their marketing campaigns. The goal was to optimize customer value under consideration of demand in the individual life cycle phases of their customers (for example business/private use; single/young family/established family/ 'empty nest' etc.). The bank was able to reduce its process costs by more than 20 percent and achieved significant sales growth through a cross-selling method streamlined to the individual life cycle of its customers. For the first time, the mobile communications company was able to recognize migration-prone customers (churners) very early on and convince a high percentage of them to stay through individual approaches, while at the same time getting rid of less attractive customers.

Thus, we see that the use of data warehouse technology can obviously lead to rapid, positive results for a company. But the enterprise should make sure, if possible, that the introduction of a data warehouse does not further increase the complexity of the IT landscape of the old system (i.e. existing financial, logistics, CRM and other systems, from which the data warehouse obtains its data). Rather, it is advisable to take measures to simplify the IT landscape of the old system, eliminate all redundant systems and harmonize the key data in the data structures and clean up the data files. Such a consistent concept improves the capabilities of IT, reduces IT spending and prevents unnecessary complexity. At the end of the day, every data warehouse is based on the sum total of its previous system, and if its data structures and data files are not harmonious and 'clean', such data problems will penetrate the data warehouse and diminish the significance of the benefit realized by the data warehouse – and with it the potential sales for the company as well as cost potential.

2.2.2   Faster product development with Product Lifecycle Management (PLM) in engineering-oriented industries

Speed and target-reaching in product development are a vital core competency for survival particularly for engineering-oriented industries. One engineering sector with particularly complex products, which is at the same time highly international, is the aero-space industry, in which IT plays a key role in the engineering and manufacture of the products. In this case, the entire product life cycle, right from the planning phase using CAD systems, through production and on to maintenance, is IT-assisted (figure 10).

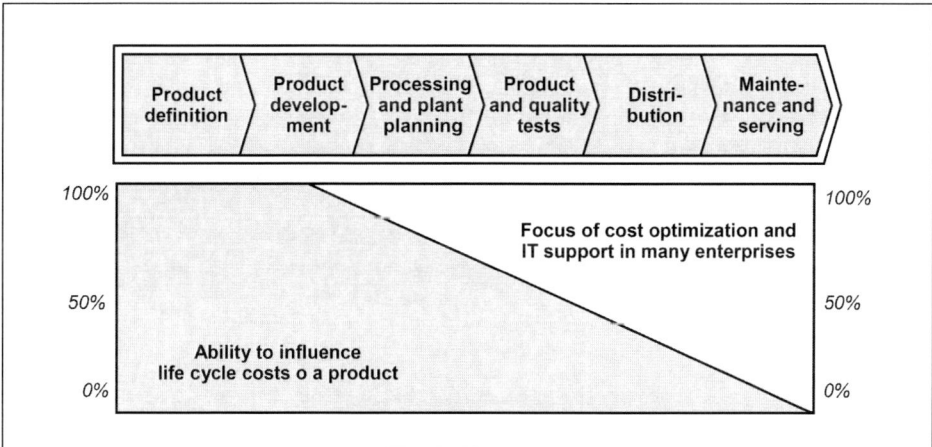

Figure 10:   *Support of the product life cycle across all phases of the value added chain; Source: A.T. Kearney*

The current trend in the aerospace industry towards shortened time-to-market for product development and production, towards an increasing rate of customer-specific solutions, for example individualized cabin designs, and towards continually growing product complexity has lead to all-new requirements being made on the engineering processes and the IT systems that support them, when a new aircraft is being developed. Even just the simultaneous working of over 20,000 employees networked in one database is no longer thinkable without modern IT solutions.

The answer to these challenges is modern Product Lifecycle Management (PLM) systems with their core building blocks 3D CAD concurrent engineering and product data management systems. In addition to the technical platform, these solutions offer concrete economical advantages, as the following examples illustrate (figure 11):

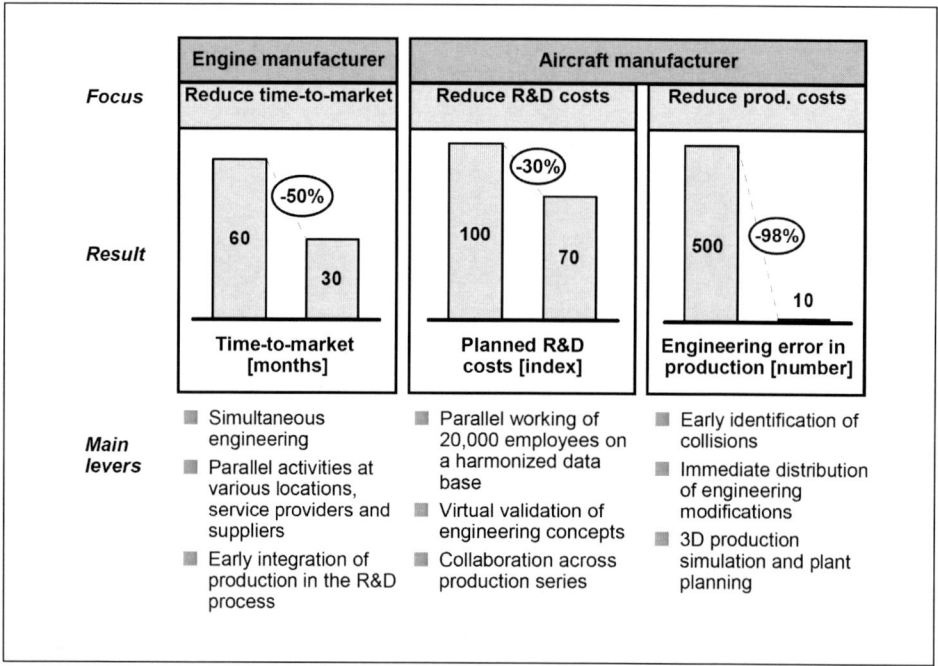

Figure 11:   *Benefit potential through systematic Product Lifecycle Management;*
                 Source: A.T. Kearney

■ When a new airplane wing is being developed using digital mock-ups – i.e. assembly simulated in 3D – the number of production defects in the wing rib assembly was reduced from 500 to less than 10.

■ Due to the simultaneous development with a common database being used by the various development locations and different suppliers, the time-to-market could be drastically reduced. For example, in an engine manufacturing company the time-to-market could be reduced from five to two-and-a-half years. In a second case, another engine manufacturer was able to shorten development time from 42 to 24 months.

■ Customer-specific aircraft design has been considerably simplified and accelerated by using modern 3D-assisted design tools. As a result, the serial production of passenger aircraft – together with other supply chain measures etc. – was accelerated by up to 20 percent faster than a comparable model.

■ The 3D simulation of the aircraft enables an efficient and early integration of production and the assembly of components in the development process. This way, in the development phase the design can already be adjusted and optimized to the requirements of the industrial process. This way, the source of errors and their consequences (defective parts, additional work etc.) can be recognized early and be prevented. On the introduction of a new airplane model, a reduction of such errors by 20 percent (a conservative estimate) can amount to savings of up to four million euros in the work costs of tail section assembly in the first production year.

■ For the development of a new airplane, one assumes that more than 30 percent of the R&D costs can be eliminated by using a holistic PLM platform:

– development time can be shortened by 50 percent
– production time for assembly can be shortened by 60 percent
– the costs for holding spare parts can be reduced by 50 percent
– maintenance costs can be reduced by 50 percent

The experiences and successes of the aerospace industry can also be put to use in other industries, for example in the automotive industry, for high-tech manufacturers, in machine/plant construction and even in the consumer goods industry.

2.2.3   Increasing sales with CRM technologies

Customer Relationship Management (CRM) is the type of IT support most often named when the goal is to increase sales and/or assure revenues, not only in the anonymous mass market but also in the B2B sector.

Of course, here too IT only supplies the basic foundation; CRM can only have an impact on the basis of systematically planned and consistently operations-oriented processes and distribution structures.

CRM is therefore a holistic concept that leads from the specified target groups and products and encompasses all interactivities of the organization and its customers – beginning with demand creation on the customer side through the marketing contact to customer service, including complaint management – and finally triggering demand for follow-up purchases of new models or additional products or services (figure 12).

CRM includes all contact points between the company and the customer and also includes approximately one marketing activity without direct customer contact. In order to efficiently record, evaluate and control these customer contacts, a uniform company-wide data model of the customer, but also of the products and all 'information objects' in connection with customer interactivities is needed – including, for example, the billing and collection data that is often forgotten in this context.

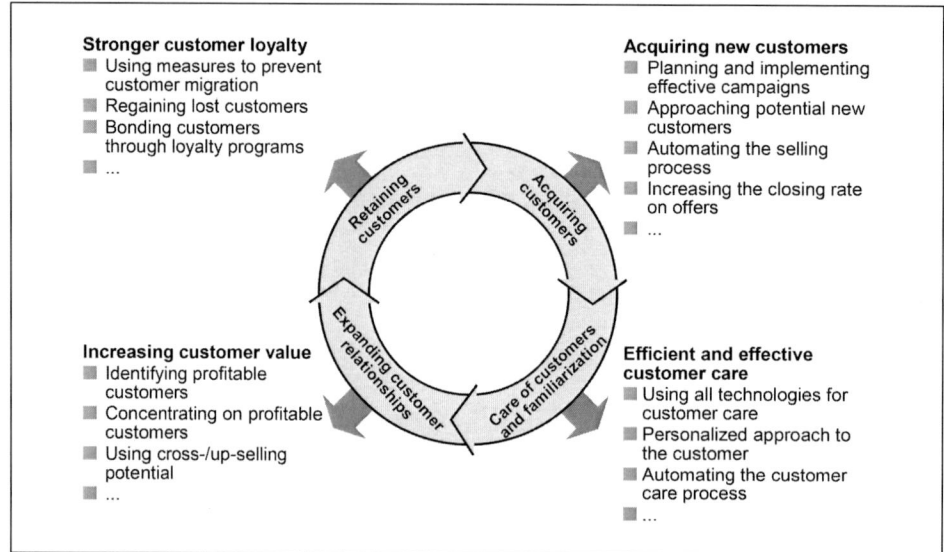

Stronger customer loyalty
- Using measures to prevent customer migration
- Regaining lost customers
- Bonding customers through loyalty programs
- ...

Acquiring new customers
- Planning and implementing effective campaigns
- Approaching potential new customers
- Automating the selling process
- Increasing the closing rate on offers
- ...

Increasing customer value
- Identifying profitable customers
- Concentrating on profitable customers
- Using cross-/up-selling potential
- ...

Efficient and effective customer care
- Using all technologies for customer care
- Personalized approach to the customer
- Automating the customer care process
- ...

Figure 12:   *Increasing and protection sales with CRM technology;*
                Source: A.T. Kearney

Customer data comprises statistical information about the customer (in keeping with data protection regulations, preferably with the consent of the customer) as well as data that is related to the products and services of the company (for example information about family status for banks or information about outings or special diet-related requirements of customers in the hotel and tourism sectors).

On the basis of this customer information, individualized or anonymous marketing activities are then carried out. If, for example, the evaluation of the sales made to a customer of a mobile communications company should show an abruptly declining tendency, this would suggest that the customer is in the process of switching to another network. In this case, the company can make inquiries about the reasons for the customer's dissatisfaction with the mobile communications company, and how these reasons can be remedied – and the mobile communications company retains the customer.

In the meantime, convincing results on the use of CRM are in evidence in numerous sectors, for example banks, mobile communications providers and financial service providers (figure 13). CRM is, however, being used equally successfully in tourism, by car makers, consumer goods manufacturers, in retail and other sectors.

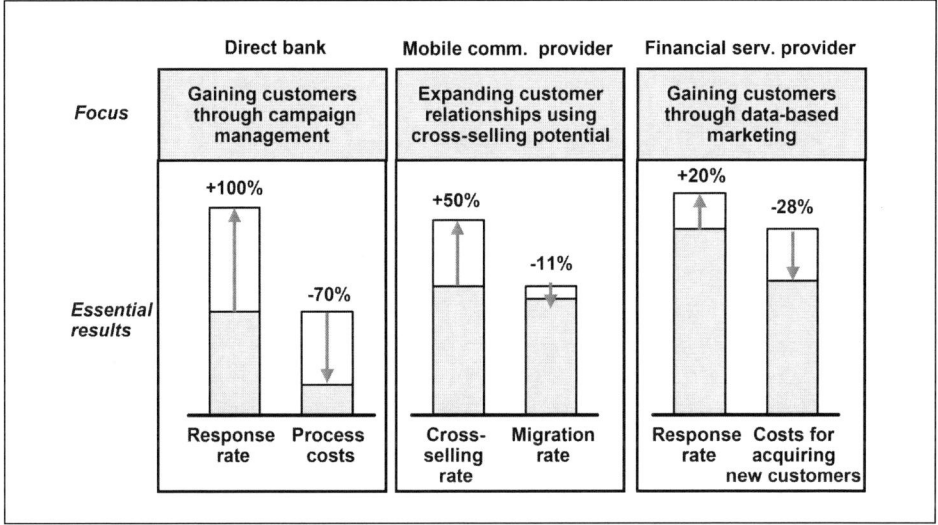

Figure 13:   *Sales potential with CRM; Source: A.T. Kearney*

2.2.4   Faster sales by shortening clinical phases until registration using IT-assisted document management in the pharmaceutical industry

It is well known that research in the pharmaceutical industry is extremely time-consuming and expensive – R&D projects usually run for more than five years. And even during the course of a research project there is a high risk of failure. Therefore, pharmaceutical conglomerations have a vested interest in shortening the research process until registration for new medications and in recognizing less promising projects early on and stopping them.

This goal is pursued by document management systems. Besides the employees of the company, others involved in the research, for example physicians in clinics and partner companies (for example CRO – clinical research organizations), who are given the task of carrying out studies, also have access to these systems. Document management systems make the research information available at the relevant locations without media breaks and double entries of the research information. In this way they shorten the decision process and make it easier for the pharmaceutical company to identify less successful projects early on, so that they can concentrate on more promising projects. Additionally, they facilitate the preparation process for the registration dossier and thereby shorten the process for registering a new drug. At the same time they improve the quality of the registration dossier.

In the meantime, global document management systems are being widely used in clinical research. However, there are as yet no empirical studies on the benefits actually achieved during the clinical phases. Merely the time needed to prepare the dossier could be shortened by up to 20 percent for some pharmaceutical companies. Expenditure for the conception and implementation of such a solution was mostly in the upper two-digit million regions (Euros), with a timeframe of one to one-and-a-half years. Even if, after such a project, the timeframe for the clinical research of a project were shortened by percent or if ten percent of the less promising projects were discovered and stopped in time, the IT investment would be amortized after only a few research projects.

2.2.5   Improved customer bonding through better information exchange in global container logistics

Organized marine transport is one of the most complex logistics systems there is. Modern container shipping connects load-carrying containers with the shipping system of the carrier. Both components have their own logistics and must be planned and controlled in collaboration with the services of harbors, associated cargo handlers, depots and secondary land and feeder transports at global level. To this end, carriers developed high-performance ERP systems at an early stage. Based on the system-controlled handling of the transport and the electronic shipping documents that are continuously being updated to reflect the current transport status, further functions were developed, such as system-generated transport route mapping, including price-finding or the really forward-looking load planning of the container fleet and also the ship capacity, the integrated load control ('yield management'). Particularly carriers that switched to globally compatible processes at an early stage and realized them in a globally homogeneous system have achieved the highest efficiency increases and are able to fully enjoy the competitive edge of operative excellence today.

The development of commercial Internet technologies ultimately made it possible for carriers to do business directly with their direct customers, the shippers and the consignees. While the early web-based services were more instrumental to the information needs of the customer and for easing the burden of customer service, and thus increasing internal efficiency, leading carriers developed electronic services that opened up additional sales potential. The basic features included everything from simple but continuously updated shipping plans and global container tracking (track & trace) with reference to transport plans and even electronically transmitted warnings for expected delays. Electronic transport booking, confirmations and payment processes rounded off the services portfolio.

Individual IT components or those still in the development stage make up an IT portfolio that stretches from the employee to the customer (see figure 14). Via the Internet platform, the customer exchanges data with the carrier, which is automatically processed and which can be viewed by the employees of the carrier in its ERP system. Leading carriers developed services that were individually tailored to the needs of their demanding customers and which were coordinated with highly advanced Supply Chain Management (SCM) systems. Some examples are the direct electronic linking of the customer-side SCM system with the ERP system of the carrier for automated transport processes, or the transmission of detailed load-related data from the shipper to the consignee, including article numbers, material numbers and number of items for the transfer in the SCM system of the consignee.

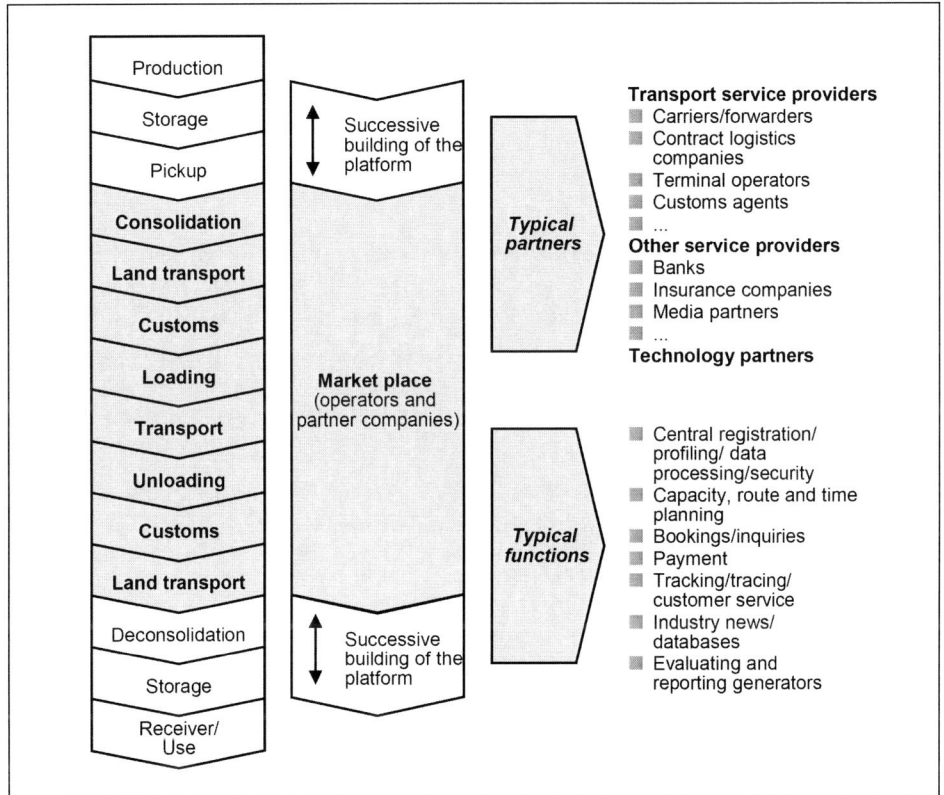

Figure 14:   *Linking all partners in the container shipping industry;*
              Source: A.T. Kearney

Shipping customers use this new data quality and up-to-the-minuteness for their part to be able to plan well ahead and thereby increase their competitive advantage. Offering such customers added value means bonding large transport volumes long-term and planning far in advance in close collaboration with the customer. The extensive availability and up-to-the-minuteness of the information provided by the IT technology has been made a clause in many transport contracts and enables the acquisition of new, technically demanding customers.

2.3   IT as a Part of the End Product

For enterprises that have already had experience in enhancing value with IT, it is only a small step further to be able to increase revenues with IT not only directly – for example through price premiums based on additional benefit, as in the example of the container shipping industry described above – but also indirectly to develop new sales potential and even new business fields with IT.

Undeniably it depends on the type of individual business, whether IT can be implemented as a component in the end product at all, and whether this proves to be financially feasible. In sectors whose products are inseparably connected to IT, for example telecommunications companies, this idea of sales-relevant IT is nothing new. The introduction of the so-called prepaid card, on which funds can be loaded for making phone calls in mobile communications networks, was almost exclusively a challenge for IT managers. It was the development of software solutions in billing and accounting systems that created the prerequisites for implementing this innovative product.

The birth of transaction banking shows how IT makes improvements to operations that open up potential for increasing sales, until IT ultimately creates new sales potential.

The birth of transaction banking

As a result of enormous cost pressures, several banks automated their transaction processes and achieved considerable improvement at operational level:

■ Error reduction by raising the STP (Straight Through Processing) rate

■ Acceleration of transaction processes (from 'T+3', i.e. completion of process three days after carrying out transaction, to 'T+1' and finally to real-time transaction 'T+0')

■ Improved overall bank control by linking front-office systems (trading systems) with back-office systems and systems for risk controlling and reporting

■ The flexible transaction systems enabled these banks to develop the further potential benefit of IT: product innovations, particularly the handling of new derivative products, could be realized more quickly. Thanks to improved time-to-market, some of the banks were able to position themselves as product innovators in retail banking and increase their sales in the area of purchase warrants and structured loans, while others positioned themselves as innovative market players in the credit sector with high-performance IT supporting automated credit processes. As a result they were able to make faster decisions than many of their competitors for granting deferred payment credit – a crucial competitive edge

And finally, several banks used IT for developing new business fields: Some of the operations systems were set up in a client-enabled way and the services of other banks were made available. With this step, entirely new customers were acquired and the result was a pure transaction bank, which made use of high economies of scale in the transactions. Through these transaction banks, other banks are able to achieve cost advantages of up to 30 percent over handling the business themselves. Why should every bank develop and maintain their own transaction systems for their clients when IT makes it possible to provide a larger number of such services more efficiently on a central basis?

In addition to IT-oriented sectors like mobile communications and banking, other sectors, whose products do not appear to be IT-oriented, are also using innovative IT to capture additional sales potential for their business.

- Manufacturers of agricultural machinery, for example, integrate information technology as an additional 'precision farming' component in their combine harvesters, fertilizing machines or chaff cutters – a component with its own sales that also achieves a high level of customer bonding. In connection with Global Positioning Systems (GPS), intelligent software in fertilizing machines can, based on the carbon content of the soil, calculate within a fraction of a second, how much fertilizer per square meter must be applied to each individual part of the land. In next year's harvest, the combine harvester, equipped with appropriate recording software, then measures the exact harvesting quantity for each field and feeds the information into an integrated database, from which the fertilizing machine can draw its information for calculating fertilizer quantities for the following growth cycles. This enables farmers to increase their earnings in kind, economize on inputs and optimize processes with improved soil cultivation and a focused control of all agricultural operations. Naturally, the manufacturers of farm equipment not only allow the farmer to pay for this software-driven feature, they also achieve valuable customer bonding effects, because the solutions of the various manufacturers of agricultural machinery are of course proprietary and not necessarily compatible, which means that if a farmer changed to a different machine he would lose valuable data for optimizing sowing/planting crops, fertilizing and harvesting – so for this reason alone the hurdles involved in switching suppliers are higher.

- Manufacturers of tractors, trucks and construction machinery can use information technology as a tool to analyze and diagnose the end product, for supporting maintenance and maintenance-related processes. For this, software programs – so-called 'machine messengers' – are integrated into the machines and deal with failures by calling up essential maintenance and maintenance-relevant information, such as operation hours, fuel consumption or average speed, in a cyclical and also need-oriented way. The information is transmitted via a 'communication controller' and a cellular antenna to a central server at the manufacturer's company. All information about the entire life cycle of the machine, with every problem that has ever occurred and all of the servicing that has been carried out, is stored here. This information is just as useful for the owner of the machine as it is for the manufacturer. On one hand, potential problems and particularly failures can be recognized and prevented in advance, thanks to the precise analysis and evaluation of the data. For this, alert logs are used, in which especially parameters that should be subject to regular maintenance are called up from the primary technology. If a failure could be prevented, then the recording of the maintenance and operational activities can be used to search for possible causes. In combination with the data on previous experiences, which have been collected in the database for the machines of other owners as well, this comprises an excellent database for the focused analysis of problems. The manufacturer achieves significantly more efficient and also more effective maintenance processes. The advantages for the owner lie in a higher level of availability of a restricted number of expensive machines: On the one hand failures can be prevented. On the other hand, unavoidable failures can be corrected faster. This way, in addition to the original product, the manufacturer can build up a competitively differentiated position via the implemented IT solutions.

■ A completely different sector – in which the value-enhancing use of IT in the products seems hard to imagine at first glance – is the furniture industry. Behind the terms 'roomware', 'ubiquitous computers' or 'smart artifacts' technologies are hidden that aim at the direct and invisible integration of computers in our living spaces. Talking walls, at home and particularly in the office, is intended to give people the information they need in whatever context, every moment of the day. For example, a particular wall color or shading in an office can indicate that e-mails are waiting in the mailbox, or for example in the controlling division, it could mean that available funds have sunk below a defined threshold. In private quarters, the wall color could, for example, indicate that electronic appliances such as the washing machine or the dryer have a defect. A manufacturer of office furniture recognized the changing work forms and processes in enterprises and has developed new, IT-assisted products. As today's average employee spends some 30 percent of his work time in meetings and managers spend even 60 to 90 percent in meetings with colleagues, customers or suppliers, the resourceful furniture makers concluded that more highly professionalized tools and equipment could achieve considerable boosts in the efficiency and effectiveness potential of communication. Who hasn't seen them, the banks of notebooks set up round the table at every meeting, supposedly for communication, but actually blocking communication between participants rather than promoting it? The company built interactive 'electronic walls' (DynaWall), interactive conference tables (InteracTable) and systematically prepared the use of collaboration software (Basic Environment for Active Collaboration – BEACH). Without going into great detail, common to all of the products was that facts are more readily available for viewing – literally 'on the table' – and can be processed by all participants online with a stylus or by hand. The furniture company had thus created the prerequisites for inventing new customer needs and developing new sales potential. Today there is already a competitive advantage: for example, the company was the only representative of the furniture sector invited to exhibit at the CEBIT – an excellent platform for approaching customers and penetrating new market and market segments.

▨ A further example of the integration of IT in products is the 'smart home' – the German federal office for promoting security in information technology speaks of 'integrated building systems'. These systems equip building components such as lighting systems, blinds, window and security systems or household appliances with sensors, actuators, control units and software, and then network everything together. Based on this, systems are developed that integrate this hardware and software and offer services for improving the quality of life in various types of building utilization scenarios. For example such services enable an increased level of comfort (everything is remote-controlled), the optimization of energy consumption or the improvement of building security. Enterprises from a variety of sectors could profit from this technology. For the makers of the technology, the benefits lie in the expanded functions of the devices, in retaining and/or regaining higher profit margins through various price segments and in the possibility of integrated device and content offerings. For telecommunication companies, integrated offers for home services, Internet and cellular communications would be considerations. Utility companies can offer new services like load management, individualized energy consulting or the consolidation of services, utilities and devices, an already widespread method used today in heating systems.

All these examples show that many enterprises are already achieving success today with the use of innovative IT. Leading enterprises like Rank Xerox have already initiated comprehensive research programs, intended to deliver the expected revenues by using IT in the product at an early stage. Thus, it makes sense to think about seemingly 'impossible' and innovative integration possibilities in primary products because soon as the first company in a given sector has begun using IT to develop new market potential and create competitive advantages, it will be difficult for 'latecomers' to make up for lost time.

Checklist: Is your company ready to maximize the value of IT?	Yes
Is your corporate strategy clearly defined?	
Is your IT strategy oriented long-term to corporate strategy? Do IT benefits have clear priority over IT spending?	
Have business units and the IT department identified the potential benefit with IT together?	
Have business units and the IT department decided on an IT innovation portfolio for developing IT potential benefit together? Are the business cases calculated and positive?	
Is there a systematic IT implementation plan, and has this been discussed with all parties involved?	
Is there willingness to use innovative IT to assure revenues and increase sales and to develop new sales potential by integrating IT in the product?	

3.   Enterprise Transformation –
Ensuring the Benefits of IT are Achieved

Identifying value-enhancing IT projects in IT strategy is an important step towards promoting the innovative power of the company and increasing its market share and competitive chances. Whether or not the benefits of future-oriented IT projects are achieved, however, depends on whether the users actually take advantage of the possibilities of IT in their daily business.

In the 1970s, when the first accounting systems were introduced to automate accounts payable departments, which up to that point had been paper-based, the structures and processes of only one unit had to be changed to realize the benefit of IT. With today's IT systems, however, this adjustment is no longer restricted to one closed unit within the company. The IT technologies mentioned in Part A, Chapter 1, e.g. Customer Relationship Management (CRM) and Product Lifecycle Management (PLM), are holistic concepts that necessitate a complete modification of views pertaining to the handling of customers (in the case of CRM) or in the orientation of engineering, production and after-sales services (in the case of PLM).

The greater the significance of IT for the performance output of enterprises (regardless of the industrial sector or size) and of public institutions, the more these changes in the company also call for modifications to the IT system, and vice versa: if the IT system is modified, the company must also adjust accordingly. A company can only realize the benefit of IT for its business operations if the mindset of the employees and their working methods, its operations, structures and often even its interface to customers suppliers are all oriented to the new IT applications and infrastructure. We refer to these changes as IT-driven enterprise transformation.

Such enterprise transformation addresses strategic and operative aspects, as opposed to business process reengineering, which deals primarily with the processes. Contrary to restructuring, which in practice often only takes place as a reactive alignment in the event of a crisis situation, but which is intended to represent a proactive alignment of the changing external framework conditions of the company, enterprise transformation is an extensive, fundamental modification of the company, which is generally initiated by strategic decisions made by the proprietor/CEO. A classic example of enterprise transformation is the transformation of an in-house service provider, which to date served only one customer, the parent company, into an independent company that is to successfully acquire and develop business in an outside market. In such a case, it is necessary not only to create operative conditions (e.g. client-enabled systems), but also to ensure a fundamental transformation: Away from an in-house service provider focused on one customer, who is also the owner, and towards a company with distribution competence, service orientation and competitive cost structures (*cf.* Part C, Chapter 2, 'In-House IT Service Providers').

It has been our experience that not all enterprises combine IT modification with enterprise transformation. There are still IT projects being carried out without planning the necessary changes to the business. This can only lead to conflict: On the one hand, the time and expense for coordinating IT and the business as well as the extent of such adjustments are often underestimated. On the other hand, the potential of IT is not taken into consideration in the planning – and therefore cannot be delivered. IT then earns the reputation as a cost driver and becomes a hindrance for meeting company goals, because at a certain point in the IT project the question inevitably arises of whether the planning should be changed so that the IT potential can be developed, or whether a sub-optimal implementation should continue – with too few IT benefits, but too high IT costs.

In a concrete example, at the end of the 1990s a capital goods manufacturer decided to switch from SAP R/2 to SAP R/3. The reason given by the IT department was a technical one that SAP R/2 was going out of service, and so the migration from SAP R/2 to SAP R/3 began. As IT capacities were tight, they decided to leave operations and structures essentially unaltered, except for some minor improvements, i.e. integrate them into the new SAP R/3 system status quo. Three years and a good 40 million euros spent on IT/SAP projects later, senior management was wondering about the sense of this exercise and what had actually been achieved. Although the SAP conversion resulted in many small and also some larger improvements, the company had thrown away decisive potential benefit by not using the migration as a chance for a systematic improvement and for streamlining their business processes and business structures, as well as altering thinking and behavior patterns (for example for faster processes in production and the consequential possible reduction of inventories). As a result, the enterprise anticipates a repeat performance: the business processes and business structures will be systematically modernized and then integrated into SAP R/3 and based on that, the thinking and behavior patterns of the employees will be altered – which should amount to the same expenditure as introducing SAP R/3 the first time around.

The better, more modern procedure consists of installing IT as a trigger mechanism, driver and designer of the transformation process. Naturally, IT is in this case not an end in itself: The goal of enterprise transformation is always the impact on the business operations of the company. Nevertheless, the trigger for transformation does not necessarily have to lie in the business operations – on the contrary: Often it is already too late for successful changes if the business is forcing them. Therefore, changes in IT technology that will open up new markets or customer potential for the company should be used as a reason for enterprise transformation.

A good example of this is a beverage bottling company making IT-driven changes in the area of route planning for its maintenance and deliveries. In the past, the employees did maintenance work on beverage vending machines, following routes that were mapped out first thing in the morning; they delivered beverages to restaurants, hotels etc. and other businesses and restocked the vending machines. If a customer required a delivery on short-term notice, several telephone calls had to be made between the office and the drivers of the various locations to inquire about the available quantities, in order to then decide who should make the delivery. Delivered quantities were jotted down on paper and in some cases paid for on the spot in cash. These transactions frequently contained calculation errors or manipulations in the invoices and the information about the quantities actually delivered was rarely available immediately.

In the meantime, however, IT offers a solution that has widespread effects on business processes: The maintenance staff and drivers of the delivery trucks now have handheld computers, which automatically transmit the location of the driver to an IT application in the main office. Possible changes to the planned route are transmitted back to the hand-held, which immediately connects to the beverage vending machines to check on their quantities. In addition, the handhelds enable cashless payments to be made with debit or credit cards, they prepare and print delivery notes and invoices and transmit the data on delivered quantities to the inventory and distribution systems in the main office. This eliminates the time-consuming follow-up checking of routes at the end of the day, including correcting errors, the drivers are able to use their time for deliveries and not for paper work, and information about the delivered quantities is available immediately. Intelligent vending machines, which automatically send out refill orders as soon as they drop below a predefined quantity level, enable even greater optimization of the route planning, and lost sales due to empty vending machines can be prevented.

Extensive, IT-driven enterprise transformation achieves not only increased efficiency on the level of the business processes, business structures and improved thinking and behavior patterns, but also creates value enhancement potential for the company through increased sales. On the level of business processes (and of the business structures as well as thinking and behavior patterns) enterprise transformation enables a more efficient execution of the daily business, for example by increasing the degree of automation. This in turn makes it easier for employees to carry out routine tasks and at the same time decreases error rates. Additionally, the transformed business processes enable better cooperation with customers and suppliers. For example, the time-to-market for new products can be shortened for manufacturing companies or the decision time and quality for approving credit applications at financial service providers can be cut down, so that new customers can be more easily acquired and existing customers bonded more closely to the company.

Additional sales and profits are made possible by the fact that previous back-office areas are independent and can offer their services to third parties – on the basis of a suitable IT platform for this. This is done, for example, by installing an IT service provider in such a way that, for example, the IT of a machine/plant engineering can also do work for other manufacturing firms, or by opening up the IT transaction platform of a financial service provider in order to work together with other financial service providers with similar or identical transaction types, in order to realize economies of scale.

However, achieving improvements in business operations with IT requires a new understanding of the function of IT in the company, and places far-reaching demands on those in charge, not only in the IT department but also in the business units: IT managers must be in a position to actively introduce innovative IT solutions with suggestions for organizing business processes and business structures, and consequently to instruct management personnel. Naturally this creates conflict potential with the business units, as they must come to believe that the IT department is not merely a 'support feature such as the system in finance and accounting, but rather that IT as an enabler for business has an active right to have a say or even an obligation to reorganize the processes and structures, as well as the thinking and behavior patterns of the staff in the business units.

But honoring this position also requires additional skills on the part of management personnel and the staff of the IT department. They must consider themselves to be the creators of the business. Therefore, to a growing extent not only specialist knowledge about IT technology, but also fundamental strategic and operative know-how about the long- and short-term organization of the business is key. Only then can the IT department play this role competently – and also implement it in a credible way. If the capability profile and training program for IT managers and IT employees are redesigned, then the technically competent 'IT fiddler' will be superceded by someone with a degree in information management, who is well-versed in business and social skills. The professional development of such a person would consist, for example, courses in the logistics module of standard business administration software provided by the software manufacturer, visiting strategic logistics conferences and relevant sector conferences. This would facilitate an evaluation of the potential benefit of the logistics module for current and future competitive requirements (also in terms of today's possibilities) and a best practices comparison with other logistics users, so that it can be implemented for the success of the company.

3.1   Planning and Controlling IT-driven Enterprise Transformation

In today's world, introducing a future-oriented, innovative IT system is no longer just a question of the right project management. Planning an enterprise transformation must be part of strategic corporate strategy. Transformation alters the entire enterprise including the interfaces to external market partners, and often entails changes for customers or suppliers too. The planned changes are not to be oriented to the existing environment, but rather must include creative new solutions. Due to the long time needed for enterprise transformations and their scope, it should also be expected that the external framework conditions will change during enterprise transformation implementation, and it must be ensured that the IT benefit can also be realized on unplanned developments. It is also absolutely necessary to actively control enterprise transformation and ensure its sustained success through risk and benefit management.

3.1.1   Strategic planning of enterprise transformation

The changes necessary for implementing IT benefit must be systematically planned across the entire value added chain, including all interfaces to customers and suppliers as well as, if necessary, supervisory authorities and other interest groups. Of course both the value added chains itself and the vertical scope of the company should be checked as part of transformation planning.

Besides the necessary external orientation, enterprise transformation means that fundamental changes are necessary throughout the entire company, and also beyond the borders of business units and subsidiaries (at least if the company has a close solidarity with mutual suppliers and service relationships and is not merely a collection of financial interests). As a rule, related business units develop their own information technology solutions and specific business processes. The standardization of such partial solutions eliminates the processing of redundant data so that the business processes, and often also the business structures, can be harmonized.

In the case of an aircraft manufacturer, the engineering department had the goal of introducing new software to make product development more efficient. Although important and practical, the goal of better customer orientation could not be reached with this measure alone. The information about the contractually agreed design options as well as any modifications to the design desired by the customer after the product launch were held up in marketing and usually reached the engineering department after a delay, by which time new plans for the design had already been drawn up.

By linking the engineering data with the data of the marketing department, the engineering department was immediately informed about the wishes of the customer, unnecessary reengineering and design modifications were avoided and the product development process was accelerated.

Tips for planning enterprise transformation:

- ▪ Effective involvement of external partners: Obviously, only the most important customers are integrated in the transformation project, so that their requirements can be taken into consideration as fully as possible. In this respect, the most important suppliers should also be involved in order to eliminate unnecessary, cost-incurring back-up inventories from the supply chain through better demand management.
- ▪ Courage for 'creative destruction': When looking for improvement potential in its structures and processes, a company should always be open to new, innovative concepts and not restrict its creativity to optimizing existing components. Developing the possibilities of IT requires the courage to analyze, and even remove existing structures and to try out new solutions, even if they appear unusual at first glance.
- ▪ Only those who have big plans will achieve big objectives. IT enables revolutionary improvements not only within the company but also externally. Small, marginal improvements cannot realize sustained IT benefits.

Similar successes can be realized in many other sectors. IT also supports optimizing the vertical scope in enterprises. Improved data storage and data transmission enable the outsourcing of (partial) processes particularly in cross-section functions (called 'business process outsourcing'), but also in the operative area, as the information is available independent of company limits. For example, the outsourcing of administrative human resources processes is gaining increasing significance, as many firms do not see their core competence in this area of work and therefore pass their human resources issues on to specialized service providers. The relevant human resources data, of course, are available to the enterprise at all times. Financial service providers also frequently use the possibility in the operative area, to focus on certain segments of the value added chain (for example product development and marketing) and pass on other segments (for example transactions) to third parties. This concentration on selected parts of the value added chain would not be possible without efficient IT systems, as a close connection between transactions and marketing is essential. Thanks to IT, such a connection can even be successfully realized outside the boundaries of the enterprise.

Considering the IT requirements of customers and suppliers is an important step in successful enterprise transformation. However, experience has shown that the creative involvement of customers and suppliers often delivers requirements that are oriented to the status quo. This limitation must be eliminated jointly – whereby changes made by the company to the interfaces of its customers and suppliers will lead to further transformation projects in their IT departments and business processes, and this 'snowball effect' then triggers an avalanche of IT-driven enterprise transformations – with potential benefit for all parties involved. This happens, for example, when a large automobile or logistics group transfers it's purchasing to a marketplace in the Internet, forcing its suppliers to either go along with this step – or, worst-case scenario, to lose its turnover with this group.

As part of the transformation of a mechanical engineering company, its customers were specifically asked about their IT and process requirements. Most of the customers, when searching for improvements, were not able to mentally divorce themselves from existing IT solutions and essentially proposed smaller, 'evolutionary' changes. For example, one customer wanted information that had been circulated in paper form as one copy to be circulated in future in quadruplicate copies. The company, however, had already planned the elimination of paper through the close, inter-company linking of information. The customer could only be convinced of the advantages of such IT-assisted information transmission after he had evaluated the potential benefit that would result for him. In order to achieve benefit enhancing changes with IT, it is necessary to confront external market partners, such as customers and suppliers, with IT solutions that are perhaps completely new for them, and to give them time to come to terms with these 'revolutionary' changes.

When planning IT-driven enterprise transformation, IT managers are aware that evaluating future framework conditions (which planning is based on) will cause uncertainty. Therefore, as a rule, several planning scenarios are drawn up that take into consideration the various possible developments of the framework conditions and which mostly have a similarly high probability of occurring. All the more surprising it is to see that, in practice, of the planning based scenarios of future framework conditions, often only one scenario is chosen to be used as the basis for the IT solution. All too often, a different scenario of corporate development occurs during IT realization, for which the IT has not been programmed. This ruins the IT benefit if the IT department is not in a position to deal with the new scenario – which in the meantime has already become a reality.

Choosing a robust IT solution to cover several future scenarios can counteract this danger. At the planning stage, the elements that represent the goals of enterprise transformation must be carefully chosen to allow for easy modification if the framework conditions are changed. IT solutions that can be parameterized leave many options open. For example, in planning the transformation of a distribution company it was not possible to determine in advance in which countries of Eastern European the company operated. The IT department opted for a multi-language solution, to enable later use in other countries. Flexible IT therefore means planning security for the company.

3.1.2   During implementation pay attention to results, rather than aiming for perfection in every aspect

In view of the abundance of requirements that are to be converted as part of a transformation process taking place over a considerable period of time, there is great danger of the managers in charge not being able to 'see the wood for the trees', and in their efforts to convert all the requirements simultaneously, they lose sight of the target.

This applies particularly when external market partners are involved in the planning. All the IT requirements of important customers are classified as 'absolutely necessary'. In striving for perfection, the development and introduction of a new organizational and technical IT solution keep slipping further away. In view of the enormous work involved and the time needed to do it – particularly in the case of large individual software projects – the result can easily be resignation. Experience has shown that IT-driven enterprise transformations with a timeframe of more than two years often become endless projects, without the goal ever being reached.

In order to achieve the targeted benefit quickly, while also allowing for feedback loops, a good solution is to start with 'Version 1.0', which obviously does not cover all requirements, but which can be implemented in a manageable timeframe. Shortening the project timeframe with a focus on the most important requirements also has the advantage that in real use 'Version 1.0' delivers positive and negative empirical values at an early stage, which can then be successively integrated into later IT transformations – for example in a roll-out via several business units. In many cases, the communication of initial successes gives employees and management staff the courage and energy to persevere along the long and often rocky road to complete IT implementation and enterprise transformation. Additionally, the IT benefit that is realized in 'Version 1.0' (for example cost-cutting) contributes to financing later versions for further IT-driven enterprise transformation.

3.1.3 Using risk management

Even when the IT transformation process is prepared as carefully as possible, there are still some implementation risks. These can either have their origins in the company and therefore can be influenced – or they can be caused by external factors, upon which the company has no or limited influence. In the latter case, it is important to remain capable of reacting strategically. To better recognize the risk factors, setting up a Program Management Office (PMO), especially for larger IT-driven enterprise transformations, has proven to be worthwhile.

The PMO supports project management in the operative control of the transformation project. Depending on the complexity of the project, it comprises several employees from the IT department and from the business units, who evaluate how important interim goals are reached and the individual project status objectives achieved. Additionally, the PMO enables extensive project communication – especially important for managing changes in enterprise transformation – and, together with those in charge, draws up measures for dealing with project interference factors.

One of the most important duties of the PMO is systematic risk controlling. Risk controlling is responsible for proactively evaluating and prioritizing project risks, and when risks occur, of actively initiating counter-measures and then monitoring the effectiveness of these measures (figure 15). The foresighted assessment of risks increases the time available for implementing counter-measures.

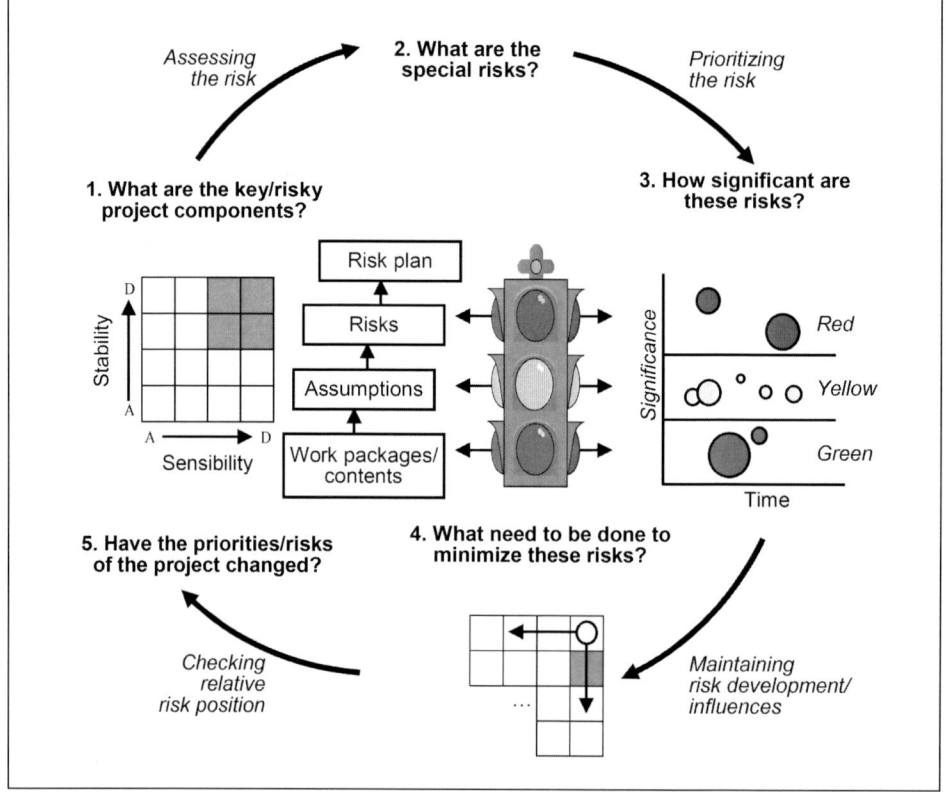

Figure 15:   *Cycle of proactive risk controlling*

The significance of proactive risk management is illustrated perfectly by the Y2K example: at that time there was a very real danger of important IT and process control systems carrying out incorrect comparisons as the date changed from '1999' to '2000', triggering failures or simply causing the system to break down. Proactive risk management meant systematically evaluating the essential components of the IT system and the process control technology of the company, in the weeks or months before changing over to the new year on 1 January 2000, to determine just what a breakdown would mean for the company and its customers, and how high the probability of event was. Then, assuming the highest damage potential with the highest probability of event, precautions were taken, i.e. the probability of event was verified or falsified with IT-assisted tests, and in the event of a verification precautions were taken, for example by buying new PCs, adjusting programs or modifying process control technology.

At a major airline, for example, all central programs for booking flights and for the 'flight ops' were systematically tested and corrected. The mainframe was made 'Y2K safe' with the necessary hardware upgrades and software patches from the manufacturer, the PCs, fax machines and printers were replaced, in case they were too old and therefore more susceptible to damage. Even more important was that the aircraft manufacturers published very precise statements in their maintenance manuals stating from which version the flight computer and other safety-critical IT components in the aircraft were 'Y2K safe' and to which version a replacement was necessary. Even the process control technology of the airports were checked and modernized. Through this it emerged that, for example, the fueling equipment of a major European airport was not 'Y2K safe': Triggered by the change to the year 2000, the controls would have assumed a failure and for security reasons closed all valves, so that aircraft that had landed could not have been refueled. Systematic preparations for the 'year 2000' and risk controlling at airlines, in the power and telecommunications industries and other sectors prevented major problems from occurring at the millennium. This example shows how successful risk controlling proves that nothing happens – although the 'year 2000' risk caused national damages of billions of euros.

3.1.4 Carrying out benefit management

The opposite of risk management is benefit management. Its goal is to maximize the benefit, not to minimize or eliminate risks. To this end, the total targeted benefit of IT transformation is broken down into partial benefits. From a technical perspective, the criteria for this stem from the modules of the IT solution and from an organizational perspective from the business processes involved and/or their individual stages or from the affected organizational units. The partial benefits are evaluated according to their size and according to the necessary expenditure for transformation (= the sum of the expenditure for IT realization plus the expenditure for aligning the business processes and structures plus the expenditure for modifying the thinking and behavior patterns of the senior executives and employees involved). They are sorted according to highest partial benefits and lowest transformation expenditure. The reflection of this classification on the technical and organizational IT dependencies results in the fastest possible – and therefore optimum – transformation sequence.

Thus benefit management draws up a benefit realization schedule and controls the transformation process to ensure that the targeted benefits are actually delivered. To this end, a controlling cycle is also run through, consisting of 'defining the objective for partial benefits', 'defining measures for realizing partial benefits and necessary transformation steps', 'initiating transformation steps', 'evaluating transformation steps in terms of achieving partial benefits' and finally in turn 'defining a renewed objective'.

In many transformation projects the reality is a different one. Frequently, the technical regulations of the installed software package dominate in which order the steps of the transformation project are executed. Not seldom, companies begin with relatively unimportant transformation phases, for example in financial accounting, with the argument that all further configuration of the software package is based on the settings for the financial accounting department. The result is that, in the first weeks and months of the transformation project many senior executives and employees invest all their time and energy in working on the IT transformation of a business unit that in most cases is not relevant for competition, with the result that high project costs with no relevant potential benefit are incurred – instead of working on the logistical core processes or on the interface to the customers. Systematic benefit management helps to find the right method for optimizing the benefits of IT-driven enterprise transformation, while at the same time efficiently using tight resources for the most important key functions in competition.

E-government: Transforming a government body (pensions agency)

In many government offices, the administrative processes have not really changed much in the past few decades. Handcarts full of files and circulation folders characterize the landscape, data is not available as the files are stuck somewhere between archives and the office, and of the few existing PCs some were brought in by the employees themselves so that they would no longer have to type in data on a typewriter. The employees spend a large part of their time searching for data and cannot get all of their own work done. There is enormous improvement potential with IT here for optimizing the business processes. However, the pure installation of IT systems without changing the decade-old, historically-grown work processes and the thinking and behavior patterns of the staff would not make sense. The necessity here for IT-driven enterprise transformation is obvious.

The organization and processes of the pension's office of a neighboring European country were no longer able to cope with demand. Complaints about poor service, unfavorable office hours, complicated procedures, long waiting times and frequent errors were on the rise. At the same time, the cost pressure on the government agency was steadily increasing, and particularly the central location of the pension's office was under considerable pressure to rationalize. The state government had also clearly recognized the challenges of the coming decades: the shifting of the age pyramid results in fewer employees (due to budget restrictions because of long-term declining tax revenues) having to take care of an increasing number of pensioners. This development will peak when the high birthrate generations of the 1960s (baby boomers) reach retirement age, at which time there will be about two pensioners for every contributor to the pension plan.

An extensive reorientation of the entire agency with modern IT technology was needed, particularly under the aspects of 'customer centering and 'focus'. The IT backend systems of the pensions office ('legacy systems') were over 30 years old and the programmers also soon reaching retirement. Even the IT frontend systems were fairly ancient: screen masks on special input terminals with complex data input and insufficient transparency. If adjustments or changes to the existing systems were possible at all, then only under high cost and time expenditure, combined with high risk, as all data structures and system parameters were no longer completely documented and the extent of their effectiveness was no longer known. Replacing the IT systems was urgently necessary, not least of all because these IT systems not only calculated the pensions but also controlled most of the weekly payments of pensions and social security benefits via post offices and therefore a considerable money flow.

As a solution, the IT-driven transformation of the government agency to 'e-government' was planned. Based on the new processes and organization possibilities that were opened up by the use of IT, the tasks and goals of the pensions office were analyzed, a vision was drawn up for e-business-centered processes and structures, and for the future relationship of the government agency to its customers and for the type and quality of the services, and a strategy was defined. Its core claim being that thanks to 'e' the citizen is placed on center stage like a customer, and processes and organization structures are oriented to their needs and requirements. The use of modern IT components should enable all employees to be able to answer more than 80 percent of all inquiries promptly. In addition, the case-workers were specially trained to guarantee fast, error-free processing of inquiries and applications.

Based on these goals, the future IT systems with their processes and organization were redefined and re-planned. A completely new 'frontend' – a customer contact center with 500 employees – was developed on a green meadow very far from the old location of the pension's office, with the idea of also enabling a new psychological beginning. The planned IT systems, processes and organization were implemented step by step, gradually 'loaded up' through the step-by-step transfer of more and more customers, and continually tested and streamlined. Finally, the finished concept was expanded through the establishment of up to 26 country-wide customer contact centers, situated close to the people, replacing some 620 local offices that had been used before.

The local employees at the various locations were given the option of transferring to a customer contact center, which, thanks to a newly-introduced incentive program, also met with a positive response. A newly developed training concept quickly put the employees in a position to serve the customers of the pension's office with a full range of services. The pleasant working environment made it easy to motivate the staff for their new duties.

IT characterizes the three core processes of the pensions office – for one, the one-off processing of the pension application form, secondly, the application for social security benefits in old age, and thirdly, adjusting to new living conditions (admittance to hospital, move to a senior citizens' home, change of partner etc.) – as well as parallel internal processes for controlling customer satisfaction and ongoing improvements, and for researching changes in the market and in requirements. For the processing of these core processes a comprehensive CRM system was developed, which set down new working methods and organization structures. For example the CRM system led to a dialog between employees and customers based on predefined dialog procedures, which gave the employee the questions in advance, recorded the answers in predefined fields and branched off the interview, depending on the answers of the customer, into specialized sub-dialogs. This guaranteed that the employee received all information necessary for the processing of the application form. An agency-wide Intranet including an information infrastructure, knowledge management, search tools and other features further supported the staff.

The results were clearly positive: the echo from the political and public sides – particularly from the customer – also increased the level of employee satisfaction. The project is today considered to be the best reference project for the transformation of complex organizations with IT.

3.2 Using External Partners for Accelerating Transformation: Build – Operate – Transfer (BOT)

IT strategy, IT benefit, enterprise transformation are all very well, but how do we implement it all? How do we ensure that – as in many enterprises in the past – the planning does not prove to be unrealistic by the next project that deadlines are met, costs do not explode and the users are not annoyed by the IT system? Principally speaking, there are two possible procedures here: traditionally the company takes charge of providing (in the case of standard software, purchasing) and installing the IT system, as well as the transformation of the enterprise. IT consultants and other externals (for example change agents) are often called in to contribute the necessary know-how, make up for lack of experience and insufficient resources and to cope with the burden peaks that are part of every project. This means that the company is also responsible for the success of the introduction – with all of the project risks.

There is, however another way to do it: for example in the construction industry it is customary for the client to hire a general contractor for the complete construction of a building ('Build'), while in plant construction the manufacturer of the system also takes charge of putting the machine into service until regular operations have begun ('Operate') and the machine can be handed over to the owner ('Transfer') – this model is also referred to as the BOT concept.

Payment is made in installments after the completion and inspection of clearly-defined construction phases and/or after operations commence and responsibility has been transferred to the client.

Such a BOT concept can also be used for enterprise transformation through the introduction of comprehensive IT systems in major projects. An external IT partner is chosen (often a consortium). This partner ensures the success of the enterprise transformation, by first identifying the technical and organizational modifications necessary for enterprise transformation ('Build' phase), then introduces the IT systems and adjusts the organization (change management) and carries out the IT operations until stabilization of the new processes has been achieved ('Operate' phase), after which the responsibility for the new IT solutions and processes is transferred to the company after a stabilization phase ('Transfer' phase). BOT projects take into consideration the necessary IT and organizational transformation measures right from the planning phase and ensure holistic goal-achieving implementation.

Tips for implementing the BOT concept:

■ *Pay attention to the partner management capabilities:*
Only consider large IT companies or consortium leaders for assuming risks. Smaller IT specialists are contracted and controlled by the consortium leader. Therefore, if the contractor is a consortium, the consortium leader must be capable of managing and controlling his consortium partner. When the job is being contracted out, it must be clearly regulated to what extent the consortium leader is responsible for any reduced output or even failure of his consortium partner to deliver.

■ *Integrate the employees in the transformation project:*
When selecting the contractor it is advisable to involve the staff and representatives of the workers' council, in order to eliminate unfounded fears of the staff members and to integrate any ideas they may have in the BOT concept. Integrating the employees in the 'Build' phase ensures the transfer of know-how and paves the way for the enterprise to manage the system after the IT solution has been completed. In the 'Operate' phase the employees are successively integrated in the operation and the maintenance. An immediate structured shift from the 'Operate' to the 'Transfer' phase takes place, so there is no abrupt transition that could prove too much for the employees.

With BOT models, the IT partner not only installs streamlined software, but also assumes all of the risks of enterprise transformation. He carries the responsibility for the realistic planning and implementation of the cost and potential benefit of the business case and avoids unrealistic expectations.

The enterprise is not obligated to pay the IT partner as soon as the first operative milestones of the project have been reached (for example: 'the server is installed'), but only when the services have been transferred over to the IT user. This can, if necessary, include the customers and suppliers of the company.

Before the transfer is complete, functionality tests are carried out and the solution must perform perfectly in the 'Operate' phase. Therefore, this is not only a simple shifting of liquidity flow, but rather the actual transfer of risks by the IT partner, because in the theoretically worst-case scenario, it will only come to light later on in the project that the goals on the business level are not being met, and therefore the initial work done by the IT partner may not recompensed.

This assumes clearly-defined and measurable goals, to which the payment obligation is linked, for example operation over a six-month period with 99.9 percent availability, the reduction of IT system-related resources in operations to a defined number of staff members and the acceleration of business processes, for example the handling of a transaction within a certain length of time. The organization undergoing transformation thus avoids implementation risks, can be assured of a high level of commitment from its IT partner and guarantees that the expected results are actually achieved. This concept is also suitable for government offices and other public sector institutions when converting to 'e-government'. They are about to undergo considerable changes in services, processes and structures.

Tips for implementing the BOT concept (cont.)

- *Select the right contractor* (often a consortium of IT suppliers and supporting companies): As the contractor plays a key role in BOT projects, in the contracting process the focus should not only be on information technology-related criteria, but rather the chosen BOT concept and the willingness and capability of the contractor to assume risks should be evaluated. The role as constructor and temporary operator poses high demands on the management of the client organization, because the responsibility for the transformation process that must be borne is much higher than on classical IT projects.
- *Safeguard transfer of risks to the contractor:*
  In order to ensure the commitment of the IT partner, payments should be made on reaching strategic milestones – as opposed to the way payment is handled in classical projects. This obligates the contractor to provide services over a longer period of time. This is not only a matter of postponing payments, but particularly a postponement of the payment obligation, as it may be necessary for an IT system to be rebuilt if the benefit promised by the IT partner is not delivered. Many IT partners are entering unknown territory here.

One must, however, keep in mind that in such a role the IT partner has the right to demand more influence on the decisions of his client than would be usual in a client-contractor relationship. The IT partner can, for example, demand that the company or government office make decisions vital to the progress of the project within a predefined time, or that he is temporarily integrated in his clearly-defined role into the top and middle management of the client organization, including a temporary transfer of management duties. Otherwise the IT partner will be able to control the project risks.

BOT is particularly suitable for major IT-driven projects and enterprise transformations. It is to be expected that in future a collaboration will exist between the organization and the IT partner similar to that which is the norm in plant construction, including the issues of financing and liability. There are great opportunities for both partners in this new kind of cooperation. The organization can assume a faster and higher-quality enterprise transformation; the IT partner receives a high order volume and has a more comprehensive and demanding role as well as the responsibility for the success of the transformation. A win-win concept with high potential.

Transformation of a payment service provider

A payment service provider founded a business unit as an independent subsidiary, in order to foster growth through the acquisition of new customers and to lower unit costs. However, this business unit possessed no marketing or distribution competence, no competitive IT (among others no client-enabled or ready for release IT systems), neither standard offerings nor customer-tailored solutions. If the newly-founded subsidiary was to have achieved all the necessary improvements on all fronts independently, it would have been in danger of running aground, due to the high level of complexity.

There are basically two possibilities for making the newly-founded subsidiary competitive. Either the enterprise tries to achieve transformation alone over a longer period of time, or it hires a partner to take care of implementing transformation according to the BOT concept. After having talked to various potential partners, five suppliers were invited to submit a Request of Intention (RoI). For the subsequent Request for Proposal (RfP) process, the suppliers were selected according to a scoring model, which in addition to information technological aspects, took into consideration its suitability as a BOT partner in particular, its capability and willingness to assume risks as well as proof of qualifications for successful enterprise transformation.

The ultimately selected BOT partner safeguarded the assumption of risks by streamlining the existing IT platform to the specific requirements of the newly-founded subsidiary, thus limiting the risk for himself and for the subsidiary. The subsidiary was given an IT system, which was an essential prerequisite for its outside market capabilities, was able to concentrate on the market development while the platform was being introduced, and also won the trust of its target customers, as the name of the BOT partner in the relevant market stood for quality and performance. The parent company also reached its goals: the BOT partner carried the implementation risks, as its payment would not be made until after the parent company had taken over the system and after the subsidiary had won new customers. The BOT partner for its part profited from having its entire IT platform introduced, which would only have been possible in partial units in traditional project procedure and which would have meant a smaller order volume.

Checklist: Is the organization of your company ready for the necessary enterprise transformation?	Yes
Has all the creative potential been taken into consideration in the planning of a change and are your customers and suppliers integrated in the organization of the new IT systems, business processes and business structures?	
Is attention being paid to strategic flexibility on major projects?	
Is IT a driver of enterprise transformation? Are the managers and employees of the IT department strategically and operatively competent enough for the business, as well as socially competent enough for change management?	
Is the success of enterprise transformation safeguarded through proactive risk management?	
Is the progress of enterprise transformation being controlled through systematic benefit management?	
Can the company concentrate on its core competencies during enterprise transformation by using BOT partners?	

4.   IT Merger Integration and IT Carve-Out – Fostering External Growth and Disinvestment with IT

Acquiring enterprises and streamlining the portfolio during an external growth strategy are just as much integral parts of the life cycle of large enterprises as innovation and customer orientation are the supporting pillars of internal growth. Just as IT as an enabler for business strengthens the innovation capability of the company and increases customer bonding – thereby forming the basis for internal growth – it is also a success factor for external growth. The merger integration of enterprises always means integrating IT as well, and divesting a business unit always means that the IT system of this business unit is de-integrated from the overall enterprise as well – also called IT carve-out.

As soon as a sector has entered into a consolidation phase, companies are forced to pursue growth through mergers as well as the goal of internal growth or they face becoming the object of a takeover themselves. A comprehensive A.T. Kearney study illustrates the development of consolidating sectors based on a 'Consolidation curve' (figure 16). Here the sectors are listed according to the degree of concentration in the individual sector as a percentage of the sum of the market share of the three largest enterprises of the relevant sector in relationship to world markets, as well as their position in the consolidation life cycle. In each of the four phases of the 'merger endgame' of an industry, IT plays a decisive role:

▤ In the opening phase, there are numerous start-ups, spin-offs of major enterprises or industry segments, which have been liberalized or deregulated. In this phase the number of market participants in an industry increases, until by the end of this phase the highest number of enterprises in an industry has been achieved. For the enterprises in this phase, the issue is to win market share as fast as possible and at the same time build up market penetration barriers to keep out other companies and to obtain first mover advantages. In all this IT plays a decisive role – not only for start-up enterprises.

▤ With the transition to the accumulation phase, enterprises begin to encounter growing cost pressures caused by consolidation, and with rapid growth they reduce their high costs through economies of scale. With the numerous acquisitions that must be integrated in this phase, the capability to integrate IT in the merger integration is essential for the company's survival.

▤ The third phase demands focus. After the rapid growth of past years, most global corporations are now streamlining their portfolios, to divest themselves of divisions not belonging to the core business. The number of acquisitions is on the decline, but their complexity is considerably higher. This also increases the requirements on IT merger integration and calls for the capability of disintegrating the IT of individual business units before a sale.

■ The last phase of the consolidation wave reaches only a few market giants of a given industry. They face the challenge of constantly having to reinvent their core business, in order to survive this phase. Innovative IT investments and at the same time the lowest possible IT spending are key success factors here.

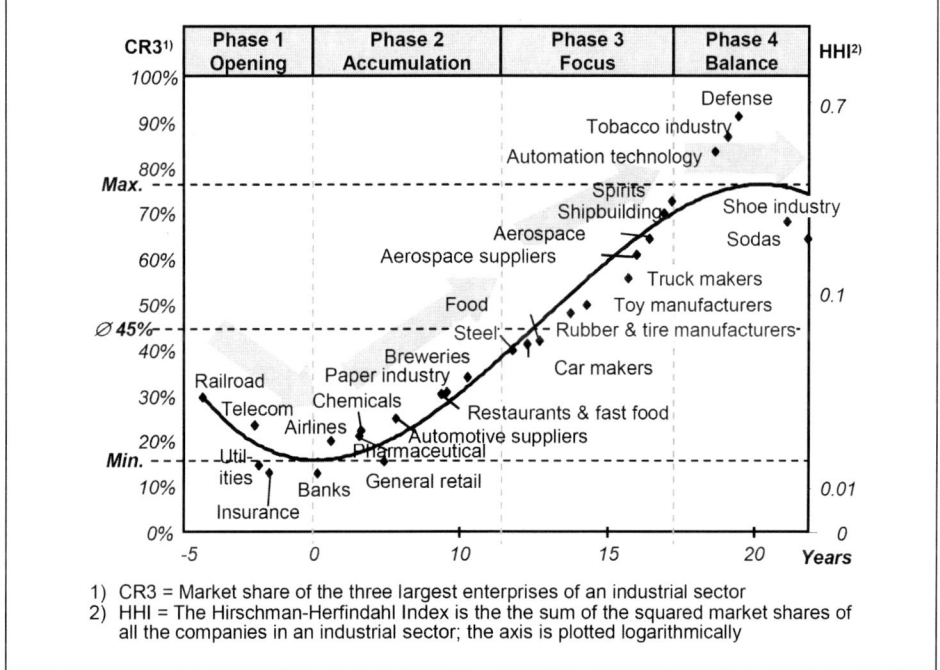

1) CR3 = Market share of the three largest enterprises of an industrial sector
2) HHI = The Hirschman-Herfindahl Index is the the sum of the squared market shares of all the companies in an industrial sector; the axis is plotted logarithmically

Figure 16:   *The consolidation curve; Source: A.T. Kearney*

Fostering growth through mergers and acquisitions is a risky business. 52 percent of mergers destroy the value of the company instead of increasing it. However, one-quarter of all enterprises realize value increases through mergers and subsequent merger integration that which clearly lie above the sector average.

A similar pattern can be seen with disinvestment – the divesting of company assets or business units. Especially for enterprises that grow rapidly and extensively through mergers and acquisitions, the subsequent portfolio adjustment is an important building block for the success of the company. With professional disinvestment management, the strategically correct disinvestment candidates in the enterprise are identified, removed from the company and sold to the highest bidder – and this is all carried out within a manageable timeframe. IT carve-out is a critical process for severing entire parts of a well-functioning unit without having a negative effect on the operations of the company, and at the same time giving the newly-founded company full capacity to act.

Transformation processes of this scope are not possible today without also modifying IT systems. Thus, the evaluation of IT should be an integral part of mergers and disinvestment:

- In the case of fostering growth through mergers, the compatibility of the IT of the company being acquired is already analyzed with the IT-assisted business processes of the acquiring company in the preparatory due diligence phase (for example one company uses Baan, a different SAP application – incompatible!), the synergy potential (for example by consolidating computer centers) must be assessed for IT efficiency, and the hidden chances and risks through large up-and-running or abandoned IT projects must be realistically evaluated. Although many buyers devote themselves to evaluating products, financial situations, company location, synergies and other factors with a lot of commitment and thoroughness, they fail to adequately involve the IT department. Over the course of the integration, IT then often proves to be an important factor for successful company integration – or a hindrance. As part of merger integration, the business processes of both business units must then be linked together – at least whenever the acquired business unit is to be "melted" with the buyer company and not just temporarily kept as a financial investment. As the majority of business processes are usually IT-assisted, a common IT landscape is formed. The building of a comprehensive IT platform ensures the success of the external growth strategy down the line.

- As part of divesting a business unit, in the preparatory phase of the sale the previously integrated IT of the business unit being sold is severed from that of the parent company, thus creating an independent company. This includes, for example, the separation of an SAP system as an independent client or the separation of e-mail and other IT infrastructure systems, including the separation of important contract agreements with the most important suppliers of hardware, software and IT services.

As varied as the requirements on IT merger integration and IT carve-out are in various company situations – it is important to analyze and solve the issues from four IT dimensions:

1. *IT organization:* Step and process organization, distribution of duties/responsibility, process depth/outsourcing, management, application development/maintenance etc.

2. *IT systems:* ERP systems, mail systems, special applications, databases, operating systems etc.

3. *IT infrastructure:* LAN, WAN, server, operations systems etc.

4. *Agreements and licenses:* Software licenses, IT service agreements, maintenance agreements, user rights to company's own and third-party owned soft-ware, rights to data files etc.

As the type and scope of the necessary activities are strongly dependent on the back-ground situation of the IT system and the organizational complexity of the merger or disinvestment, the timeframe for the IT merger integration project can be from 3 to 18 months. Close collaboration with the IT specialists right from the initial phases of acquisition planning and due diligence and/or the disinvestment planning and carve-out will keep down existing risks and accelerate the subsequent integration/disintegration process.

4.1 Successful Mergers with IT Merger Integration

In the past, the greater the strategic significance of IT became– not only for the efficiency of the business processes but also for success on the market side – the larger the role of IT became in the preparation and implementation of company integration. The strategic goal of the merger and the extent to which the IT systems of the merging companies overlap will determine the focus of IT as part of merger integration. Depending on whether the merger is 'horizontal', i.e. the products and markets strongly overlap, or whether the goal is expansion of the product, or geographical expansion or making full use of IT synergies with low market and product synergies, IT will be allotted different tasks (figure 17):

▪ *Same market/product overlapping:* A merger in the same market with strong product overlapping is usually motivated to achieve cost synergies in purchasing, production and administration. In this case IT efficiency gains are top priority. If the merging companies have identical activities, often one of the two IT platforms will form the future platform for the joint company and the other platforms are 'switched off'. If a total IT merger does not seem right for the specific company situation, cost-cutting can nevertheless be achieved in the IT infrastructure (computer centers, networks, e-mail systems etc.), at the IT suppliers (hardware/software/services) as well as standardization of the applications particularly in the financial area.

▪ *Product expansion:* If the acquiring company sees the goal of the merger to be product expansion in related markets, an IT concept similar to those used in mergers with product overlapping is suitable. It should be first determined whether the new or supplementary new products can be supported on the existing IT platform, possibly with lower, product-specific IT expansions.

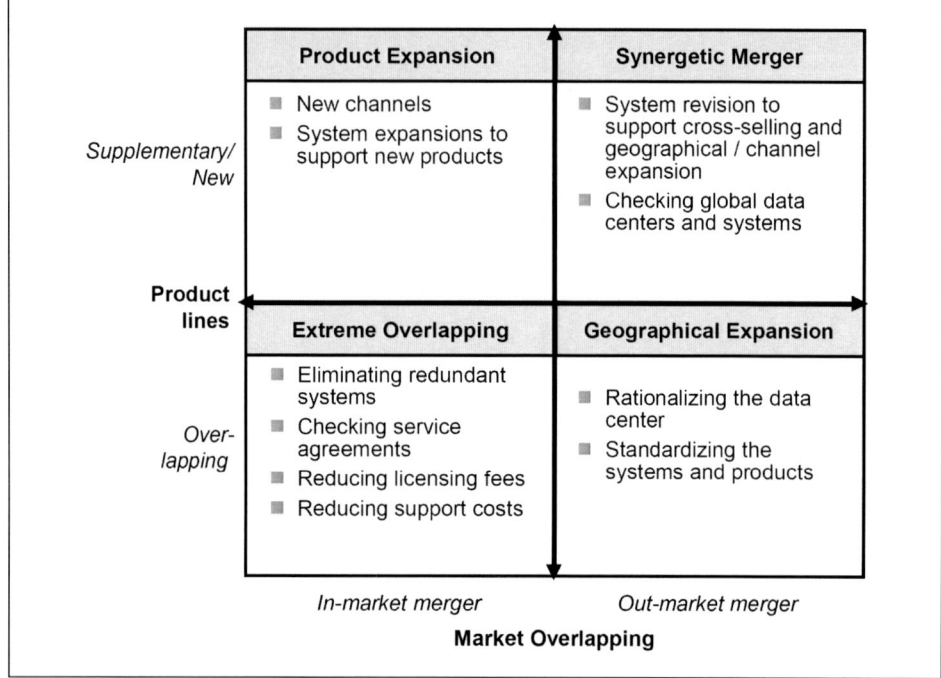

Figure 17:   *Technology focus in the context of a merger;*
                 Source: A.T. Kearney

■ *Geographical expansion:* For mergers with product overlapping in a geographical market that is new for the company, there are often great differences in the requirements on the IT systems in individual markets. Particularly if the new market is also culturally very different, difficulties can arise, for example in consumer behavior or in the taxation and legal framework conditions of a consolidation. This applies, for example, to market penetration in China when acquiring a local company with a similar product range. It would then make sense to look for synergies in the IT infrastructure as well as in the IT systems for the same products in both markets. However, due to the objectively existing differences and great geographical distances, the decision is often made in favor of differing IT systems, each of which covers the special country-specific (for example legal) requirements particularly well. The benefit of such country-specific applications often surpasses by far the impact on costs due to IT standardization. Synergies can therefore only be achieved selectively via IT interfaces or cross-functional IT systems – particularly in the areas of financial consolidation, controlling, purchasing and sales/revenues planning and production program planning, and depending on the sector also in inventory systems and logistics.

■ *Synergetic merger:* New business fields, which show somewhat lower synergies to prior company activities, can, for example, aim at approaching new customer groups, for example if an automobile manufacturer takes a stake in end customer business. Here the possibility of using common IT systems is often restricted to finance management (especially cash flow management and balance sheet consolidation) and to controlling and purchasing. An exception is entry in the upstream or downstream value creation phases. Here the value added chain of the company being acquired is directly connected to the value added chain of the acquiring company. Here IT synergies can be expected in particular at the interfaces as well as in comprehensive planning and capacity utilization control systems (for example comprehensive yield management systems in integrated tourism service providers for the revenue-optimized capacity utilization control of travel agents, flights, hotels and on-the-spot services). Efficiency gains in the scope of IT in a synergetic merger are restricted to general IT infrastructure synergies (for example WAN, computer centers) and joint IT suppliers.

Common to all forms of mergers is the necessity of an integration process to reduce the loss of customers or employees – naturally this also applies to IT employees. Time is an essential factor here. Therefore, as early as the preparation phase of a merger the three important tasks of IT merger integration should be taken into consideration as part of merger integration, and enough time planned for them (see figure 18):

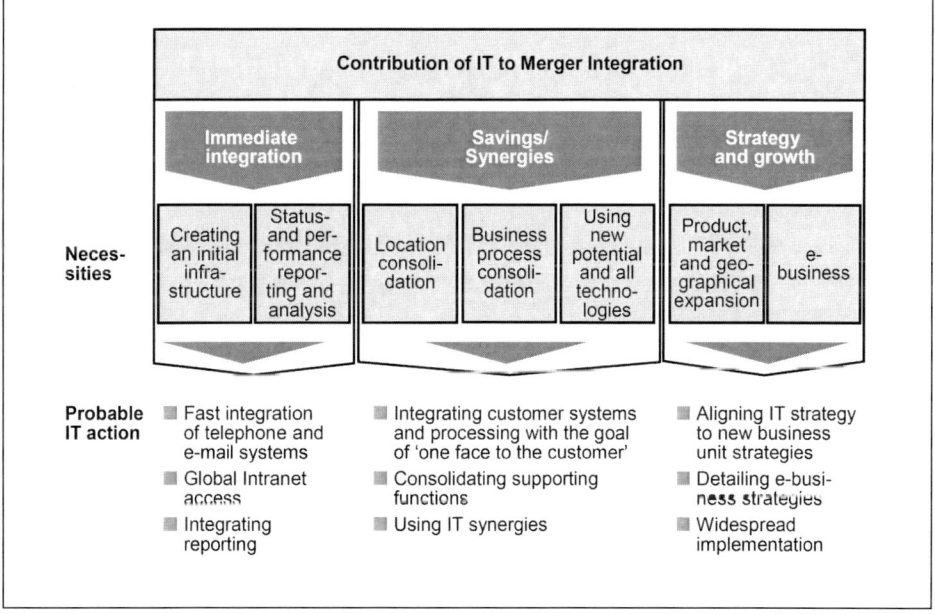

Figure 18:   *The role of IT in merger integration;*
             Source: A.T. Kearney

1. Integration in the IT landscape of the acquiring company, to ensure communication and work capability in the merging companies from 'Day 1' of the merger.

2. Cost reduction and realization of IT synergies, among others through the harmonization and standardization of business-neutral IT processes and IT systems, as well as IT infrastructure, support in consolidating the location (particularly computer centers and help desks) and the consolidation of IT organization.

3. Support of the long-term strategy and growth goals of the company through rapid adaptation of IT strategy to new company goals, to ensure the success of the merger down the line, as well as building a comprehensive IT platform as the basis for further external growth.

IT integration not only supports the primary goals of the merger, but also functions as a driver during the entire integration process, as it also has a positive influence on the other success factors of merger integration:

■ Lack of communication is one of the most frequent causes of mergers failing. IT creates the prerequisites for effective communication with all the parties involved in the merger – both inside and outside the company – from 'Day 1' of the merger.

■ Delays during the integration process are another main cause of mergers failing, as uncertainty about the sense of the merger among the employees of the company and among external market players, as well as not least of all investors and analysts, can have disastrous consequences. Rapid IT merger integration can lead to rapid success, which counteracts this danger and also enables up-to-date and realistic reporting on the implementation progress of the synergies in the business processes, in purchasing and in marketing.

■ If product quality deficits arise after the merger, this can endanger customer satisfaction and lead to losses of market share, which would have almost irrevocable consequences for the company. These are often a result of non-standardized processes and systems, due to inadequate IT merger integration.

■ The loss of important carriers of know-how and other experts in the company can also lead to quality deficits and irritations with customers and suppliers. IT merger integration, which opens up new perspectives and possibilities to act, is an essential contribution towards being able to retain valuable employees in the company.

4.1.1   Ensuring capacity to act from day one through rapid IT integration

Immediately after the acquisition and as one of the first integration measures, an IT 'start-up infrastructure' is set up. It integrates the newly-acquired company in the communication of the acquiring company and opens up the communication channels for the installed change management program. Additionally, it facilitates the transition of the control functions to the new top management personnel through regular, comprehensive reporting and controlling as well as performance and status management of the operational integration efforts (for example the implementation of synergies in purchasing).

Tip for rapidly ensuring ability to act on Day 1:

Fast availability is more important than perfection: The initial IT infrastructure is essentially temporary in character; thus more attention should be paid to rapid availability than perfection and performance.

Communication channels for sending out e-mail to all employees, e-mail circulars, telephone directories and Intranet are considered a matter of course in most enterprises today. But in times of a merger they are not. One of the first duties of IT merger integration, therefore, is to ensure that from the first day of the corporate merger onwards, the senior executives are able to inform all the employees about the strategic orientation of the company, the status quo of the merger and the chances and risks in the market with memos sent through a standardized e-mail and telephone system with a directory.

At the same time, an important issue for the senior executives is to receive complete information about the up-to-the-minute business operations and financial situation of the enterprise, to be able to make strategic decisions, develop cost-cutting potential and, if necessary, comply with instructions from the supervisory authorities. At the same time, it is important to prevent future risks to the integration process early on, in order to maintain their accountability towards external market partners. To this end as well, the in-house reporting must already be fully functioning from the first day of the merger and optimally supported by the IT system.

In the preparatory phase of the merger the central short-term IT requirements must first be identified, which is necessary to ensure the capacity to act of the new senior management staff. The processes for the final balance of the acquired company must be completely supported and the reporting department for the new company management must be in place. For the period of transition to the new management, communication strategies and organization plans must be developed for IT and, not least of all, the prerequisites for realizing cost-cutting measures in the medium-term and supporting corporate strategy with IT must be established.

4.1.2 Realizing cost cutting and synergies

IT merger integration makes an important contribution to merger integration through the generally high cost reductions that can be realized through the synergies of the merger. This applies first and foremost to the business processes after the merger as well as purchasing volumes and sales.

The goal of supporting the implementation of the synergies should be top priority during IT integration activities. Particularly with mergers between enterprises having similar products, the managers of the acquired company strive for cost synergies across the entire value added chain (research and development – purchasing – production – marketing – customer services as well as in administrative and supporting processes). As IT supports all these processes, it makes sense to use it in the implementation of organizational and process synergies as an enabler for the integration. Only if one of the companies simply 'superimposes' its existing process and system landscape over the other company – which seldom happens – will the processes and organization of IT remain as they are. In all other cases major IT adjustments are necessary, even to the point of completely replacing old systems and introducing new IT systems. This leaves 'no stone unturned' in IT after a merger.

Tips for achieving cost savings and synergies:

Concentrate on rapid results, not on technological perfection:
It is also important here not to strive for a perfect IT solution, but rather for implementing the doable quickly. By modularizing the existing IT landscape that supports the integration requirements, we can avoid a sequence in the processing of the IT requirements that is technically-driven and removed from the realization of operational synergies, possibly even opposed.

Financing initiatives for business process integration from IT optimization:
With a sufficient IT budget, generally speaking IT can easily finance the necessary initiatives from its own cost savings. The IT cost potential after a merger lies among others in a reduction of various existing IT products, particularly in the area of software development, in joining and standardizing software licenses, in standardizing the office environment and in consolidating data, IT services and the IT infrastructure, if necessary through outsourcing (*cf.* Part 3 of this book).

During the preparations for 'Day 1' the existing and planned IT initiatives for the integration of the two merging enterprises must already have be identified and evaluated. As the resources and budgets for implementing IT integration are generally limited, the initiatives must be prioritized and implemented in the correct order. Two goals of the new company management are key here: Besides the realization of cost-cutting potential it is important to achieve fast and visible success, in order to make all interest groups – particularly supervisory boards, shareholders and analysts – clearly aware of the value of the merger. An important matter is signaling continuity to external market partners. Integrating customer systems and processes of both merging enterprises with the goal of a standardized market presence ('one face to the customer') is an important step here. Of course this also applies to the interfaces to suppliers and other interested parties, for example supervisory authorities.

The employees are also a critical target group in the first period after integration. The existing resources necessary for implementing future IT projects and any gaps must be recognized right away, in order to show existing employees new perspectives and to retain know-how within the company.

In the area of reducing costs after the merger, IT has two 'construction sites' to work on: the IT initiatives that aim at delivering cost reductions in business processes, as well as the cost reducing potential within the IT department itself – whereby the former should have clear priority here. Through the support of the business-oriented goals of the merger – be it location consolidation, business process consolidation or the market-side utilization of targeted growth and new technologies – in the first period after the merger IT merger integration can make the best contribution to the long-term success of a merger.

The measures for integrating business processes incur varying levels of expenditure and promise varying levels of synergy potential. IT should give priority to supporting those which have the highest potential. This operational prioritizing criteria leads to a number of changes in the scope of IT, for example shared suppliers of both merging enterprises can only be recognized if the IT of the enterprises each provides an appropriate database. To begin with, IT should therefore support the new company initiatives through a rapid IT merger integration (particularly of the IT organization and IT systems), through a rapid alignment of the business processes, harmonization of the information flow, and joint project planning and control instruments, before cost cutting in the IT department can be realized.

Takeover of an international manufacturing company by a German conglomerate

A German conglomerate took over the majority stake in an international manufacturer headquartered in France. There were production locations in France, Asia and in the USA. As is usual in this industrial sector, there was no order-based production. The company's inventories often lasted for many months. Due to the tense market situation in the specialized market segment of the newly-acquired company and the negative revenue contribution to the group results, it quickly became clear that the purpose of the acquisition – profitable market development in a short time – could only be achieved through better company management and a closer relationship to the proprietor.

Without integrating the IT landscapes, managing and controlling the manufacturing company with the existing human resources was not possible. Additionally, the systems used by the manufacturing company and the quality of the installed IT services were far from corresponding with the standard in the rest of the conglomerate.

The task of IT merger integration consisted in harmonizing not only the group processes, particularly the inventory management, billing and controlling, with the group standards, but also improving the communication between the enterprises through the integration, in particular, of e-mail and directory services, thus cementing them more closely. As part of this, the French ERP system was replaced with only marginal modifications by the standard SAP template of the conglomerate. The technical infrastructure – particularly the operating system and the e-mail system – were standardized, and the locations of the new company were linked via VPN technology and smaller locations via DSL to the group network. Comprehensive training measures assisted the French employees in their conversion to the new IT systems.

After only a few weeks the technical integration of the infrastructure, including the standardization, was complete. The introduction of the SAP template, however, proved to be more complicated than planned. The head office of the group had seriously underestimated the scope of the enormously important user training courses for aligning the business processes at the location. Only after head office had intervened with support could the initial difficulties be overcome.

4.1.3 Fostering long-term external growth strategies

After the first cost and potential benefit from a merger have been realized, the IT department can devote its attention to setting up an IT architecture, which supports all the strategic and operative requirements of the new company down the line. For processes with strategic relevance, e.g. for securing market shares or for distinguishing the company from the competition, for operative and transaction processes and databases, middleware and IT infrastructure, the existing IT solutions must be checked, evaluated and if necessary new solutions initiated.

IT strategy is aligned to the new corporate strategy, to identify new solutions that will foster further growth in the long term. Depending on the focus of the merger, these solutions can apply to e-business or cross-selling. These also include unavoidable trivialities like the multilingualism of the systems or transaction-oriented online processing in 24-hour operations, which is possible due to globalization (loss of backup and maintenance windows), and also more fundamental business-driven changes, for example in the acquisition of additional country units with marketing and production units with connected European or global production and logistics.

Aligning IT strategy is a suitable occasion, regardless of the current necessity of IT integration, to also secure any future merger plans of the company with suitable IT projects. Particularly if the enterprise has geographical expansion plans it is a good idea to systematically develop IT into an international platform for realizing product or process innovations – i.e. to pursue a 'platform strategy'.

Contrary to the standardization of processes, a platform strategy orientates itself to IT at the product and/or customer segments and allows not only similarities but also specific dissimilarities (for example a product that is the same all over Europe, but which has a different name in each of the countries, with different marketing and pricing). Realizing the IT platform therefore aims at achieving synergies without complete standardization.

This task becomes more demanding, the more a company grows into a globally thinking and operating corporation. The country-specific orientation still evident in many industrial sectors must make way for a global structure with universal global responsibilities for individual business units, to be able to offer identical products and services all over the world. A correspondingly worldwide uniform IT architecture with worldwide uniform business processes is the prerequisite, for example, for developing the advantages of a global customer management from uniform coordination and universal organization – with the lowest possible level of country-specific individuality.

The telecommunications industry is currently following such product or customer segment driven IT platform strategies in the area of cellular communications. Based on the goal of pan-European branding and therefore universal customer bonding as well as a high level of recognition, Vodafone, for example, with 'Vodafone Live!' creates a uniform product in Germany, Ireland, Italy, the Netherlands, Portugal, Spain, Sweden and the UK with increasing system networking in the background. Similar goals are achieved by MMO2 with its 'XDA', as well as Orange with 'Orange World' and KPN/E-Plus with 'i-mode'. Deutsche Telekom aims to realize IT platforms, for example in the area of billing. All these telecommunications providers harmonize major parts of their product-related IT as well as the accompanying business process-oriented and administrative IT systems, in order to realize such an IT platform. Other parts of IT, which have no direct relation to such European telecommunication products, are not affected by IT platform building.

The effectiveness and efficiency advantages of a product-driven or customer-segment-driven IT platform will become clear in these examples:

- The telecommunication provider is given more strategic options for marketing its products (for example, simultaneously in several countries vs. in only one country) and can increase customer bonding as well as the turnover per customer (for example through pan-European availability of the product for business travelers).

- The time-to-market becomes shorter because the development resources are consolidated and solutions can be shared. This means that sales can be realized sooner.

- Cost reductions arise from avoiding multiple developments and from consolidating demand according to joint IT solutions for building IT platforms.

It is equally important that, particularly in European or global enterprises, establishing common products and IT platforms has the positive side effect of improving the mutual understanding of the senior executives and employees of the individual country locations, thereby strengthening cultural integration.

When such a comprehensive IT platform is established, a picture of the IT landscape is created that is differentiated according to products and customer groups. Based on a common IT system for products or customer groups, the business processes and IT systems in further areas can also be harmonized and integrated, for example, financial processes by realizing a comprehensive financial shared services center on the basis of uniform IT systems. Whether or not this makes sense in individual cases is determined by the portion of standardized products and/or customer groups there is. For example, in a European conglomeration with 20 percent (or less) international and 80 percent local products, the comprehensive European IT platform is oriented to the support of the comprehensive 20 percent, while the IT support of all other processes is more locally oriented. If the relationship should shift in the medium or long term, building a pan-European standardized IT platform would seem the obvious choice, in which any peculiarities of the local products and country-specific differences can be taken into due consideration.

It is not only the telecommunications industry that is building European or global IT platforms. Globally operating automobile manufacturers also already have such IT platforms or are in the process of creating them, not only in passenger cars but also in the commercial vehicle segment. And the major aerospace manufacturers and suppliers are also creating these kinds of IT platforms, for example to shorten product development time through 24-hour development according to the 'follow-the-sun' principle, or for shifting specific manufacturing jobs to low-wage countries. Many other industries are also working on the basis of global IT platforms on such globalization themes.

Checklist: Does your company use IT for smooth integration of mergers or takeovers?	Yes
For 'Day 1':	
Are the existing IT structures of both enterprises analyzed and are short-term opportunities as well as medium-term needs for action identified?	
Has a plan for fastest-possible realization of a comprehensive reporting for control of the merger progress been set up?	
Have data network connections between important subsidiaries and locations been set up?	
Are the e-mail directories consolidated so that the employees have a uniform system to work with?	
Is access for all employees to the Intranet assured?	
Can a controlling/merger control tool be implemented?	
Are the legal requirements, among others from the financial and taxation point of view, supported and/or fulfilled by IT?	
For implementing merger goals:	
Have the strategic goals of the IT merger integration been approved?	
Are the IT implementation measures for fulfilling the synergy goals clearly outlined and prioritized, responsibilities allocated, milestones date-planned and implementation budgets allocated?	
Are the roles and responsibilities coordinated in the scope of the IT of the new organization?	
Does continual and non-conflicting communication take place with all internal and external parties?	

4.2 Divesting Operations Successfully with IT Carve-out

Regularly checking corporate strategy, evaluating the current strategic positioning and the chances for growth are normal measures that are taken in most enterprises. In the past few years the search for cost-cutting possibilities and improvement potential was high on the agenda of many senior executives. It is especially important to check all business units for their strategic contribution to the overall success of the company, to verify their proximity to the core business as well as their growth potential and the sustainability of market success. If at the same time disinvestment candidates are identified, the question arises of their value and growth potential and not least of all a potential buyer who would be prepared to pay the highest possible price for the business unit.

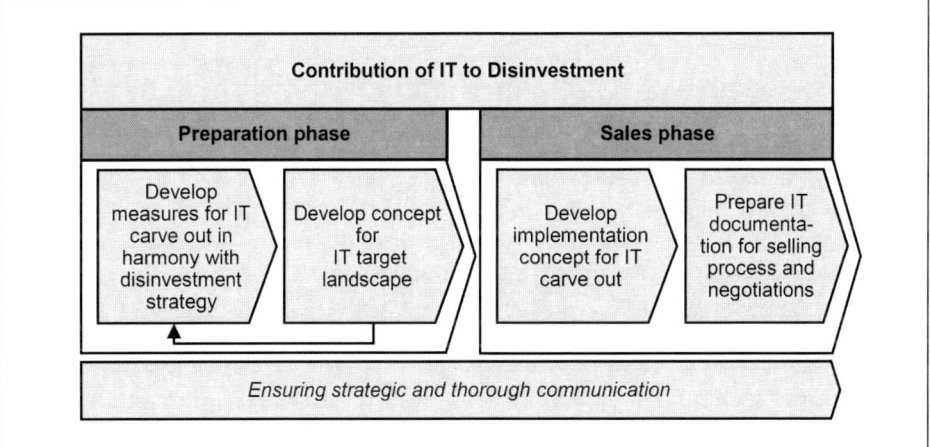

Figure 19:   *The role of IT in disinvestment;*
                 Source: A.T. Kearney

IT carve-out plays a critical role in this process – not only in the preparatory but also in the selling phase of disinvestment (figure 19). It must ensure that the company being divested is already independently capable of doing business before the sale is completed, to enable rapid integration with the buyer. An insufficient IT carve-out in the preparatory phase can considerably reduce the value of the company unit for a buyer.

4.2.1   Preparing business units for disinvestment

Before the actual selling process begins all necessary measures must be in place to make the company being divested independent and capable of doing business. In the preparation phase of disinvestments, the IT department has to identify the IT dependencies between the divesting company and the disinvestment candidate in accordance with the disinvestment strategy of the company, and to define the requirements on IT carve-out. This also includes the analysis of the IT cost structures for the company to be divested and the evaluation of possible risks arising through the removal of the business unit, to avoid possible conflicts with the buyer after the sale.

Tip for preparing a disinvestment:

Pay attention to apparently unimportant factors:
For carrying out IT carve-out, you need correct and up-to-the-minute service and cost data for the business unit being divested. Apparent trivialities gain enormous significance here, for example the establishment of a precise measuring procedure for the use and billing of telephone and network services. Advisable is a separate contract with the telephone/ network operator. Here again, cost breakdowns after a disinvestment are often the cause of disagreements – particularly in the case of major changes to the breakdown of human resource expenditure.

From the perspective of a company-wide optimized IT support, generally speaking it is advisable to carefully weigh up doing without partial solutions and redundant structures in individual business units and rather to consider harmonizing and standardizing IT applications and infrastructure as well as procurement processes in IT. In the case of a disinvestment, however, shared hardware and software, as well as common network resources hinder the divested business unit's capacity to do business independently. Before the sale, therefore, assets such as hardware and software licenses must be transferred to the business unit being divested in accordance with requirements; jointly used agreements must be distributed. If the business unit being divested continues to use the centralized IT resources of the parent group, e.g. the computer center, service agreements must be drawn up to bridge the time gap until the IT integration into the divesting company and the switch to its centralized IT resources have been completed. If possible, however, the company being divested should avoid continued use of the assets of the former parent company, as the proportionate calculation of the costs for the use and maintenance of these assets often provides reason for disagreements with the new owner after the sale.

In the preparation phase, the divesting company sets down the necessary measures in a disinvestment concept and prepares an implementation plan. At the end of this phase the disinvestment is prepared to the point of ensuring that a smooth disinvestment of the business unit will ensue. It is the task of the IT department to prepare a concept for the future IT landscape of the business unit being divested and to identify some initial solutions as well as potential 'quick wins' for the disinvestment. For the business unit being divested the IT requirements must be set down and prioritized according to operational benefit criteria. The existing IT infrastructure and IT systems must be checked and compared with the best practices of the sector-specific IT landscape.

Divesting four business units of a technology conglomeration

A conglomerate wanted to divest its fully integrated technology unit. When preparing the disinvestment the company unit was divided up into four parts, which would clearly fetch a higher selling price when sold to investors than the entire business unit together. Up to that point, a central IT department was responsible for the entire infrastructure as well as the commercial applications (SAP R/3) and the office communication of all of the locations in Germany.

Before the disinvestment took place, the central IT department was outsourced to an IT service provider. To control the situation, the position of CIO was established in the company. While the foreign companies, who had access to their own IT systems, simply allowed themselves to be allocated to one of the newly-created business units, the six locations in Germany were closely interwoven. Therefore, the IT landscape had to firstly be divided into four independent units, which were then to be integrated into the IT landscapes of the individual investors to maximize value.

To begin with, the IT landscape was analyzed: Which commercial and scientific systems were present? Which IT costs arise where? Which inputs (users, end devices etc.) exist? What is the IT organization like? What technical infrastructure is there? Next, in each of the new business units a lean CIO organization for IT planning and controlling as well as control of the IT service providers was established.

The existing operative SAP systems were copied for the new business units and the data distributed accordingly. One system was segmented through a client copy, which technically speaking was the simpler solution, although in retrospect there were high SAP operating costs and a more complicated archiving system. The second system was completely reinvented ('green meadow' concept) and preselected data was entered.

In retrospect, this concept proved to be the best practice. For economic reasons, both of the new small, low-staff business units introduced slimmer 'package' ERP systems such as Datev or Navision. During the segmentation process the SAP system was spared a release change – these investments were not covered by a higher sales price.

The division of the infrastructure was an issue at the locations that were used by several business units: every business unit should only have access to its own data and applications. This of course meant foregoing the IT synergies. To avoid a cost explosion, particularly expensive infrastructure components like firewalls, servers, routers, etc. were to be shared as before.

To begin with, the existing IT assets such as PCs, servers etc. were distributed as well as possible among the business units and the shared components were left with the residual company. The local networks, including the user structures, mail, server, etc., as well as the WAN and the telephone infrastructure, particularly the billing, were severed and the data files also distributed to the business units.

In addition, existing software, hardware and IT service agreements were distributed among the business units and inputs and requirement structures were adapted, whereby the original conditions were to remain the same for the business units for as long as possible. This proved to be especially difficult in the case of the service agreement with the IT outsourcer, as the contractual risk had risen for him for one, and for another it had become difficult for him to realize synergies between the four business units. In particular the specification of inputs – decisive criteria for profitability – shrunk considerably. Together with the IT service provider, therefore, consolidation activities were carried out that permitted him to offer the four business

units new agreements at normal market conditions. Additionally, new service agreements were completed for utilization of the infrastructure overlapping more than one business unit between the residual companies and the business units at normal market conditions.

Chiefly due to regulations and legal reporting obligations, the electronic archiving of historical data – particularly marketing, product and personnel data remained IT activities. For the remaining commercial activities of the residual companies (processing, pensioners etc.) a simple Datev ERP solution was set up, which was transferred to the ERP system of the disinvestor after the entire business unit was dissolved.

4.2.2   Supporting the sales phase with IT carve-out

During the actual disinvestment of the company, IT disintegration plays a special role. A 'disinvestment highway code' sets down the necessary steps and differentiates between short-term necessary measures and those activities that are only carried out in response to specific requests from the buyer, in accordance with his conditions. In the short term and in any case it is essential to sever the e-mail system. The more complicated and far more important separation of, for example, the production planning and control systems as well as further logistics or R&D systems should, on the other hand, be discussed with the buyer. It would be ideal to switch from the former IT landscape directly to the IT systems of the buyer, while safeguarding the disinvestment item's capacity to act, without having to set up a temporary IT landscape of their own, particularly for logistics and finance systems.

In order to safeguard the disinvestment item's capacity to act, the new company must avail of autonomous IT services. For this, the IT department must ensure not only IT services that are vital to survival, but also guarantee their payment. In framework agreements for hardware and software as well as for maintenance, an agreement is made to keep the existing contracts for the interim period. For billing and reporting, however, a separate system as well as a separate accounting cycle for the divested company is an absolute must. This can be done within the framework of an SAP system that is, as before, shared.

Tip for the selling phase of a disinvestment:

Ensure continual communication:
The migration of important carriers of know-how can considerably reduce the value of the business unit being sold. Therefore, continual communication between the staff and between the IT department and the disinvestment team in the company are absolutely essential.

If the number of users and employees and the revenues and complexity of the divested company are not critical for the ERP software used to date, there are two alternatives:

- Selecting a simple, less complex but sufficiently functional package software and the migration of data from the old system

- Sharing a simple ERP system, which is made available by an IT service provider, for example as part of a workstation (ASP) operation model.

- If it makes economic sense to continue using the existing ERP system, there are two feasible alternatives:

- Creating a client copy and selectively erasing data that is no longer needed. This is less complex in terms of technology and content, but means that use of the system is basically the same as before.

- Setting up a new client on the basis of a template and input the old data. This is more complicated in terms of content, but enables the adjustment to the requirements of the divested company and helps get rid of 'dead wood'.

For the actual sales negotiations and the transition of the disinvestment item to the buyer it is the job of the IT department to make the various IT options for the new company, including a cost outline, and the data structures of the new company transparent for the buyer, here again in order to avoid the danger of later conflicts.

Checklist: Can you avoid the most important risks of IT disinvestment?	Yes
Does the business unit being divested have capacity to act alone?	
Is the IT organization of the disinvestment item prepared for future requirements in terms of the number and qualifications of its employee?	
Are the ERP systems of the divesting company and the business unit to be divested separated from one another?	
Have all necessary licenses, assets and agreements for the business unit to be divested been prepared?	
Is the transition of IT services to the buyer of the business unit contractually safe-guarded?	
Are all rights to data and programs clarified?	

5. Green IT –
Meeting Social Responsibility through IT

There is wide agreement in research and science, as well as in society, politics and economics, that increasing CO_2 emissions are a major cause of the climate change: While CO_2 emissions amounted to 21 billion tons worldwide in 1990, more than 36 billion tons are forecasted for the year of 2020. At the same time the global temperature is rising significantly, regardless of the particular scenarios, which vary gradually at best but not by trend. CO_2 emissions are not getting positive mentions by science and politics anymore. The German Bundesregierung therefore set a CO_2 reduction target of 40 percent until the year 2020 and demands likewise a contribution from society and industry, for instance through saving energy, avoiding unnecessary traffic or using renewable energy sources. On the other hand, an increase in CO_2 emissions in the IT-sector by more than 200 percent is expected for the time span of 2000 to 2020.

Reason for this is first of all the increase in internet usage, a higher IT-penetration level through special solutions like CRM (Customer Relationship Management) or SCM (Supply Chain Management), the rising distribution of computer-intensive architectures, e.g. SOA (Service Oriented Architecture), or the rising IT performance capability (better response times, higher degree of availability etc.). CO_2 emissions caused by IT constitute by all means the most significant amount of 600 million tons worldwide per annum (basis 2007). This represents the annual CO_2 emission of almost 320 million small cars. 60 billion trees would be needed for compensation. A.T. Kearney verified this through the results of a study conducted in the year 2008.

First and foremost, the IT-industry needs to create innovative concepts and solutions for decreasing their energy use. At the same time IT is stuck between a rock and a hard place right here:

- IT can cause considerable savings of CO_2 emissions: IT-based innovations and active participation of IT on the CO_2-strategy can reduce the costs of CO_2 emissions. This leads to the sustainable improvement of a company's as well as entire regions' total energy balance. And this holds true especially for production and logistics in energy-intensive industry-sectors, such as energy, steel or chemistry.

- IT can cause a substantial increase of CO_2 emissions: customers of internal and external IT-services always expect top-performing applications, shorter response times, higher security and global availability. Additionally, the rising competitive pressure has more and more impact on a company's IT. In this way and because of the challenge in dealing with new technologies and their capabilities, companies of almost all industry-sectors increasingly depend on IT to hold or extend their competitive advantages.

Exposed to this pressure the majority of IT-organisations will change significantly – and already did change to some extent. Taking the right direction towards business requirements is important for a company, even if this leads to an increase of CO_2 emissions caused by the energy need of the electronic data processing centres (EDPC). However, it is important for the energy balance to cut the CO_2 emissions down at the same time. But there are ways to "square the circle:"

- IT as an object of climate protection ("Green IT"): Through consequent implementation of, as already mentioned, well-known energy-saving concepts IT can cut its total CO_2-emission in half.

- IT as an enabler of climate protection ("Green Business"): Besides its own CO_2-reduction-potential, IT is one of the important levers to create a green, emission-reduced Core Business of the entire company.

Green IT becomes a CIO issue: With the help of Green Business the *obligation* to even better protect the climate can be reached, and at the same time remain a *pleasure*.

5.1   Green IT: Turning IT into a "Green" Object of Climate Protection

If IT wants to halve its CO_2 emissions through consequent implementation of energy-saving concepts, the most important act is to reduce the amount of physical servers through the virtualisation and harmonisation of applications. Since servers empirically are used to less than one third of their capacity, this would mean a reduction of five million tons CO_2 emissions p.a. in Germany alone. Energy-efficient cooling-solutions for existing systems and an optimised building-design for future EDPC's could save around half a million tons of CO2 emission.

Green IT in some cases means also outsourcing of hardware and operations to energy-efficient services, which can use idle capacities more efficiently. These actions could reduce the CO2 emissions to an additional of four million tons p.a., if IT services can manage to meet the rising ecological requirements of their customers.

Exhibit 20 shows the ten most important activities for IT-related CO2 reduction:

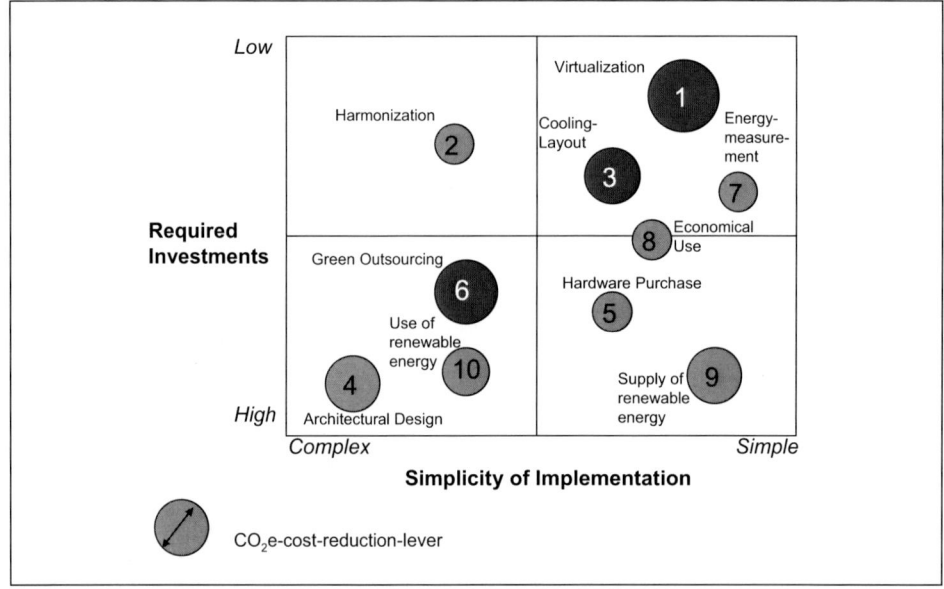

Figure 20: Ten actions for IT-related CO2-reduction

5.1.1 Actions for IT-related CO2-reduction

Server Consolidation

A substantial driver for energy use and CO2 emissions is the amount of EDPC-driven servers – if the amount can be reduced, this means a significant low energy use at the same time, less IT-caused CO2 emissions and – as spin-off – less IT costs as well. Two major levers can be used here, the lever of *1) virtualisation* and the lever of *2) application harmonisation:* virtualisation is a process, which partitions one and the same hardware-resource into several independent working units. One physical server can therefore simulate several independent-working virtual servers. This decoupling of hardware and software enables improvement of the server's utilization and respectively a reduction of the amount of physical servers. Reduction of physical servers through harmonisation of applications is more difficult: Many business departments make use of for their requirements optimised IT applications. Such applications are often isolated and lead to a heterogeneous, unmanageable application landscape. Application harmonisation reduces the amount of applications through migration to a broader ERP system. The underlying infrastructure can equally be consolidated and therefore be reduced.

Energy-efficient Cooling Solutions and Building-Design

Depending on whether an existing EDPC has to be reconfigured, or a new EDPC has to be built, the possibilities differ in size to influence energy-efficiency through *3) cooling-layout solutions.* Even in existing systems there is room for creativity: modern cooling solutions use row-based cooling systems. In this process heat exchangers are placed between the rack rows to chill the IT equipment down from front to back. The equivalent partition into warm- and cold-periods avoids the mixing of warm and cold air and offers a much more efficient cooling, than the traditional room-based cooling solutions. Even more opportunities generate when a new EDPC is to be built, ideally as "passive-computer-center." EDPC is understood as an element of passive *4) building design,* in which a major part of the heat requirement is covered by "passive" sources, such as insulation and rejected heat of persons or technical equipment. The waste heat, actually a fall-out, enables savings through reduced heating costs of other parts of the building. However, such a concept requires enormous structural measures.

Hardware-Purchase and Green IT (Out-)Sourcing

The *5) purchase of various hardware components* in combination determines the power consumption of the end device. Old hardware cannot compete with new energy-efficient technologies and should be replaced wherever possible. Currently the energy-use is irrelevant in purchasing IT-equipment since Total Cost of Ownership (TCO) is not taken into account. Flat screens for instance use two third of energy less compared to CRT displays. With daily eight-hour use, the purchase price will have paid off in less than two years. If *6) Green Outsourcing* of hardware and operations is carried out by an energy-efficient service, energy-efficient infrastructure services, which recognised the issue of "green EDPC's" at an early stage and implemented those through intelligent EDPC-controlling, can perform in this way instead of trimming the own EDPC into "green" through several measures and investments. There are several suppliers, as for example T-Systems and IBM, which advertise their initiatives in a media-effective way.

Energy-efficient Consumer Behaviour

Changing consumer behaviour can also make users more aware by *7) energy measuring and energy transparency*. Following a survey of the Chip-manufacturer Intel, 80 percent of companies are not aware of their office equipment's energy use, although up to 75 percent of energy use can be saved in the office. Guidelines and communication measures in terms of energy use where consumers put hardware in cause rethinking and change of behaviour. Also EDPC-Benchmarking should be taken into account. Further there is *8) energy-efficient hardware use* (turning-off, power management): IT-users also play an important role here: IT equipment often is not turned off by the user, who leaves his workplace for a longer period of time (e.g. at the end of a workday). This wastes a lot of energy needlessly. An intelligent power management can reduce the energy-use within a working day by turning hardware components, which are not actively involved in the manufacturing process, into standby mode. This can reduce the energy-consumption by up to 90 percent.

Adopting and Using Renewable Energies

With *9) adopting renewable energy* for IT-power supply: during power plant-operations for power supply CO_2 emissions are generated. The amount of emissions depends on the power-mix of the electric energy-supplier (nuclear power, brown coal, stone coal, gas). By switching the supplier of the traditional power-mix to an electric energy-supplier of renewable energies (e.g. water- or wind-power), the so-called green electricity and the volume of emissions of climate-hostile CO_2 can be reduced. By *10) using renewable energies,* such as a solar heating systems on the roof of a data processing service center, electricity-use out of domestic production becomes possible, instead of purchasing electricity from external suppliers with traditional power-mix. In this way the user of the EDPC invests into the construction of a systems for electricity generation out of renewable energies, as for instance a solar heating system on the roof of the data processing service center, and therefore demonstrates personal responsibility concerning environmental-friendly and sustainable development and uses electricity from renewable energies.

Case Study STRATO:
Green Data Centre at a Hosting Service Provider

The hosting service provider STRATO AG already kept up with the times at an early stage. Today, Damien Schmidt, CEO of STRATO AG, is proud of his CO_2-neutral data processing service center. "A computer cannot operate without electricity, but without CO_2 emissions very well." And STRATO shows, how it goes. Since the beginning of the year 2006, the responsible persons concern themselves with the issue of saving electricity and costs in the computer center but also with reducing the STRATO-caused CO_2 emissions at the same time. In doing so, three areas of energy-reduction were identified: hardware, building services engineering and software.

- **Hardware** – energy-efficient and powerful: besides performance new computer center components are evaluated regarding their energy-efficiency. For example the shared webhosting platform of STRATO AG in Karlsruhe is saving up to 90 percent energy on the central processing unit (CPU)-level with the help of the Sun Microsystems T2000-Server with UltraSPARC "Niagara" processors compared to the forerunning system.

- **Building Services Engineering** – cooling on the spot: warm and cold periods allow highest energy saving-rates: beginning at the front the servers are fed with cold air, drawn in and heated at the hardware-rear side and then delivered back to the climate control unit. Special covers and measuring-sensors provide a precise supply of cooling air during cold periods. In this way only individual server and rows are chilled down and not the entire EDPC.

- **Software** – focused on energy efficiency: in search of energy efficiency STRATO discovered energy-saving potential in the less obvious software area as well. Important savings today are generated through performance-optimised, custom-fit and machine-oriented software. The operating system Solaris 10 is precisely justified toward the requirements of the STRATO AG-shared webhosting platform and nearly saves 30 percent of energy in comparison to the forerunner. Even the self-developed Spam filter manages on a tenth of the resources, which standard systems require. The principle is clear. The fewer steps in calculations are needed to achieve a result, the lower the electricity use will be. Subsequently, the goal of STRATO-software-development is its highest efficiency.

With the help of different measures, STRATO was able to reduce the energy use per customer by around 30 percent within 18 months. Since 2008 STRATO is purchasing the entire electricity-amount (ca. 13 percent of the performance of an average power plant) from NaturEnergie AG which is generated from 100 percent CO_2-free and environmental-friendly water power (TÜV-certificated). The vision of a CO_2-free computer center became reality.

5.2 Green Business: Using IT as Enabler for Climate Protection

Besides the effect of its own CO_2 reduction potential, IT is one of the crucial levers for the creation of a green, emission-reduced core business for the entire company. By acting in a consistent way, IT can in this way turn into a climate-saver, since more than 97 percent of a company's CO_2 emissions are caused by core business, depending on the industry-sector.

Taking adequate actions in the core business have a much higher effect, as if IT would be treated as an isolated unit. Since IT itself is responsible for only three percent of emissions, CIO's should think outside the box by taking the entire company's perspective and deal with the CO_2 problem in a pro-active, constructive and cross sector way.

IT has the chance to actively co-develop a company's CO_2 strategy and to strengthen all areas of the core business with the help of IT supported innovations for CO_2 reduction. Communication- and collaboration technologies help decreasing the business volume cross-functionally, as for example through video conferences. New technologies and a powerful infrastructure led to fundamental improvements in quality, which enabled an atmosphere of video conferences, in which it seems as everybody would be in the same room. Together with user-friendliness of the conference-solution this leads to higher user-acceptance and to stronger use of video conferencing – with the result of less time and cost intensive meetings. This is how high savings can be made and more productive working time can be generated.

Detailed Recommendation for Reducing CO2 Emissions

Also sector-specific there are several possibilities to reduce CO_2 emissions of the core business with the help of IT:

- With the promotion of Online-Banking financial service providers achieve less customer traffic and reduce the paper use. Cashless payment transactions in the long term mean less production of cash and less cash transport.

- Telecommunication companies should make use of central services more often, such as the T-Net Box, and therefore avoid the use of complex local hardware. Also the increasing use of energy-efficient network-hardware and power management – especially for base stations – would lead to sustainable energy savings.

- For car manufacturers the use of software-based energy-saving functions in cars pays off, e.g. through auto-start-stop functions. Computer-based design and simulation in production as well as climate-efficient controlling of the value chain in the areas of capacity utilisation, network-design and transportation with the help of "Best-practice"-PP-systems.

- In the trade-area, effective controlling of branch- and central warehouse-supply as well as local provisioning means less traffic and in turn causes less emissions. Further with the provision of trading platforms IT can use the existing cargo effectively to full capacity.

- Power suppliers benefit from an optimised IT-control of generation through intelligent Merit Order systems, less manual reading of the meter by intensified use of "Smart Metering" and a CO_2-optimised control of the material flow during power generation.

The consulting firm A.T. Kearney undertakes "Green Business" within the scope of its global sustainability strategy as well, i.e. climate-neutrality of the company within two years. This shall be achieved through cutting its own emissions down (a major part of those emissions arises from the travelling of the consultants) as well as through investing in climate-protection projects, which meet highest international climate-protection standards. A direction which could be taken by many small and medium-sized companies.

5.3   Green IT and Green Business Mean Ecology and Cost Minimising at the same Time

There are several ways for companies, which are interested in Green IT and Green Business. First and foremost, it is all about safeguarding the energy-efficiency. Most of the companies still have to get some homework done in this area. Thereto the goal of "energy-efficiency" has to be set in the IT-strategy at first and lines of communication with the core business have to be opened, which pave the way for collective measure-taking and evaluating. On this basis IT-energy-efficiency can be increased through virtualisation, Green (out-)sourcing and intelligent cooling solutions. Therefore, innovative IT-solutions for the reduction of CO2-usage in the core business have to be determined. All those approaches can – implemented in action plans – quickly be realised.

Companies of the IT-industry find themselves in a different situation. They have to focus on innovation to grow in the environment of Green IT with the help of innovative offerings, to determine market potential for green IT-services and software solutions as well as to develop client-specific offers. Therefore, investments in the development of green products have to be extended. In this way a major contribution to offer energy-efficient solutions for IT-users can be made and on this basis new ideas and solutions can be developed and brought to market.

Sustainability is becoming more and more important for all companies. The numerous examples of Green IT show that – not least because of constantly rising commodity prices – ecological optimisation of business processes can often facilitate cost reduction. By means of IT, companies can control those initiatives much more efficiently. In this way they improve their profitability and protect the environment.

Case Study Chemicals Industry: IT Decision Support for Optimising CO2 emissions of a Company's Network in the Chemicals Industry

Optimising production networks is a crucial strategic challenge for companies. In which manufacturing bases should be invested? Which warehouses and transport connections will be needed? In which strategic supplier and sales markets should be invested? Within the chemicals industry company-network-decisions go hand in hand with high investments and determine the cost structure and the competitive position of the company middle- to long-term.

So far location- and network-decisions are made on the basis of primarily economic criteria: The objective is to maximise the reduced revenues. Influential factors are of economic nature: purchase-costs, production, distribution and marketing, sales volume and prices, country-related tax and subsidiary differences for location alternatives, qualification and availability of a suitable workforce, sticking around suppliers and sales markets is important here. IT and especially IT-supported optimizing-software already bolstered this optimisation-problem and the management-decisions in the past. "Strategic network design"-tools can support decision-finding with many location-alternatives, suppliers, clients and products more efficiently than this would be possible with manual calculation and subjective evaluation: simulation, optimisation on different targets, analysis of sensitivities and visualisation of complex quantitative results are supported customer-friendly and lead to a quantitative decision support for the management.

A company that obliged itself to Green Business in the narrower and to sustainability in the broader sense has to optimise the company-network on the economic and additionally on the social and ecologic dimensions: Not longer the "single bottom line" – the maximum tax revenue is the goal, but the balance of the "triple bottom line" – the sustainable balance from economic, social and ecological performance of the company. Balance, because it is not about maximum performance, but about a sustainable performance-level on behalf of present and future generations. The CO_2 emissions in a company's network in particular, especially in production and distribution, are significantly determined by strategic network decisions and investments.

In the chemicals industry the value chain-networks of leading companies are often characterised by a structural disequilibrium: traditionally the manufacturing bases and markets of the chemicals industry are located in Europe and the US. Globalisation and the opening of markets led to an increased growth, especially in Asia, while markets in Europe and in the US are getting more and more saturated. This leads to rising network decision-making of companies in the chemicals industry to supply Asian markets from Europe and the US or to raise regional manufacturing bases and distribution networks in Asia and therefore to re-optimise their companies' networks. Additionally many companies in the chemicals industry, such as BASF, DSM or Bayer, have contributed themselves to sustainability and reduction od CO_2 emissions and take part in emission trading.

In this context, these companies can balance their network decisions concerning sustainability aspects and can optimise economic goals in terms of CO_2 emissions with the use of IT. CO_2 emissions can be integrated in the existing optimisation schemes and IT-tools: The ratio of CO_2 as parameter is comparable to cost parameters and can be defined for the same structures – for manufacturing bases and locations, transport connections or warehouse locations – and in this way can be directly applied on the optimisation problem. As a result cost-minimal vs. CO2-minimal scenarios can be compared and the appropriate balance between revenue and carbon footprint can be estimated. The constitution of regional production-capacities with short ways of transportation, e.g. in Asia, only can be decided on economic and climate-protection-aspects by use of IT-related optimising tools.

Checklist: Where does your company stand?	Yes
Is there an idea and suggestions for a sustainability strategy or objective or rather energy efficiency in your company?	
Have general company targets been transformed into operational sector targets for IT?	
Is energy-efficiency set as a target within your IT-strategy?	
Are there conversations between IT and the core business and have collective action plans been created and developed?	
Could energy-efficiency of IT be improved through virtualisation, green (out-) sourcing and intelligent cooling solutions?	
Have innovative IT solutions for reduction of CO2 consumption in the core business been developed?	
Have more than half of the discussed and planned actions been implemented?	

Part B: Controlling Performance – Value-Oriented IT Management

There are a number of possibilities for using IT to increase value, and companies from many sectors are able to give good reports of their positive experiences of using IT as an enabler for their business operations. IT's new role is changing the face of our companies. IT departments are emancipating themselves from the status of being pure technology experts and are starting to feel responsible for business processes. Users and decision-makers in the other business units and at group management level are beginning to appreciate IT managers as valuable sparring partners when it comes to discussing strategic issues.

In some companies, this kind of relationship between IT and operational business units is already a reality, but in most companies IT and business units find themselves on either side of a deep divide. It is not just that the IT department has a reputation for being a cost driver, whose benefit for business operations is highly contentious or at least incalculable, but that IT staff and IT users simply speak a different language. As long as the IT and business sides of the enterprise do not pull together, it is virtually impossible to realize the benefits of IT for the company's operations and equally impossible to realize the considerable potential for reducing business process costs using IT.

Companies wishing to use IT to increase value will have to create a number of conditions for integrating the IT and operations departments. The chapters in Part A clearly showed that IT can only add value if it is planned and implemented in close connection with company strategy. When introducing innovative IT systems, it is also crucial to re-think the company's business processes, corporate structures, and its ways of thinking and behaving: IT can only fully realize its value for the company if it is an integral part of strategic changes, e.g. mergers and divestments, from the beginning. It is also important to firmly anchor the IT department into the management and control structures of the company in order to measure and steer its contribution to the objectives achieved by the company.

Although the number of companies that fulfill the requirements for value-oriented IT management is on the increase, the figure is still surprisingly low. In A.T. Kearney's annual study, only 35 percent of companies accorded the IT department equal status with other strategic projects in terms of corporate planning. 40 percent on the other hand, only involved CIOs in corporate planning if IT projects were involved and 25 percent only involved them when planning how to implement IT projects or even didn't involve them at all. These findings are surprising as it is only by linking IT closely with strategic objectives that companies can realize the benefits of IT for their operations.

Value-oriented IT management calls for a organizational framework that allows IT to bridge the traditional divide between the IT department and the 'business side' of operations, especially between the technology specialists in the IT department and the IT users in the other business units. It is only this kind of structural framework that will allow IT to exert the required influence on the decision-making committees within the company. And to create it, we need *IT governance* – by defining how IT is managed within the company. 'Managing IT' involves answering two questions in particular:

■ Which tasks should be carried out by the business units and which must be primarily established in the IT department?

■ Which IT tasks can be carried out centrally and in which cases would it be better if they were decentralized?

A number of innovative concepts have been developed over the past few years to provide answers to these questions that will lastingly improve the productivity of IT management and provide a reliable basis for implementing value-adding innovation. These concepts provide an integrated framework and also involve structural recommendations alongside procedural solutions.

The committees concerned with IT governance, in particular that of Chief Information Officer (CIO), not only fulfill an important function in implementing and managing IT benefit for company operations, but above all, they are vital for IT planning. For many companies, *IT planning* means assigning IT budgets for the various business units from the top down. The next step is for the business units to assign the funds to services such as PC support and – if there is anything is left over – to then allocate the rest to innovative projects. In this manner, a lot of the potential for adding value through IT is 'wasted'. Leading companies, on the other hand, use IT planning to identify innovative processes and methods for adding value in IT operations, and also in IT project portfolio management, and to ensure that these are developed by using suitable motivational measures.

From the perspective of a great many boards of directors and specialist business units, IT is still a technology that – provocatively speaking – seldom works and is too expensive to boot. As a result, the 'success' of IT is managed almost exclusively in terms of costs. Typical ratios used are costs in relation to sales, costs per user, number of IT employees in relation to the number of users and other similar cost ratios. To get the whole IT picture however, we need to augment the cost side with the performance side. But how can we measure IT's performance? Is it even measurable? *IT performance management* provides all the answers to these questions and is both an innovative concept and one that has also proven its worth in practice.

A company's ability to measure and manage IT performance depends on the maturity of its IT organization, IT planning (including existing cost and performance accounting systems) and the IT management mechanisms that it uses. There are four levels:

■ *Uncoordinated IT management (Level 1):* On level one, it is the technology specialists in the IT departments who are responsible for developing IT projects. At top management level none of the members of the board are responsible for IT. The business units are only involved in IT planning sporadically or for specific projects, and IT managers and users often talk at cross purposes, one group speaking 'techie' language and the others using business terms. Accordingly, those IT projects that are initiated without bearing any reference to corporate planning are fragmented and uncoordinated. IT is chiefly managed on the basis of the cost categories and cost centers laid down by IT controlling methods – and these are rarely complex enough for the needs of IT departments. Furthermore, larger companies with group-like structures often use standard cost categories and cost centers for all divisions. At this level, a number of aggregated IT ratios can be established, for instance IT costs as a percentage of sales. Yet although they make IT costs more transparent and help to establish global management and cost controlling, they do not provide a great deal of information about the efficiency of the IT support that has been provided. IT performance is then measured by the criterion of whether it stays within the prescribed budget – a large part of which has to be allocated to day-to-day business.

■ *Cost-oriented IT management (Level 2):* At the next level, IT projects are initiated by the IT department as before, but a member of top management is responsible for supervising activities. This usually results in at least some of the IT employees using business language and generally means that at least some of the most important users are involved in planning IT projects. Some business units have already introduced IT cost categories and definitions, however the focus is on reducing costs, not adding value. The costs are still focused on technology and allocated and managed on the basis of hardware platforms (e.g. desktops, servers, mainframes etc.) and passed on to the user. One example of this is 'costs per server'. In this case, the costs can be evaluated and compared for each technology platform, but meaningful benchmarking at a later date is still difficult because there are no detailed performance categories. For example, the maintenance costs for applications servers differ considerably from those for file servers, although they are sometimes operated on similar server platforms. These kinds of differences can only be made rather inadequately at this level. IT is managed using sector-oriented cost benchmarks, which do not provide any meaningful information on IT's individual performance capability.

■ *Service-oriented IT management (Level 3):* At this level, the focus is shifted from technology to the IT services that are provided to the individual business units of the company. A member of top management is involved in IT decision-making, users are involved as IT coordinators in prioritizing the projects for their unit, and the responsibility for larger IT projects lies either with the IT department or the business units. For managing IT, the costs planned in terms of cost categories and centers are based on services, which are categorized according to the types of services provided, and which then provide a basis for allocating the services used. The most important variables used for measuring are usually the single user and the IT services, service levels and applications that he uses. This makes it possible to allocate the costs in terms of IT usage and to then benchmark this against services that are standard on the IT services market, for example an ERP workstation.

■ *Business-oriented IT management (Level 4):* At the highest IT management level, a number of other IT governance committees are integrated alongside top management, which supports the user-side of IT in making decisions. Planned projects are prioritized and implemented in terms of their impact on the business activity of the company. Cross-functional teams from the IT department and the business units share responsibility for developing and implementing projects and materializing the anticipated benefits. Calculating the costs on the basis of transactions makes IT costs and services more transparent, thus creating the connection between IT costs and the main parameters of each business unit. Typical IT ratios at this level are for instance costs per flight booking, costs per credit card transaction and costs per bank transfer. This facilitates 'proper' benchmarking with external IT services and in the case of IT outsourcing, allows variable cost allocation. Developing benchmarking to include benchmarking business process outsourcing services is then possible as a result.

IT governance, IT planning and IT performance management are important components of a value-oriented IT management approach. Whilst they do not single-handedly create value directly, they are essential for recognizing the potential of and implementing IT utility increments (described in Part A of this book) and IT cost reductions (described in Part C).

1. IT Governance – Creating the Organizational Framework for Value Enhancing IT

The cost and benefit potential of IT can only be fully developed if the IT department is aware of the needs and objectives of users and is able to make proactive proposals for meeting those needs. This requires active cooperation between the IT department and users, and this must be firmly anchored within the organization of the company. IT governance lays down the 'IT highway code' with the aim of managing the deployment of IT effectively and efficiently. Controlling IT begins on the demand or business side, which sets the priorities for IT investment in its role as a recipient or customer of IT services and as such reaps the benefit of the value enhancement, and ends on the supply side, usually the traditional IT department, responsible for providing services such as PC support, running data processing centers or developing software. Holistic IT governance integrates both perspectives and coordinates them perfectly with one another.

In practice, this is still not the case in many companies today: Our experience of the *demand side* shows that IT competencies and responsibilities are not assigned systematically and important strategic IT processes are often defined in an arbitrary manner or entirely by coincidence. One example of this is the following: In a survey of a large group, each of the subsidiaries was asked who, in their view, was responsible for the eminently important (in terms of its contribution to enhancing value) process of IT innovation management. The answer was as baffling as it was sobering: 42 percent considered that they themselves were responsible, one fifth considered it to be the CIO's job and one fifth thought it was the responsibility of top management, whilst some 16 percent thought that if fell to other units such as corporate planning, controlling and others. There could be no question of a homogeneous understanding of the role of IT within the company, let alone of concerted and controllable processes. This lack of concerted effort results in business units carrying out the same work in parallel and at best, with less than perfect results.

This example shows the typical dangers for conglomerate-type companies, where IT is in use in several business units in parallel, not only on the demand side but also on the *supply side*. In one large, international group, consisting of a management company and several regional subsidiaries and affiliated companies, there were more than ten internal IT service providers and three internal IT departments, all offering largely identical services at the same time, such as developing and maintaining complex individual software, introducing SAP, running data processing centers and providing network and frontend services – sometimes even competing with one another internally.

The repercussions for the whole group are clear:

▪ Cost-intensive efforts to develop innovations are carried out more than once. Scare staff resources are not bundled but 'wasted' by doing the same work twice.

▪ Upgrades or new versions of standard software are carried out twice and use a great deal more resources than coordinated or concerted procedures would.

▪ As far as the data processing centers are concerned, the subsidiaries and affiliated companies do not achieve the critical mass so essential for efficiency. Concerted efforts would achieve considerable economies of scale.

▪ Each IT company or department buys its own IT services separately and often uses the same supplier. By bundling volumes, significant savings could be made here.

The list of negative effects for all the subsidiaries is even longer. Effectively controlling IT as part of a comprehensive system of IT governance aims to prevent such erroneous developments, but to do this a number of structures and rules have to be developed so that IT can be managed in a comprehensive and balanced way. The following issues have to be clarified as a priority:

▪ What are the *basic principles* of IT governance? This also involves defining how roles are assigned between the business units and the IT department.

▪ How the basic areas of responsibility are assigned in IT governance and which *organizational units and committees* play a role in managing and controlling IT? Based on each company's individual IT service portfolio, how are decision-making competencies and responsibilities for IT planning and controlling assigned within the group?

■ Which *processes* are used for IT governance? To answer this question we need to define suitable IT governance processes, lay down clear escalation procedures and distinct instructions for action.

1.1 Separating the Organization of IT Demand and IT Supply

At the center of debates on IT governance these days is the question of how roles are to be allocated among the business units and the IT department: Should the so-called 'delivery units' (supply organizations that develop, run and maintain systems) also be responsible for controlling IT? Or should control be carried out by the business units, i.e. the business side of operations that points IT in the 'right' direction – a direction that supports the business? Neither alternative is ideal:

Controlling IT via supply organization leads to a conflict of interests, since we have noticed that in the majority of companies the IT department is managed in the interests of the supply organization and not in the interests of the core business of the company. Here is an example: The IT department of a mechanical engineering company (now divested and a company in its own right) was no longer working to full capacity following the completion of its Y2K project and currency conversion to the euro. The IT team, which had taken on more staff to cope with these two large-scale projects and in view of the e-business hype of the late 1990s, was suddenly 'unemployed' for a lot of the time. To keep his team occupied and prevent his team from being realigned, the inventive IT boss initiated a number of IT development projects, however without a business case. He also omitted to discuss with the business units whether his IT projects were relevant for the core business of the company. After the software development was completed, the upgrades were announced and implemented. The consequences were obvious: The IT staff had plenty of work to do; the business units were provided with a new solution, whose purpose and relevance was unclear, and after the monthly overall costs were allocated, the units were burdened with high IT costs – a solution which suited the IT department fine.

Tips for setting up a demand organisation:

Appoint decentral CIOs to the business units: Larger companies should establish decentral CIOs in addition to central CIO positions in order to provide a powerful counterpart to the supply side.

Position the demand organisation towards the top of the hierarchy:
To be able to work effectively with the supply side, the demand organisation should be positioned high enough up in the hierarchy.

At first glance, it would seem that *controlling IT via the business units* is a better solution because this ensures that IT departments must orient themselves towards the core business. However, the question is, just who exactly is supposed to be responsible for it – a member of the board responsible for IT, or all the top managers interested in IT, or just a selection of them? This variant has often failed in practice on account of the member of the board and top managers frequently not having the necessary IT competence to effectively control the IT department. Furthermore, they also do not have the time or the interest to really get to grips with the IT issue.

How can we solve this dilemma? For most companies, the second option is generally the better solution. To tackle the problems outlined above, a 'demand organization' is set up on the business side, headed by a CIO, who usually reports directly to the CEO or an 'IT board'. The CIO's chief priority is to control and manage the IT department and also the supply organization.

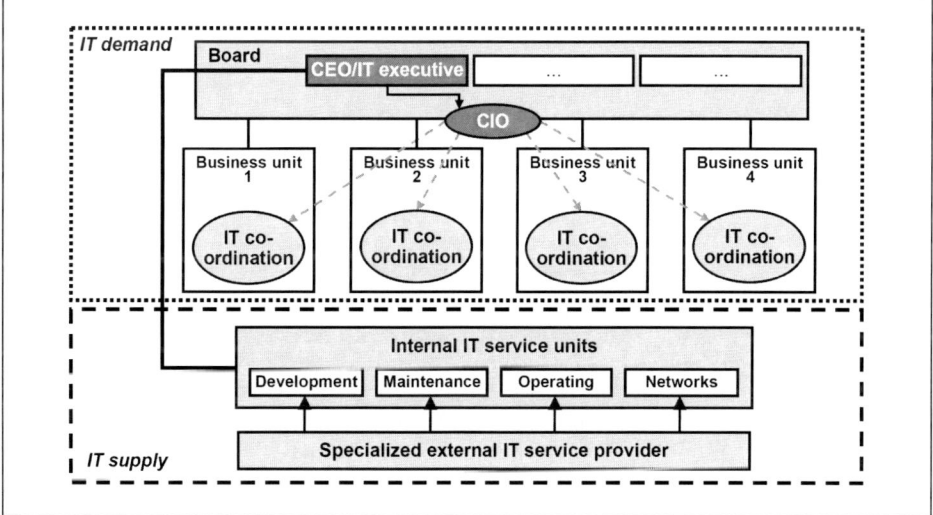

Figure 21:   IT demand and IT supply organization (example)

Depending on how large the company is, the CIO can fall back on decentral staff: In smaller companies, these are usually IT coordinators, who devote part of their duties in the business units to working under the CIO and controlling IT (figure 21). These IT coordinators are subordinate to their own supervisors for disciplinary and technical matters (see solid line), but for IT-related matters they also answer to the CIO (see dotted line).

1.2   Establishing Centralized and Decentralized Areas of IT Responsibility and IT Control Structures

In larger companies, especially those with group-like structures, i.e. with a central holding company and decentralized subsidiaries, there has always been the question of whether to centralized IT services or not. Opinions differ between the champions of a centralized control system, for instance via top management, and the champions of a de-centralized system of control, for example, via the subsidiaries. The advantages of standardization (uniform solutions company-wide), harmonization (exploiting economies of scale) and efficiency all speak in favor of a centralized system of control. The champions of a decentralized system on the other hand maintain that IT might be more expensive this way, but it is a lot more effective, because 'local' IT units know what their business units need and can adapt IT better to local problems.

Tips for assigning responsibilities:

Open communication:
Centralizing areas of responsibility often leads to conflicts of interest. They must be dealt with and discussed openly.

Involve all those affected:
When deciding on responsibilities as part of IT governance, it is important to involve all those affected directly or indirectly.

In practice it has proved sensible to neither central nor decentralize all the areas of responsibility. In fact, it is a good idea to weigh up the best approach for each IT service in turn. When doing so, both of the criteria applied when prioritizing IT services at group level are important (see also Part B, Chapter 2, IT Planning): (1) The strategic relevance of each IT service and (2) The synergy potential if coordinated company-wide. On one hand, IT services that strongly impact cost and quality of service or show a high potential to stabilize sales or boost turnover growth are of strategic importance. One example of this is the billing system of a telecoms company: its workability and flexibility when setting up new pricing models was a strong factor in the success of sales. On the other hand, high potential synergies are promised by IT services where the costs can be significantly reduced by bundling volumes, and where the required IT know-how can be bundled into supply centers company-wide. A typical example of this would be the data processing center services, whose costs can be primarily reduced using economies of scale whilst retaining the same standard of quality. Analyzing portfolios from the two perspectives of 'strategic importance' and 'potential synergies through company-wide bundling' produces three fields of action:

- *'Strategically important' and 'synergistic company-wide':* IT services of high strategic importance and high synergy potential should be controlled centrally. Enterprise Resource Planning (ERP) or Customer Relationship Management (CRM) are often among these IT services. When introducing an ERP or CRM system in each of the decentralized subsidiaries of a group, up to 30 percent of launch costs can be saved as a result of 'template effects' during development and implementation .

- *'Non-synergistic':* IT services that do not create synergies if coordinated company-wide should be decentralized – regardless of their strategic importance. These are often services developed by the subsidiaries themselves for individual purposes or applications that are only important for a specific area of the business. This is often the case with groups that include one or more 'untypical' companies amongst its standard subsidiaries. For instance, in a construction group that is made up of a number of building contractors and a construction subsidiary, the special construction systems are best left under the jurisdiction of the construction company. If however the IT service in question is of strategic significance for this business unit, the CIO of the holding company should be kept regularly informed by the CIO of the group management company and involved in key decision-making, for example, in the form of steering committee meetings.

- *'Strategically unimportant' and 'synergistic company-wide':* Typically, commodities – such as managing PC workstations or running data processing centers – are not strategic, yet promise a high degree of company-wide synergy potential. In such case, the question is less one of responsibilities, and more one of finding the right vertical scope. These kinds of commodity services are often bundled and outsourced. If they are to stay within the group however, it makes sense to assign one subsidiary the responsibility of providing the service for the whole group.

If the areas of responsibility are clear within the supply organization, suitable committees should be set up to ensure smooth cooperation between the demand organizations themselves and between demand organizations and the IT supply organization side. It is their job to identify innovative, strategically relevant IT projects and to undertake planning and controlling IT. In practice, a three-tiered structure of responsibility has proven to be the best solution, ensuring that duties are carried out in a timely fashion and the necessary decisions can be taken:

- *The CIO circle* represents the interests of the demand side and is the committee for dealing with company-wide IT issues and those issues that need to be coordinated. In this circle, the company-wide 'IT development plan' is drawn up as part of IT strategy (see Part A, Chapter 1, IT Strategy) and the IT budget for each business unit discussed and consolidated. (see also Part B, Chapter 2, IT Planning).

- To keep the CIO circle workable, it is important to delegate content and operational issues, for example, evaluating business cases. *Working groups* are ideal for this, headed by representatives of the demand side and if need be, supplemented by representatives from the supply organization.

■ CIOs often do not have enough decision-making powers to take far-reaching decisions such as adopting longer-term innovation portfolios. For this purpose, it is a good idea to set up an *IT decision-makers circle*, consisting of the board members responsible for IT in the holding company and also those in the subsidiaries/affiliated companies. In smaller companies, business unit heads from the main applications areas could also be included in this circle.

This multi-layered committee structure ensures the horizontal cooperation between the representatives of the demand organization. It also guarantees integration into the linear organization with relevant decision-makers at management level. In sum, it interlocks efficiently and effectively with the organization of the company.

It has proven to be a good idea to use the instruments of standard customer-supplier relationships for cooperation between the demand and IT supply organization, rather than setting up a separate body to do this. This also includes regular performance meetings, at which the Head of Supply demonstrates the quality of performance to the CIO using the ratios defined in the service level contracts, such as availability or response time behavior. Another example would be setting up planning rounds which decide on project proposals and determine which resources are needed on the part of the IT supply organization.

1.3   Defining IT Management Processes

The basic areas of responsibility must be consistently anchored in the IT governance processes. The processes necessary for managing IT do not vary a great deal in practice. In our experience, the following IT governance processes need to be defined:

■ IT innovation management

■ IT project planning and project management

■ IT controlling

The aim of *innovation management* is to identify and evaluate innovative IT issues throughout the company that are relevant for implementing corporate strategy. This process is a cyclical one, generally occurring at intervals of one to three years. 'Best practice' is a process that investigates the IT requirements of the whole company by using the cross current process:

■ *From the top down, from the 'whole-company' perspective:* Coordinator and process owner is the CIO, who puts together relevant issues along with senior executives from the main management company and evaluates them in terms of their cost-benefit ratio as part of a 'mini' business case (see Part B, Chapter 3, IT Performance Management).

■ *From the bottom up, from the perspective of the subsidiaries and affiliated companies:* Coordinator and process owner are the decentral persons responsible in the demand organization, i.e. the IT coordinators or decentral CIOs. Accordingly, it is their job to put together relevant issues along with senior executives from the subsidiaries or business units and to evaluate them in terms of their cost-benefit ratio as part of a business case.

The outcome of both currents is an individual IT roadmap – these are then consolidated into company-wide IT roadmaps at joint workshops in the demand organization and passed on to the management body responsible for approval. Any new IT issues that emerge are integrated into the IT services portfolio in order to determine competencies and areas of responsibility.

The aim of *IT project planning and project management* is to anchor control mechanisms to ensure that any innovations planned are implemented and coordinated company-wide. But only when it makes sense:

■ For all 'universal' issues, joint projects are conceived for implementing innovation projects. It is the CIO's job to draw up a company-wide portfolio of group-wide projects on the basis of the innovation plan and to coordinate this with management. Project managers have to be stipulated for each of these projects to control the implementation of the projects and monitor their success. Control (not the operational management!) of the group-wide projects is usually carried out by the CIO, sometimes supported by the decentral representatives of the demand organization depending on the object of the project. The IT supply organization receives the order and is responsible for processing it. The control lies with the demand side.

■ For all 'individual' issues, no joint projects are conceived for implementing innovation projects. The decentral representative of the demand organization will integrate such projects in the project portfolio specific to his unit. Project processing on the supply side is controlled decentrally only. The central CIO is only informed on the status and progress of the project in exceptional cases.

■ For issues that need to be coordinated, case-by-case decisions are made on whether an individual or a coordinated solution is needed.

The benefit of this step-by-step procedure means that a project can then be developed individually if it does not make any sense to coordinate it for corporate reasons or on account of efficiency. On the other hand, the projects that are truly worthwhile from a corporate perspective can then be controlled centrally. By coordinating these development services, we can avoid the wheel being reinvented in several places simultaneously.

IT controlling involves controlling IT from two perspectives – cost and performance.

■ On the cost side, budgets are planned from the bottom up in the business units, and then consolidated and checked by the CIO. Budget items for measures suitable for group-wide coordination are recognized, discussed and can then be implemented jointly if need be. The budget is reflected back into the business units where it must be approved by the person responsible for the outcome or the budget (see Part B, Chapter 2, IT Planning). After budgeting is complete, the CIO cost controls the overall budget, the central units in the demand organization monitor their own specific budgets and if there are discrepancies then counter measures can be taken.

■ On the performance side, indicators that provide information on the quality of IT need to be defined as part of a universal IT control system. Ideally, this would be carried out as part of IT performance management (see Part B, Chapter 3, IT Performance Management).

Via the performance side, the demand organization is fully informed of the status of IT at all times and has a valid information base for controlling performance through the supply side.

Designing and implementing an IT governance concept in an international group

A major international group with a typical group structure, consisting of one management company and several hundred subsidiaries at home and abroad, was looking to develop and implement a group-wide IT governance concept. IT was structured very differently in each of the subsidiaries: Some of the subsidiaries had their own, internal IT. Others had disincorporated their IT into a separate company. All in all, the group had over ten of its own IT service providers, a large number of internal IT departments and also worked together with nearly all of the key IT vendors. In the group holding, there was a corporate CIO for controlling IT from the group perspective and in the subsidiaries there were decentral CIOs for controlling IT from their own company perspectives.

The group was faced with the challenge of developing a group-wide model of governance that clarified the roles of the subsidiaries and institutionalized them in processes and a suitable structure of management committees. The aim was to:

■ reorganize IT group-wide in accordance with universal rules and standards,

■ establish cooperation between the subsidiaries on the one hand, and the subsidiaries and the management holding on the other,

■ consolidate and optimize the organization of the service providers, and

■ identify potential for optimization and bundling in the cooperation with external IT vendors.

Specialists from the holding company and staff from representative subsidiaries were involved in developing the system of IT governance. The remaining subsidiaries were involved in the coordination workshops. Thus, the new group-wide IT governance concept was created with the involvement of all those responsible and all those affected and could therefore make a considerable contribution to improving IT effectiveness and efficiency:

■ By carrying out a differentiated IT performance analysis, the central and decentral areas of responsibility in the demand organization were clearly defined.

■ The responsibilities were anchored in the IT governance processes. The various process variants were designed according to whether an IT service was under local or group responsibility, and anchored in an organizational guideline.

■ To coordinate all universal IT issues at group level, a CIO circle was set up, consisting of the CIO of the holding company and the CIOs of the subsidiaries, which met monthly or if any special matters arose.

■ The top decision-making body for all strategic IT issues was made up of all the members of the board responsible for IT in the holding company and in the subsidiaries.

■ On the basis of the newly defined responsibilities, coordinated development initiatives were implemented, which amongst other things were able to contribute to using standard templates to reduce project costs.

■ The strategic IT service provider was selected from amongst several internal IT service providers, and the IT services were stipulated which were to be bought exclusively from the strategic provider. In addition, a consolidation roadmap was set up to clean up the IT provider landscape.

Key to the success of the successful introduction of the new IT governance was the intensive integration of all those involved. A sober, emotion-free discussion based on cost-benefit ratios and the distribution of attainable effects lead to the decision-makers giving their much sought-after approval of the decisions made.

Checklist: Does your company have a value-oriented system of IT govern-ance?	Yes
Is there a coherent and universal concept on IT management with a clear distinction between IT demand and IT supply?	
As the demand side of your company, do the business units possess the required competencies and powers of decision to manage IT?	
Does the demand side have the last word on IT investments?	
Are the areas of responsibility between the supply and demand sides clearly differentiated and are there a 'proper', formalized customer-supplier relationship?	
Are decisions to centralize or decentralize taken carefully in your company and based on fact and not taken simply on principle?	
Have clear processes been defined for IT innovation management, IT project planning and project management, and IT controlling and have these been clearly communicated?	
Do the IT governance processes really work in practice?	
Does cooperation between the business units function well in relation to IT?	
Do the demand and supply sides work together smoothly and without problems?	

2. IT Planning – Integrating IT Planning into Corporate Planning

IT governance forms the structural framework for effective IT management and thus also for implementing a value-oriented IT strategy. One key success factor is planning IT 'properly'. But: IT as an 'overhead department' always has a budget that it must keep to. Balancing the necessary IT innovations laid down in the IT strategy with the funds available during the planning period is a characteristic of best practice IT planning.

What does the reality of this look like in companies? For many companies, *IT planning* means planning IT costs on monetary variables. Non-monetary aspects such as organizing the business or prioritizing development projects are not taken into consideration. Budget caps are typical for this type of process, set by many companies as an upper limit for the IT budget following excesses due to e-hype and the millennium, yet without really achieving lasting success.

On the contrary: Limiting the IT budget without reducing costs will simply lead to ageing IT systems in companies. Since IT operating costs increase by one or two percent annually in line with inflation, their percentage of the overall budget will get bigger year by year. The consequence being that there is less and less money left for innovation. It is much easier to save on new projects rather than reducing expenditure on operationally critical IT operations. If, however, existing IT systems are not continually adapted to changes in business requirements or new technical standards by constant reinvesting, then the IT will age so that business processes are no longer supported by state-of-the-art technology, and IT operating costs will increase on account of ageing tools.

Top-down planning based exclusively on monetary variables does not lead to the desired results, but to developments in the wrong direction: i.e. IT provides ever poorer support for the business, yet IT costs continue to increase. But is there an alternative that links IT cost reductions with the specific use of value enhancement potential for future strategic positioning? In our opinion, this question can be answered clearly with 'yes'. It is the job of the CIO and the IT managers to make the best of the situation and to create the basis for effectively deploying funds at the IT planning stage. This requires a suitable set of instruments: Innovative methods and a best practice procedural framework create the scope for using IT to enhance value even if funds are limited.

An important basis for the workability of the planning methods is a differentiated, and functioning, cost and performance accounting system for IT. This provides the adequately differentiated information necessary for quantitative processes such as bench-marking.

2.1 Using Cost and Performance Accounting as a Basis for Planning

An effective market, product and customer-oriented cost and performance accounting system is an important condition for successful IT planning. Fundamental components are a cost category structure tailored to IT requirements and a cost center structure oriented towards the responsibilities in the demand and supply organization.

This requirement sounds particularly trivial in the case of cost category structures. Companies however often have situations where all the IT costs are booked using two or three cost categories, because the types of cost categories needed are not available in an accounts code that is primarily oriented to the needs of core business but not those of IT. These results in the actual costs that are entered not providing sufficient basis for analysis, making it difficult to draw conclusions about how funds are used. Cost-type accounting and cost center accounting are key elements of a functioning cost and performance accounting system.

For the kind of IT planning that we will be introducing in this chapter, we also need to structure cost units in a way that faithfully represents the IT services in line with market conditions and is tailored to customers needs. The planned costs are allocated to concrete IT services on the basis of standard IT operations performance categories (for example, the number of users assisted by help desks) and appropriate service levels (e.g. 7 x 24-hour availability). At the latest, companies need this kind of information if they want to investigate the competitiveness of an internal IT service provider or are even thinking of outsourcing IT. If holding talks with external IT vendors, it is not the costs of a cost center that are important but products. A LAN workstation equipped with specific features comes at a fixed price per month.

Even if the IT service is an integral part of the products of a company, the company should be in a position to disclose the IT costs of its products so that it can take the customer perspective of the IT costs into account. For example, the core business of a company selling credit card transactions on the basis of technical processors can only be run on high-performance IT. If this company wishes to expand its business to new markets, for example in Eastern Europe, it will not be very successful if it cannot calculate the costs of its transactions – i.e. costs per credit card transaction – in marketable dimensions. Since IT costs make up a considerable block of the costs in this business, a cost-unit-based system of cost and performance accounting is essential – i.e. a system based on IT services.

A forward-looking cost and performance accounting system with cost category, cost center and cost unit elements also creates the basis for effective IT controlling. It is able to provide the records needed for IT planning and should work on the following principles:

- *Principle 1:* All the costs directly attributable to one product must be booked directly – cost categories could be outside services, direct material, etc.

- *Principle 2:* All the costs created at team/business unit level are directly attributed to organizational cost centers. Cost categories here could be personnel costs, work-station costs, vehicle pool costs, telecommunication costs, office space costs, etc.

- *Principle 3:* Personnel costs and overheads at team/business unit level are allocated to products/orders via internal cost rates.

- *Principle 4:* The remaining costs are allocated (depending on who caused them) for the use of the services by charging an all-inclusive standard price or levies.

For the IT planning methods introduced in the following chapter, a forward-looking cost and performance accounting system is highly desirable. The planning methods and techniques conceived of can be implemented all the better if the base system for cost and performance accounting performs well and the more smoothly it can be used in day-to-day operational business. For a number of methods – we have already mentioned benchmarking – elements such as cost unit accounting are absolutely crucial.

2.2   Establishing Procedural Frameworks for Best Practice

A company-wide integrated IT planning process facilitates the systematic planning of IT budgets, the optimization of IT operations across the company and the prioritization of IT initiatives. For companies that are able to realize synergies across a number of business units, there are several additional processes that allow an aggregation of individual plans and a targeted analysis of synergies.

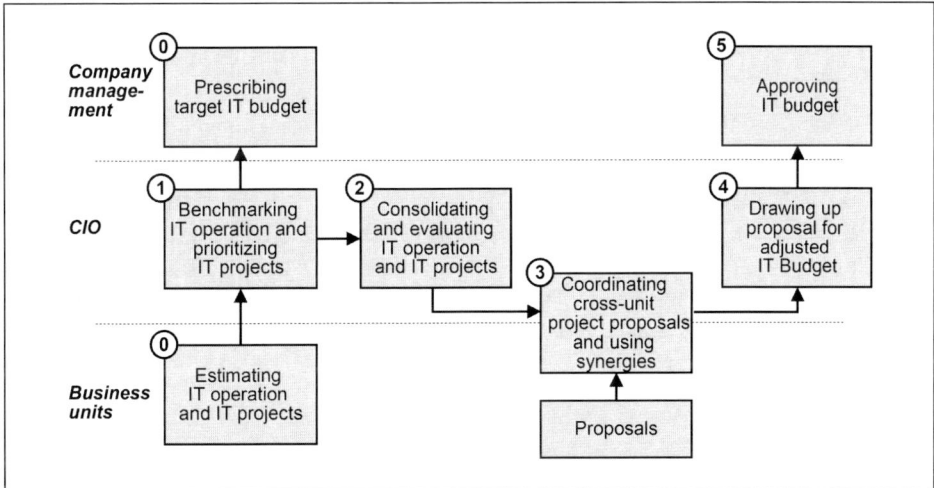

Figure 22:   *The integrated IT planning process*

Although the procedural frameworks for best practices introduced here (figure 22) promise the most potential for large, complex companies with group-like structures, the planning processes and selected methods can also be used successfully for SMEs.

Before the actual planning of the future IT portfolio and the dimensioning of the IT budget takes place, the anticipated costs and the quality and scope of the IT operation and IT projects must be assessed at the business unit level (in figure 21: 0). This information flows into the IT budget proposal, which provides the basis for top management's IT budget decisions.

The provisional estimate is bound up with a high degree of uncertainty. When planning for the current operations, the IT controlling team can assist those responsible for IT in the business units in carrying out a realistic estimate of costs and performance by providing them with transparent cost and performance catalogues. But on account of the requirements that the business units have in terms of innovative IT solutions, a great deal can change between the planning and the implementation stages. It is precisely for this reason that close cooperation between those responsible for IT and the business units is key to the success of IT planning. Otherwise, IT would find itself in the unpleasant predicament of having to react 'suddenly' to changes in the market with IT that it could not finance out of the budget. Companies that have valid targets thanks to IT performance management do not have to fear imponderables such as this nearly as much (see Part B, Chapter 3, IT Performance Management).

With its targets for the IT budget, top management sets the IT planning process in motion in the business units (0). Based on the cost estimates for IT operation and IT projects, the business units plan the distribution of the IT budget in two stages:

- IT requirements and budget proposals from the business units are examined and assessed by a central IT management unit (for instance, the CIO). For this purpose, the IT operations are benchmarked and the IT applications and IT infrastructure projects are prioritized (1). The aim is to reduce costs in the area of IT operations and to identify the planned IT projects at business unit level.

- IT planning in the business units is then consolidated at management company level and assessed with the aim of achieving cost synergies throughout the company (2).

After the CIO has approved the IT budget, the outcome of the process for top management and the central controlling department is a plan for IT operation and subsequent IT projects that has been coordinated with all the business units and consulting management departments. Based on the consolidation and assessment of IT operation and projects, IT project proposals are developed, and company-wide IT projects for implementation decided on and prepared in readiness for decision-making (3). Following the decision by the business units and the CIO, a proposal for the adjusted budget is then drawn up (4) and approved at management company level by the top management (5).

Companies that carry out the whole procedure using powerful and comprehensive methods almost certainly are employing the best practice method. But improvements can also be achieved by using a shorter version of the planning process with each of the steps tailored to the special situations in the company in question. The following section will highlight a few selected steps of this framework and discuss them in greater detail.

2.3   Planning IT Operation and IT Projects

In many companies, the planning for IT operation and IT projects is oriented towards two guiding principles:

2.3.1   Planning from the bottom up

From the bottom up, the anticipated total output of IT during the planning period is estimated. On the operations side for example, it is important to assess how many PCs or specific network forms are needed and which data processing center services or other services must be provided, run and maintained by the IT department to support the business units. When planning the projects it is a good idea to use the IT roadmap as a base (see Part A, Chapter 1, IT Strategy), in which the innovation and project proposals for the planning period have been established. On this basis, the costs and investments for the following period are estimated based on previous experiences and existing offers or pricing information.

The necessity of carrying out IT planning not only at the cost category and cost center level, but also on the cost unit or IT services level has already been explained in depth in the previous section on cost and performance accounting. A key instrument for a systematic, performance-oriented planning is a company-wide product and service catalogue. Two different components need to be taken into consideration in the field of IT:

- The hardware and software catalogue in the frontend field (e.g. workstation systems, applications, etc.),

- The IT services catalogue, which defines and presents all the important IT services in all the IT core functions (user support, server and application services, consulting and development). The content, quality and price of these services are usually stipulated in the Service Level Agreements (SLAs).

Specifying the hardware and software catalogue is not so much of a problem because the technology products used usually simultaneously represent the content. Drawing up the IT services catalogue is a lot harder.

Tips for bottom-up planning:

- Start in the business units:
  In companies with group-like structures, the planning process starts in the operative business units, since planning the content of new projects and business services requires a certain proximity to the operative business.

- *Use templates:*
  To ensure aggregatability and comparability of results from each of the various subsidiaries, it is important to obtain similar kinds of information from across the group. Here, it is a good idea to use standard templates.

Here it is important to ensure that the definitions of services are consistent and clearly distinct from one another. The definitions in a service catalogue are often very technical and are based on historical technical standards and definitions. For example, there is a difference whether in the case of help desks the costs are allocated according to the number of calls made or the number of users helped. Both aggregates offer a valid basis for internal or external comparisons, but the data for the former may not be available from the business units if the number of calls were not monitored there. It is best to take a pragmatic approach here and select the data that is available in the majority of business units.

A possible (rough) means of structuring benchmarkable services has been listed in the following table:

Table 1: Rough structural plan for IT applications and services (example)

Workstation Systems	Applications Services	Special Services
■ Standard workstation services (e.g. hardware/-software, LAN, help desks, local services) ■ Optional workstation services (e.g. maintenance of special equipment such as organizers) ■ Special features of service level agreements (SLAs), e.g. VIP support	■ Operating applications (including administration and support) ■ Hosting/housing applications ■ Purchasing and distributing hard- and software	■ Network links ■ Remote Service Access ■ WAN ■ Internet services ■ Content management ■ Domain management ■ Information and security services ■ Directory services ■ Public key infrastructure ■ EDI ■ Electronic payment

As part of IT planning, the volumes expected for the planning period (number of users, number of servers, number of systems etc.), the planned unit costs and the overall costs as a result must be assigned for each of these service categories. A comparison of the unit costs per service – for example the workstation costs per user and month at defined service levels – provides the basis for benchmarking the IT operating costs at a later date. The costs broken down into services add up to make the IT costs (broken down in the financial ratios into cost categories).

Just like the IT operating costs, up-and-coming projects are also planned from the bottom up. Here too, it is a good idea to structure the costs according to the information needed at a later date for the planning process. Unlike with IT services, it is the structured descriptions of the project focus that are particularly in the foreground, aside from quantitative components in the form of quantity structures – for example, the number of users affected by the project – or costs. This kind of information serves to identify cost reduction potential for further IT planning, for example, by investigating possible initiatives for using synergies.

As with the IT operating costs, the IT costs – planned in the financial ratios according to cost categories – result from aggregating the projects. Projects that are not fully planned at the time of the budget plan have to be listed in the projects as planned items, since they have to be taken into account later when the prioritization for reaching budget targets occurs at project level.

2.3.2   Planning from the top down

In parallel to the bottom-up method, the budget target for IT is stipulated by top management from the top down for each of the business units. The responsibility for how this is then filtered on down through the business units is decentralized. There are a number of ways in which top management can fix the budget. The three most important approaches are briefly outlined in the following section:

- *Strategic approach:* The IT budget is derived from earlier strategic planning. The conditions for this are that:

  - the timing of strategic planning is synchronized with the annual budget plan,
  - it is detailed enough to use as a base for IT target budgets,
  - IT provides for a counter check between strategic planning and current (cost) developments (e.g. actual costs of the previous year).

In general, this method of deriving the target budget from strategic planning is not practicable because the required degree of detail is often not available.

- *Operative approach:* The target budgets are derived from existing, medium-term plans from the business units that cover several years at once. Since these plans often contain bottom-up information from the previous year, they are usually sufficiently well founded and often include the latest planning information. This approach is problematic in that, in the final analysis, the planning from the previous year is projected forward and continued and a controlling effect is only partially achieved.

■ *Analytical approach:* The third approach is more of a backward-looking approach. The starting point is the IT budgets from the business units of the previous years. On the basis of the budget cuts prescribed overall for IT throughout the company, the cost cutting goals are passed on to the business units. Depending on their performance – measured for example by IT costs as a percentage of sales or process costs – and the comparison within the company and best practice industry ratios, poorly performing business units have to make more cuts than good performers.

In practice, we recommend a combined approach – a mixture of strategic farsightedness, sound and up-to-the-minute information and an appreciation of economic necessities and constraints. For example, the strategic planning outcomes could serve as a guiding principle for IT planning, according to which concrete figures are established as part of the operative approach and finally analytically verified.

The next step is then comparing the bottom-up and top-down IT costs with one another – the former costs being evaluated and the latter being prescribed from the top downwards: If the bottom-up IT costs are less than the top-down ones, the budgeted value can be established as the basis for further concretization. Further planning is more difficult if the top-down IT budget is less than the bottom-up IT costs, however experience shows that this tends to be the more likely alternative. The following section shows how companies can find an effective and lasting way out of this dilemma.

2.4   Identifying Cost Reduction Potential for IT Operation and IT Projects

If there is less money available for IT than is really needed, then there are a number of possibilities for adapting IT planning to suit the funds available:

■ *Alternative number one: To reduce the estimated costs for IT operation items.* Investigations can be carried out into whether the planned services such as an SAP application could be 'produced' or purchased more cheaply (see Part C, Chapter 1, IT Optimization).

■ *Alternative number two: To reduce the estimated costs for IT project items.* Companies with group-like structures can examine whether the investment projects in the business units overlap and whether or not certain projects can be carried out jointly. The project costs can be reduced overall through learning curve effects, using empirical values or template effects, e.g. where most of the work on developing a new product can be carried out in the same way by several business units.

■ *Alternative number three: Eliminating certain items* – i.e. reducing the scope of IT services – a move which requires projects in particular to be prioritized.

The impact of each of these alternatives is different. The first alternatives lay the foundation for more medium-term improvements. However, in practice it is unusual that companies are able to change their IT suppliers at short notice. Therefore, the impact on the budget is irrelevant for the planning period. The second alternative is more short-term. Part of the project costs that are planned in parallel are eliminated because of the joint collaboration – and this occurs during the planning period! The same is true for the third alternative: If IT projects fall through once the projects have been prioritized; this has a direct impact on the budget.

2.4.1 Reducing IT operating costs through benchmarking

High 'unavoidable' IT operating costs – as a result of frontends, networks, data processing centers and other elements – do not have to be accepted as given. IT operating services are commodities and do not usually add value directly to the company. They provide the conditions for innovative services in applications. And they also have to be 'available' – at a stipulated quality and reasonable price. As they are to a large degree homogenous, their level of quality and costs are a good basis for comparison, and the service provider is interchangeable due as a rule to a low level of complexity and a lack of relevance to strategy. IT operating services thus offer an ideal starting point for reducing costs. In larger companies with group-like structures, it is also possible to share the use of a cost-intensive IT infrastructure throughout the company, for example, by consolidating data processing centers, integrating Wide-Area Networks (WAN) or setting up a common helpdesk for all group-wide IT applications. The more operating costs are saved, the more scope is opened for investment projects!

Tips for reducing IT operating costs:

■ *Considering synergies in the core business:*
In larger companies, standard application systems, such as group-wide inventory management and bundling purchasing volumes, make it possible to coordinate processing customers company-wide and increasing customer value through cross-selling potential.

■ *Exchanging best practices:*
By discussing issues together, the business units can learn from each other's experiences and thus create the right conditions for transferring the best solution in the company to those business units still in difficulty.

The amount of money that can be saved is considerable. By introducing a group-wide CRM platform, one telecoms group was able to reduce annual IT operating costs by some 30 percent from 7 million Euros to just 5 million Euros, whilst cutting IT project costs by almost 25 percent from around 63 million Euros to under 50 million Euros.

In this chapter, we have often pointed out how important it is to define services in line with market conditions and that the additional amount of time and effect to achieve this is justified. Now, we will highlight the benefits of this approach: IT strengths and weaknesses can only be analyzed and improvements tackled, if IT costs and services are recorded in a structured manner in line with market conditions. Benchmarking IT operations highlights weaknesses in how data processing centers are run, desktop systems are maintained or licenses are purchased. There are three different processes for doing this.

■ *Historical benchmarking:* Within the company – in the case of decentral IT within the business units – historical data from the past is compared and validated by carrying out the relevant change and variance analyses and adjusted if need be. Any leaps in costs must be analyzed. They are often the first signs of misdevelopments and a basis for improvement measures.

■ *External benchmarking:* Comparing variables from other companies gives managers a differentiated view of what the competitive situation in their own company looks like – clearly highlighting strengths and weaknesses. The more differentiated the cost calculations are carried out, the more precise the findings of the analyses will be. Improvement measures can be started in two ways: On the one hand, internal improvement measures can be pinpointed for the identified weaknesses. On the other hand, some categories do not have the quantities for achieving greater efficiency within their own company and therefore 'stand alone' optimization is not an option. For these services, (selective) outsourcing for improving cost positions can be considered.

■ *Internal benchmarking:* This particular form of benchmarking presents itself in larger companies with group-structures and several internal and/or external IT areas. Here service quality and costs within the same company are compared with one another, provided the same service catalogue and standard templates for recording costs and quality are used. This process allows us to select the best-in-class business unit and suggest improvements for the others.

Benchmarking results in ideas for improving the optimization of IT operations. It is vital for further procedure to record these ideas along with the anticipated saving potential and the timeframe in which the saving (budget) will become relevant. In this manner, we can make a precise estimate of when the IT budget will be relieved and scope is also crea¬ted for IT innovation!

2.4.2   Reducing process costs by using synergies

IT costs that are planned from the bottom up do not have to be accepted as given either. In big companies in particular, the launch costs for infrastructure or application projects can be rapidly reduced through joint initiatives for using synergies. The advantages of this kind of joint approach fall into several categories:

■ Resources are optimized by maximizing the deployment of internal and external resources throughout the project

▓ Faster introduction of IT solutions in several business units by using learning curves and empirical values

▓ Reducing operating costs with a project for jointly using a standardized infrastructure for operation

▓ Reducing purchasing costs with a project for bundling the purchase of licenses, IT vendors, implementation resources and other components.

Depending on the size of the project, here too considerable costs can be saved. In one concrete case, the introduction of a customer accounting software with a template-based standard development and subsequent roll-out to five of the subsidiaries in a power utility group cut implementation costs per business unit by 23 percent.

Tips for identifying meaningful projects group-wide:

▓ *Only consider important projects:*
To concentrate on projects with a high potential for synergies, it is important to only consider those projects that exceed a specific investment volume or whose cost-cutting potential justifies the more expensive company-wide coordination.

▓ *Test feasibility:*
Before further analyses are carried out, it is vital to ensure that there are no technological or organizational barriers in the way of group-wide implementation.

To identify synergies in the IT projects, the IT planning in the business units is consolidated throughout the companies. In a multi-tier process, the synergy potential then detailed and transposed into project proposals. They serve as the basis for decision making for initiatives throughout the company. The anticipated savings are anchored immediately in the IT budget for the following years. The first challenge lies in identifying similar projects. Classifying the project makes it possible to identify projects of a similar size within the portfolio. Application projects can be classified according to the following criteria:

▓ *Software product:* SAP R/3, SAP APO, i2 etc.

▓ *Project phase:* Definition, development, launch or roll-out

▓ *Time frame:* Duration of developments in three-month periods etc.

▓ *Business processes supported:* Logistics, production, sales etc.

▓ *Area of application:* Customer Relationship Management, ERP, Supply Chain Management, Data Warehouse, Sales Force Automation (SFA), finance and controlling, B2B marketplace, etc.

Projects with a similar classification are fundamentally suitable for joint projects. However, one should take into account that it is very difficult to find generally valid criteria for weighting similarities. If the 'similarity check' is positive, checks should be made as to whether joint action really makes economic sense in this case. To start with, a company-wide initiative means that the project will be more complex, meaning that the risks are higher, and more time and effort is required to coordinate it. These disadvantages must be more than compensated for by the synergies achievable in this case.

Synergies can be achieved in several categories:

■ *Project synergies* through the smaller number overall of internal and external development resources, joint purchasing of software licenses or group-wide use of templates

■ *Operating synergies* on project completion through joint use of hardware and communication platforms, optimized hard- and software maintenance or a common help-desk – all these things are only possible on account of a coordinate project approach

■ *Business synergies* on project completion by establishing standardized business process and company-wide transparency on costs and services.

Irrespective of the profitability aspect, joint innovation can also be a good idea if the savings that are anticipated are insufficient. This is especially the case if strategic relevance is highly significant. The board of a German manufacturing group consisting of several subsidiaries in a number of countries all active in the same product segment was also faced with such a decision. Despite higher IT implementation costs, the board decided not only to define standardized processes for all subsidiaries but also to realize a joint project in the systems. The strategic advantages of this approach were considered to be higher than the cost disadvantage.

For assessing strategic relevance, there are also a number of possible criteria:

■ *Opening strategic* options through realizing flexible IT structures, for example fusions and take-overs or disinvestments, for outsourcing (IT, business processes etc.) or new business models such as joint ventures.

■ *Improving services* through better customer services, better internal service or greater transparency, for example via data warehouse or management information systems.

■ *Supporting business process* above and beyond business unit boundaries, e.g. by using cross-selling processes or a standardized CRM system.

■ *Implementing a corporate agenda*, in particular to ensure tighter management of decentral business units.

Companies organizing joint IT projects that go beyond business unit boundaries must keep one thing in sight: The benefit for the business units. The additional complexity is only justified if the business case is advantageous for all those involved. An attractive business case is likely to win the support of the IT managers in the business units. Experience shows that synergies projects cannot be pushed through without their help. This is why the business case must stipulate how to deal with cost-cutting exercises: Distributing these amongst the business units involved could represent an incentive to work together. Integrating the management of the business units strongly into the decision-making process for coordinated initiatives also helps to gain broad acceptance for the idea. Who is to take on the management role in the project and how the resources for the project are to be allocated are all points that need clarifying.

The synergies analysis results in those projects in which cooperation between the various business units seems feasible and makes economic or strategic sense. Like the approach for benchmarking operating costs, here too, the anticipated potential savings and the timeframe within which the cost cutting measure (budget) will become relevant must be decided upon. Unlike the operating costs however, the calculated cost-cutting measures usually impact the budget during the same planning period – as a result of the coordination the funds are not made use of. Furthermore, projects tackled by several companies at once are often carried out in stages, i.e. joint technical concept, joint template development and sequential implementation. As a result funds are often made 'to go a bit further'. Both effects relieve the IT budget and create scope for more IT innovation.

2.4.3   Prioritizing planned projects

The methods described above can reduce planned IT costs in the short, medium or long-term. However it is possible, and in practice even likely, that the bottom-up IT costs planned by the business units exceed the IT budget allocated top-down by the board. The only thing to do in this case is to cross out certain service items from the list or to postpone them. These items tend to be projects. IT operation can be optimized, but it is vital to the core of business operations, even if certain parts of IT operation, i.e. maintenance for application systems that are being phased out, can be cut back or even cancelled altogether. As this tends to be the exception to the rule, the problem is more likely to be shelving the 'right' projects. The aim must always be to gain maximum benefit for the company from the IT deployed, despite limited means.

This calls for projects to be prioritized, by systematically and purposefully assessing the planned project and creating a sound basis for decision-making. The systems for prioritizing IT infrastructure and IT application projects are virtually identical and based on the project data collected during the planning process. The key factors in prioritization are 'benefit' and the 'ease of implementation'. How benefit is defined must be decided on individually in each case. The criteria 'financial benefit', 'strategic relevance' and 'technological advantages' are tried and tested. For assessing the ease of implementation, the risk and complexity of the projects need to be evaluated.

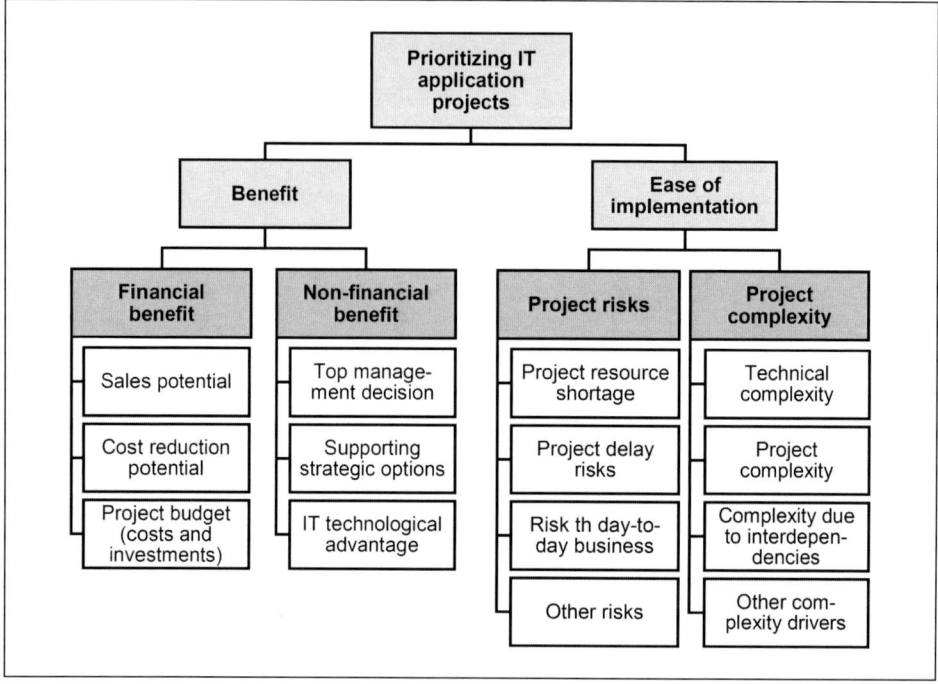

Figure 23:   *Prioritization tree for IT application projects (example)*

It is a good idea for companies to subdivide the criteria of the prioritization tree even further (figure 23), to make the dimensions more effective and evaluations as concise as possible. Each of the individual criteria are prioritized and given a high, medium or low value in the multi-dimensional portfolio (figure 24). Multi-dimensional in this case means that the information from a number of levels is integrated in the portfolio:

- The position of the projects (circles) represents the degree of benefit and difficulty of implementation

- The size of the circles indicates the volumes budgeted for each project

- The color represents the project status from launch (black) to definition (white)

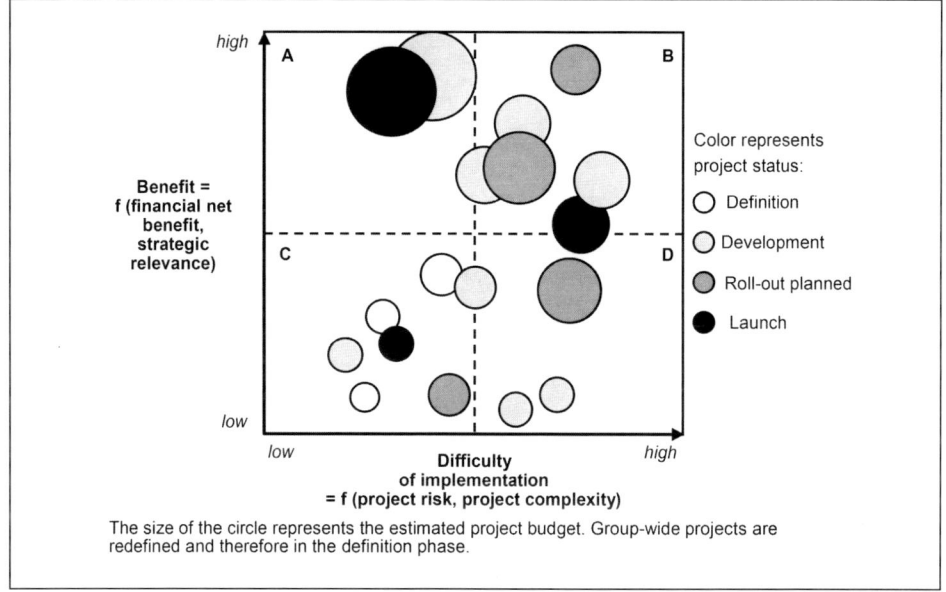

Figure 24:   *IT application portfolio (example)*

The position of a project in one of the four quadrants of the portfolio indicates the options for action:

■ *Quadrant A:* High-priority projects that are relatively easy to implement and whose implementation   is important for the success of the company. The budget should be approved.

■ *Quadrant B:* Projects that have a high benefit for the business but are difficult to implement. Each individual case needs to be carefully considered before the budget is approved.

■ *Quadrant C:* Projects that are easy to implement but are not very promising in terms of the benefit they will provide for the company should be implemented selectively – each individual case needs to be carefully considered before the budget is approved.

■ *Quadrant D·* Projects with the lowest priority as they are complex and promise to bring little benefit to the company. The projects should be postponed.

Aside from the division into quadrants A, B, C and D, the project phases and project budgets provide information on whether it is a good idea to implement a project, stop a project or cutback funding. Those projects that promise huge benefits and are also relatively advanced in the implementation phase tend to be given a high priority for implantation (quadrant A). On the other hand, projects that are of little benefit and are still at the planning stage tend to be shelved (quadrant C). Projects with little benefit (quadrants D and C) that are difficult to introduce (quadrants D and B) and are still in the middle of the definition phase with a huge envisaged budget will be the first ones to be frozen.

The prioritization sequence described above is clearly not an automatic process. Rather it is intended to create a transparency that allows IT managers to discuss – on the basis of meaningful parameters documented in later project controlling documents – IT budgets with the business units and their use in projects.

Tips for prioritizing planned IT projects:

■ *Prioritize IT infrastructure projects over IT applications projects:*
IT infrastructure projects usually arise as a result of benchmarking IT operation – for example, because new software applications are no longer supported by older hardware. For this reason, it is important to prioritize the IT infrastructure projects first and then the IT applications projects afterwards.

■ *Give projects that ensure day-to-day operations the highest priority:*
Not least in order to minimize risks: A company can manage well enough for a year without new software for booking expenses, but the same company will be in serious danger if the server is down for a number of days and no invoices can be sent out.

If successfully introduced, a group-wide IT planning process can be a springboard to considerable added value from the central IT unit. In one real-life case, IT planning was able to save the group costs to the tune of multi-digit millions.

Designing a group-wide IT planning process for an international service provider

The IT of a worldwide service provider was operating in an environment that made it extremely difficult to exploit group-wide synergies:

■ Responsibility for the IT budget had been decentralized among the business units, although IT operation for some of the business units had been outsourced by group headquarters to an external IT service provider.

■ Some of the development activities of the business units had been bundled into their own IT subsidiary.

■ Top management had set an upper budget limit for IT costs group-wide. It was the task of central IT to make sure that this upper limit was observed during the IT planning process.

An analysis of the planning processes made it clear very quickly that the budget could only be kept to by consistently optimizing IT operational services, systematically prioritizing all new projects and by achieving considerable synergies group-wide.

When introducing a new procedure for IT planning, which was aligned with the best practices outlined above, the role of central IT in identifying and developing potential synergies was strongly underlined. To gain the acceptance of each of the business units for the new procedure, they were involved in developing the concept from the beginning. The consensus-oriented process provided the business units enough (financial) incentives to become involved in group-wide issues. On the one hand, the IT managers in the business units had their own board especially set up for the purpose, where they could approve joint initiatives. In addition, a step-by-step implementation approach was selected for introducing the new system, which increases the detail of the planning every year and also provides appropriate methods and instruments. In spite of this, rapid pilot projects showing initial findings, for example a series of workshops on discovering synergies, can increase the acceptance of new systems on all levels. A further success factor was basing the introduction of new IT planning systems on existing processes and systems, thus keeping the amount of time and effort for the business units overall as manageable as possible.

Checklist: Does the IT planning system of your company enhance value through IT?	Yes
Does your company have a documented and established IT planning process and is IT planning aligned with corporate planning?	
Does the IT planning process combine planning content and monetary variables?	
Has the smooth cooperation between the IT department and business units and centralized and decentralized units been ensured for your IT planning system?	
Does your IT planning include methods that proactively analyze cost reductions for IT operations and IT projects?	
Does your IT planning include systematic methods for prioritizing the allocation of scarce IT resources 'fairly' and appropriately?	
Does your company have a cost and performance accounting system, which alongside IT-specific cost-type accounting also includes a cost center hierarchy aligned to the structure of demand and supply organization? Are IT services planned with cost unit accounting in mind and settled in terms of actual costs?	

3.   IT Performance Management – Managing IT Holistically

If IT is to fulfill its role as a value-enhancer for the company, then the services that it provides must be measurable and controllable. For this purpose, it is important to develop suitable IT systems that contribute to optimizing business process costs, enhancing or supplementing sales or possibly even adding value as a product component. The IT 'back office' also has to adapt to these changing roles: i.e. IT management, particularly the CIO, needs management/control methods and instruments that enable them to competently control IT efficiency and also the effectiveness of IT.

At the moment, however, the reality in companies is very different. In line with the old role of IT, it is purely the cost perspective that dominates the picture in most companies. IT is measured exclusively in terms of its efficiency: For example, total cost of ownership approaches, in which the overall IT costs are allocated to the terminals and their 'owners', or return-on-investment procedures, in which the anticipated inputs and pay-outs of IT investments are used as an instrument for judging their profitability. Comparing ratios, e.g. IT costs to sales ratios, is also a purely financially-oriented method for judging IT productivity.

Due to the lack of suitable ways for quantifying IT benefit and under pressure to manage the 'IT overhead' in a performance-oriented way, companies today use a selection of the following approaches as management and control instruments:

- *The historical approach:* The actual IT costs of the past have given way to new IT targets that take into account changes in quantity structures (number of users etc.) and external factors such as inflation. The advantage of this approach is that it is more realistic, which makes it more acceptable to IT employees and motivates them to achieve the targets set. The disadvantage, however, is that targets are based solely on past monetary values and do not take into account the whole picture. Thus, external factors such as competitor performances, market conditions, shareholder value or links to the core business or company strategy are not taken into account.

- *The top down approach:* Based on targets set by top management, for example, increasing shareholder value or value-oriented control variables, as many of the quantitative goals as possible are broken down and allocated to the IT department. The advantage lies in making IT goals consistent with corporate goals. However, it is doubtful whether corporate goals can be faithfully reproduced in their entirety in the guise of IT goals, as the variables under consideration are mostly purely financial. In addition, it is unlikely that IT staff will accept such targets, because they are completely detached from the content angle.

■ *The benchmarking approach:* In internal and external comparisons, best practice values from industry or other business units are ascertained and compared with the company's own targets. Benchmarking thus also offers a starting point for identifying best practice procedures. On important advantage of this method is the orientation towards competitors and the market. However, benchmarking values are often simply highly standardized financial IT targets and therefore not particularly meaningful. A detailed survey based on a questionnaire could reduce or even eliminate this disadvantage. Yet such an approach would involve a great deal of time and effort.

None of these approaches are suitable for controlling and managing IT effectively in its role as an instrument for value enhancement. A.T. Kearney's 'IT performance management' approach (IT-PM) starts out from the disadvantages of the approaches above and used the balanced scorecard method in order to prevent IT from being controlled simply on the basis of cost considerations. The assessment also includes the scope and quality of the services provided: Variables such as 'service level performance' or 'improving business processes' are included as integral elements of a holistic management and control system. These non-financial indicators are early warning signs for financial misdevelopments – developments that are often discovered when it is too late. Furthermore, the balanced scorecard allows us to take into account conflicting contexts in a 'balanced' way – conflicting, for instance, in the sense that improving service quality can negatively impact costs – and therefore serves as a good basis for simulating business decisions. Particularly in the companies with differing business models and value chains, whose strategic orientation of IT therefore also varies, IT performance management provides a framework for integrating all the business units, but is flexible enough to take into account the differences.

For the first time, IT performance management allows companies to implement and control IT strategies systematically and to realize improvements and value enhancements, be they of a financial and non-financial nature. The company and any IT service providers involved gain transparency and come to a mutual understanding of the services and value contributions that are provided by IT. This makes communication and the joint controlling of IT services between the business units and IT a lot easier. IT performance management also creates the methodological base for continuous benchmarking and the systematic exchange of best practices within and outside the company.

And last but not least, IT performance management lies to rest the perennial conflict between the business units, which are more content-oriented, and IT, which is more technically-oriented, and forges a mutual basis for communication on planning and developing IT.

3.1   Deriving IT Goals and Key Performance Indicators (KPI) from Corporate Strategy

Even when seeing IT from the value-oriented perspective, it is clear that IT is not an end in itself: All IT activities and IT projects should support the core business and corporate strategy. For this reason, IT performance management derives its objectives strictly from corporate strategy via IT strategy and quantifies them with the aid of clear, action-oriented variables – namely, the Key Performance Indicators (KPI). This approach is characterized by several guiding principles:

■ *A consistent framework:* All business units try to develop a unified concept, whilst setting great store by taking into account the differences. If one business units pursue an entirely different line of business to the others in the group, this can be reflected in the IT performance management system. Yet, one must never lose sight of the search for a 'common denominator'. Therefore, a binding, consistent framework should be used for all business units prescribing the perspectives for the balanced scorecard, definitions of standard KPIs and standard forms of documentation.

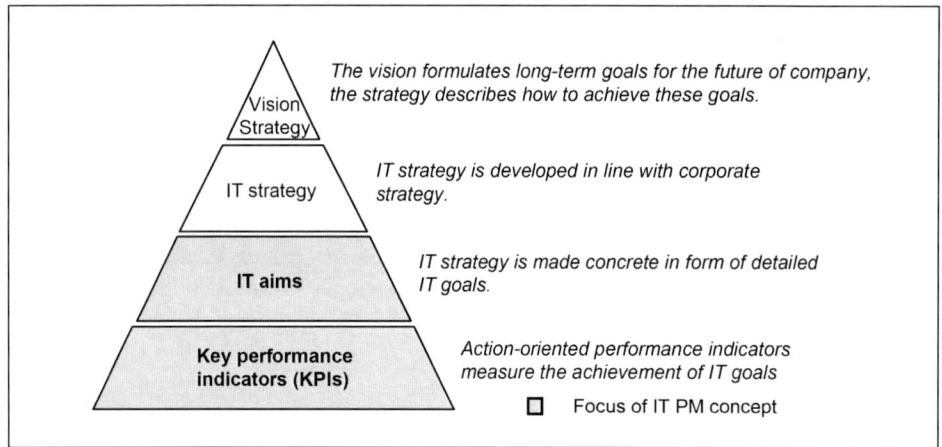

Figure 25:   *Aligning IT performance management to corporate strategy;*
                 Source: A.T. Kearney

■ *The top down approach:* Within this framework, CIOs and IT management develop IT goals and top KPIs based on IT strategy. The second step is then to cascade these down into the business units.

■ *The bottom up approach:* The balanced scorecards and KPIs from the business units are integrated into a joint reference model.

■ *The instrument-related approach:* IT-PM is established and structured – in particular the balanced scorecard and the KPI definitions – on the basis of standards developed by software manufacturers on balanced scorecard standardization committees.

On the basis of these principles, the concept starts with the strategy of the company and the IT strategy that is evolved from it (figure 25). The corporate strategy is included in the concept as a given. Areas of corporate strategy are then identified which have a direct, value-enhancing influence on IT. For example, implementing an external growth strategy via fusions and acquisitions requires the support of IT in terms of its high flexibility and technical integratability.

Tips for formulating single IT goals:

■ Formulate goals clearly and distinctly: It is crucial that you avoid any ambiguities and ensure that the content of the goals does not overlap.
■ Address the entire IT organization: When initially amassing possible goals you should fully take into account the duties and areas of responsibility throughout the IT organization, before the most important goals are selected.

Value chains, value driver models or business unit strategies are all suitable for structuring the cornerstones of an IT strategy. And it is important to take into account the varying levels of vertical IT scope (insourcing vs. outsourcing), organizational concepts (central vs. decentral) and standardization strategies (ERP standards vs. in-company developments) in the existing IT landscape. How far IT organization is evolved is also a factor that strongly impacts IT strategy: from having a systems-oriented data processing center as a partner through development partnerships with business units to integrated business partners for optimizing business processes.

To derive concrete IT goals, the IT strategy is summarized in one comprehensive top objective and broken down into smaller units (decomposition). A generic top objective of achieving a 'high level of IT efficiency and effectiveness' is then broken down into the components of 'efficiency' and 'effectiveness', in order to link these with real areas of action. The perspectives of the IT scorecard provide a balanced and complete basis for decomposing the top objective into individual goals. In practice, six perspectives for the IT scorecard have proven to be very useful: namely, personnel, projects, customers and market, infrastructure, operations, finance and costs (figure 26). The selection and designation of the perspectives is based on the balance between monetary/non-monetary and early/ late indicators, stakeholders and budget structures. When selecting the perspectives, it is important to find effective terms for describing them which all IT stakeholders can identify with and which can be used to represent IT performance to the outside world.

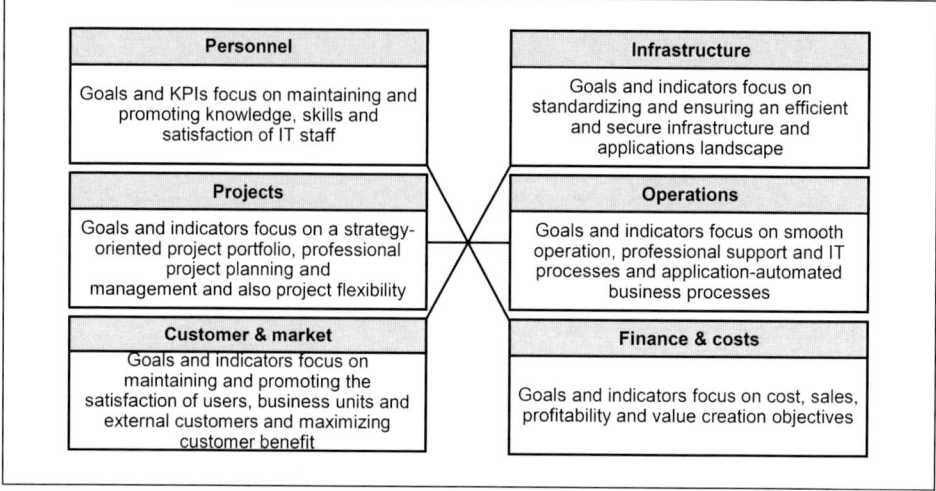

Figure 26:   Perspectives of the IT scorecard (example)

A system of goals, consisting of one top objective, a number of target areas that do not overlap and are defined in line with the IT scorecard perspectives, plus the resulting detailed individual goals – all these things form a structured basis for recording all of the relevant parameters for measuring performance (figure 27). In practice, a high degree of flexibility, detailed IT knowledge and business expertise, and an good overview of the overall process are required for developing a system of goals that is consistent with IT strategy and corporate strategy and can be controlled using KPIs.

Based on the defined goal system, Key Performance Indicators (KPIs) are developed for measuring goal achievement. KPIs must be distinct from pure reporting variables, such as monthly data processing center costs, and must fulfill a number of requirements:

■ *Measurability and comprehensibility:* KPIs must be easy to measure and to understand. As there are no universally valid KPIs, these should always be developed and specifically tailored to the concrete goals of the company, before establishing them on a company-wide basis.

■ *Clarity:* Each IT goal can be allocated only one KPI, which measures goal achievement. For the point of view of transparency and effective control, a KPI should not be allocated to several IT goals at once.

■ *Broad scope:* KPIs should represent a balanced mixture of financial and non-financial variables, and also early and late indicators. For example, employee satisfaction is a non-financial variable and also an early indicator and falling sales is a financial variable at the end of the cause-and-effect chain and also a late indicator.

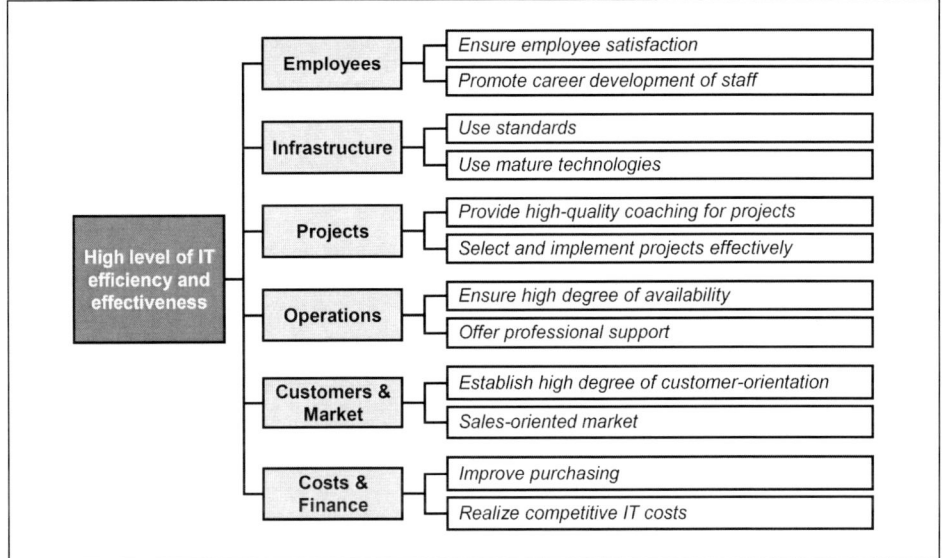

Figure 27:   IT goals system (example)

- *Responsibility:* For each KPI a KPI manager should be appointed within the company who is responsible for influencing its value. For example, the head of the SAP Basis Administration is responsible for the KPIs 'Availability' and 'Performance' of the SAP system.

- *Action orientation:* KPIs should be action-oriented; a change in its value should be a direct trigger for concrete measures. For example, time and budget problems are reflected in the 'Project' perspective as negative fluctuations of the KPIs 'Time deviation factor' and 'Cost deviation factor', and as such should immediately trigger a meeting of the steering committee.

When amassing potential KPIs for IT goals, it is important to address the duties and areas of responsibility of the IT organization as fully as possible. Only then should the most important goals and their KPIs be selected, namely according to the criteria of how relevant they are for achieving the top objective and how easily they can be implemented or rather how complex it is to measure goal achievement. This selection is important: A group-wide control instrument such as IT-PM should focus on the relevant and hard-to-implement IT goals that require special supervision. In practice, more than 130 strategic KPIs are developed and discussed to cover six perspectives, of which 40 are selected and defined for strategic control at CIO level. The most important KPIs are differentiated in line with the various balanced scorecard perspectives:

- *Personnel:* In the 'personnel' scorecard perspective, turnover rate, training days, employee satisfaction and qualifications are frequently named indicators. This perspective also takes into account legal frameworks and stipulations made by the personnel department. Important requirements are setting up an IT skills database and carrying out web-based satisfaction surveys, because this kind of information is generally not available in companies or is difficult to get hold of.

- *Infrastructure:* The 'infrastructure' perspective measures the technical basis for IT performance in terms of the degree of standardization and efficiency of technologies and security used. In this case, there tend to be less KPIs to discuss. On the other hand, the debate tends to be all the more intensive, for example, with the KPI 'Degree of implementation of standards', which frequently has emotions running high between headquarters and the business units. This also tends to be the case with security-related KPIs, which could imply restrictions for users. In cases such as these, conceptional preliminary work such as defining objects for standardization or correct asset management can be helpful.

- *IT projects:* For IT projects on developing and shaping the user landscape, important KPIs are the degree of goal achievement and cost and time deviance (figure 28). In addition, it is frequently clear in the debate over these goals that project selection ('doing the right thing'), and project planning and definition also need considerable management. For example, project activities must be clearly distinct from maintenance and small-scale developments that are assigned to operations as sustaining and not value-enhancing measures. Important conditions for management are setting up a tool-assisted project controlling system and formalizing project definition on the basis of project 'wish lists'.

- *IT operation:* After the project is completed, a finished application is put into operation. Failures or omissions in the project management will make themselves noticed later during operation in the form of higher maintenance costs and service levels that cannot be maintained. For this reason, important KPIs for the 'Operations' scorecard perspective are 'service level' for measuring availability and performance of the applications in a structured way, 'user support' via all support levels and 'managing the applications portfolio'. Depending on the productivity of the IT organization, process indicators can also be included: e.g. the duration and quality of IT processes and the measurement of automated business process applications. Important conditions for measurement are a structured process model for IT and business processes coupled with systematically structured and fully documented service level agreements from a customer perspective.

- *Customer and market:* Services in IT operation directly impact customer satisfaction and customer perception of IT. The most important KPIs in this perspective therefore measure customer satisfaction, and the quality and market success of services on the basis of non-monetary variables. Customer goals should be differentiated according to customer segments, for example, users, management or external customers, so that goal achievement measurement is done using several different KPIs. Important requirements are setting up questionnaires, web-based survey tools and important survey processes.

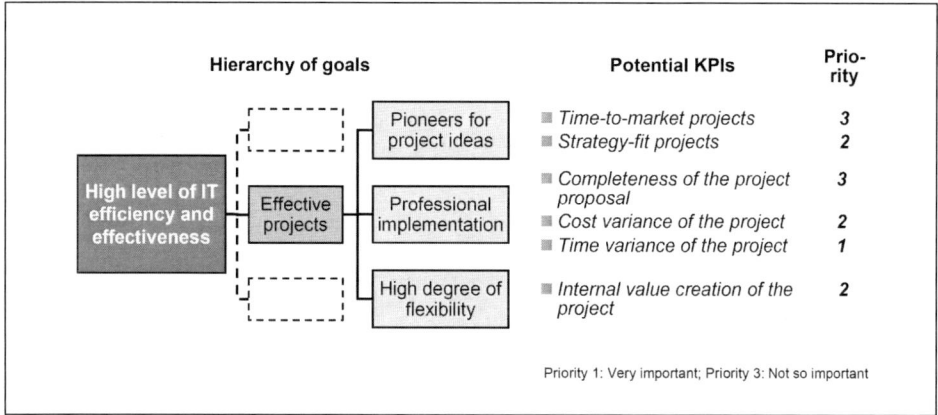

Figure 28:   *How KPIs are assigned to the goals of the scorecard perspective (example)*

■ *Cost and finance:* Finally, let us take a look of monetary indicators in the 'cost and finance' scorecard perspective. In cost center organizations, indicators such as 'IT costs to sales' ratios or 'IT costs per employee' are the most important KPIs because these are indicators for the relative efficiency of IT compared to other companies. In practice, global cost indicators are sometimes assessed as being irrelevant for control purposes because they are not action-oriented enough, whilst specific, universally recognized KPIs such as 'PC workstation costs' or 'application user costs for standard applications' are considered more advantageous in this respect. One initial challenge when defining the KPIs in this perspective lies in providing an action-oriented definition of the KPIs. At face value, an unfavorable ratio of IT costs to sales does not imply the need for immediate measures, whereas high 'SAP user costs' indicate a need for action. A second challenge lies in defining the KPIs in such a way as to make them truly measurable. The KPI 'PC workstation costs' is as concrete as it is action-oriented, but to be computed exactly it needs to be very precisely calculated, because not only hard- and software costs have to be assigned, but also those costs that result from implementation and maintenance.

After the KPIs have been developed, the CIO scorecard is drawn up. For this, all of the top KPIs are assigned to the defined perspectives. Experience shows that overall a manageable number of 10 to 15 KPIs results from prioritization (although the numbers fluctuate depending on the type of company) (figure 29).

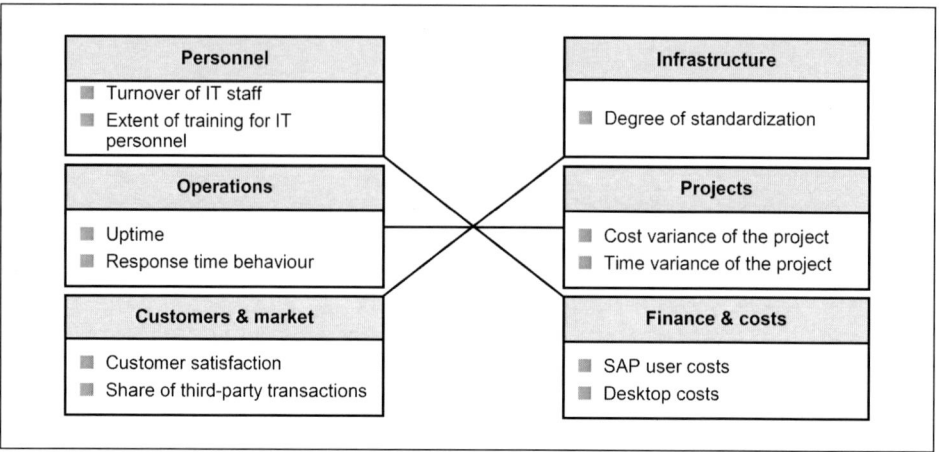

Figure 29:   *CIO scorecard (example)*

In practice, the introduction of an IT scorecard is seldom a linear process. The selected KPIs are often subject to critical reflection from a number of different sides and thus given different priorities accordingly. The process demands a high level of flexibility and a sound understanding of IT from all those involved.

3.2   Anchoring IT Performance Management within the Company

IT performance management can only be successful and meet all expectations as a management and control instrument if it is implemented and permanently anchored in the company. Anchoring is carried out via a number of different measures that are largely independent of one another.

- Detailing IT performance management for the IT organization.

- Establishing a continuous IT performance management process.

- Using tools for supporting IT performance management.

- Implementing IT performance management smoothly.

3.2.1 Detailing IT performance management for the IT organization

In medium-sized, homogenous and centrally organized companies, IT performance management in the form described in the previous section is usually sufficient. For larger companies with group-like structures, a more detailed IT performance management that cascades down into the supplying business units is recommended.

From the overall goal system, subsystems are derived for the business units that provide a basis for individually balanced scorecards for each business unit and at the same time are consistent and compatible with the superordinate balanced scorecard at whole-company level (figure 30). This method allows target values to be broken down relatively easily from the superordinate balanced scorecards into the subordinate ones. On the other hand, the degrees of goal achievement measured in the business units can also be aggregated to the level of the whole company without much difficulty.

IT scorecard and KPIs form the framework based on which the systematic improvement of performance can be planned and monitored. However, the benefit occurs only as a result of agreeing on the target values for each KPI and on appropriate measures needed to achieve the target values. Comparable to economic policy goals in the areas of unemployment, economic growth or government expenditure rates, target values are fixed for IT such as the degree of standardization, customer satisfaction or availability. These target values must always refer to a period of time – usually one year or six months – to forestall actionism that has no direction.

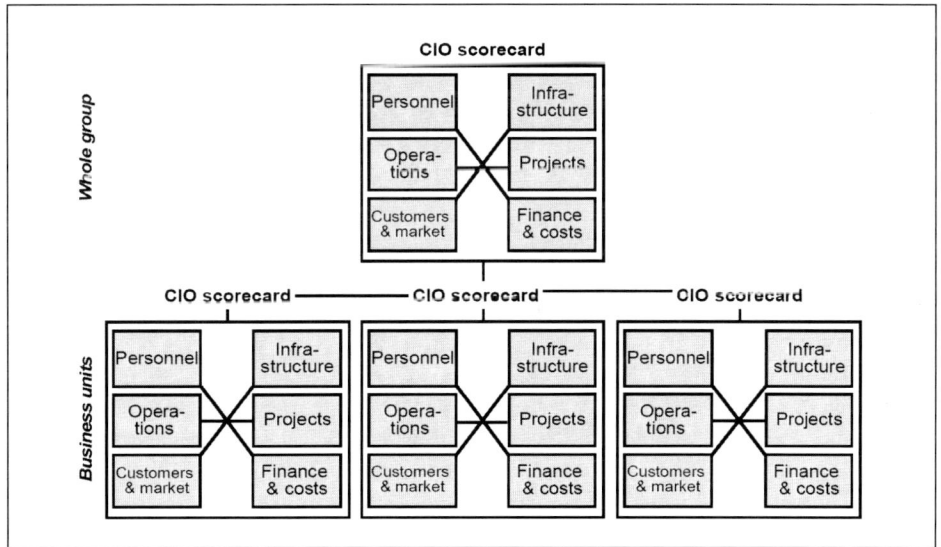

Figure 30:   Cascading the CIO scorecard down into the subsidiaries

Along with the target values, the measures, areas of responsibility and time periods must also be decided on jointly, and documented systematically (figure 31). This should not be done bureaucratically; however, a minimum level of systematic thought and structure is a basic prerequisite for being able to monitor the success of measures and KPI development and to deduce conclusions for the future from earlier decisions.

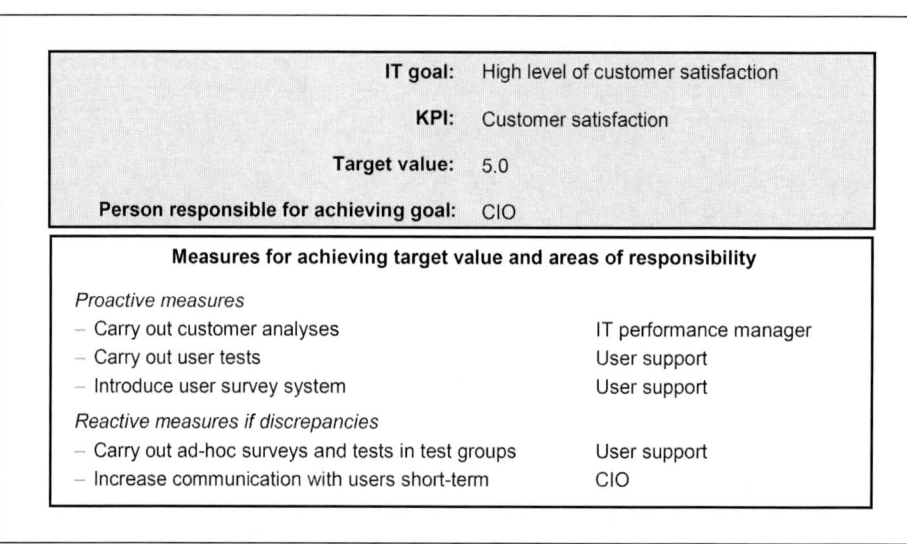

Figure 31:   Template (example)

In practice, it has proven to be a good idea to link KPI compliance to employee objectives systems. However the introduction of employee incentive systems or even linking staff bonuses to KPI developments should be implemented step-by-step and carried out with caution. These way employees can learn to associate their personal methods of working with target variables - without personal risk. This learning process can then also mean accepting a coupling of the two in the long term.

3.2.2   Establishing continuous IT performance management processes

With the introduction of IT performance management, the participating companies and business units enter into the control process. IT performance management is an additional control instrument alongside financial controlling and accountancy, and therefore it should tie in with existing processes such as budgeting, in order to ensure consistency and optimize administration. Starting from the initial concept, the IT performance management process runs through four stages every year:

- *Stage 1:* Aligning IT strategy with business strategy

- *Stage 2:* Adapting IT goals in line with the new IT strategy

- *Stage 3:* Deciding on and revising KPIs

- *Stage 4:* Comparing target values with the KPI value achieved and if need be making adjustments

The correct timing of the stages is crucial for integrating IT-PM processes into existing management and control processes (figure 32). Thus, IT strategy adjustments for the following year must be carried out in parallel or immediately after the planning for corporate strategy has taken place – usually at the beginning of the year. Within the IT itself, IT goals can then be fixed at the beginning of the year on the approved IT strategy. KPIs and target values are fixed parallel to the budget in the second half of the year, since target values and measures must be developed on the basis of the budgets that they have been allocated. At the end of the year, the agreed target values can be included in the annual employee performance reviews and staff can agree their personal goals based on achieving fixed KPI target values.

Actual KPIs are measured as a rule every quarter. Only those measurements that require more time and effort, e.g. customer satisfaction surveys, can be successfully carried out at longer intervals – for example once a year. Operational and support service levels as well as project controlling should thus be carried out monthly or weekly, so that if any deviations from the goals occur, measures can be developed to counter them in a timely manner. The actual values measured are compared with the target values – taking into account tolerance intervals depending on the relevant KPI. Any discrepancies between target and actual values are assessed and assigned a traffic light color – green, amber or red. The traffic light enables the KPI manager to analyze problem areas specifically – by drilling down the KPI to its influential factors – and to launch countermeasures

	Jan	Feb	Mar	Apr	May	June	July	Aug	Sep	Oct	Nov	Dec
Management processes		Strategy review for whole group / business units		Strategy planning for whole group / business units		*Finalizing strategic planning*		Operative planning for whole group / business units		Budget review		*Finalizing operative planning, employee interviews*
Integration into IT-PM		■ **Check implementation status of strategic IT goals** ■ **Where necessary, adjust strategic IT goals**						■ **Check implementation status of operative IT goals** ■ **Formulate new operative IT goals** ■ **Align with IT budget**				Performance evaluation of IT staff

Figure 32:   *Integrating IT-PM into the management/control process in the company; Source: A.T. Kearney*

How this is actually implemented within the company depends on the specific features of the company in question. As a rule, the CIO has ultimate power over the process and is responsible for its implementation. In larger companies, he is supported by an IT performance manager who manages the introduction and implementation of the IT performance management system and is responsible for day-to-day business - from deciding on the targeted values to reporting on actual values. Ideally, he also has fixed contacts in the business units to support him: either 'full-time' decentral IT performance managers, IT controllers or 'general' controllers, who are also responsible for local IT performance management. These contacts are responsible for collecting local values that must then be consolidated on the scorecard at CIO level.

3.2.3   Supporting IT performance management with suitable tools

Measuring and control efficiency can be significantly increased with the right tools. A central database that can be created with a tenable amount of effort collects the required information and is the core of the system. The use of a data warehouse system is ideal as the structures are flexible and there are a variety of possibilities for analyses. The KPI values can either be input via input masks where the data originates or automatically taken from operative systems lower down the line. For example, performance protocols on response times and availability can be read from the SAP system into a performance management tool using batch runs. The data cube concept of data warehouse architecture allows KPIs to be evaluated in other dimensions than the time dimension, using the concept of drilldown, e.g. the KPIS can be assessed by application, process or organizational unit. Turning the KPI analysis into graphics in the form of a dashboard and graphically displaying the balanced scorecard structure and the traffic lights makes it easier for the KPI manager to monitor and control results. A web-based interface supports the integration of the tool into the intranet or a personalized staff portal and thus makes access quicker.

The demands on applications logic and functionality are less complex. Setting up, changing and erasing KPIs should be possible within a very short timeframe due to authorization concepts oriented to the roles in the IT performance management system. It ought to be possible to fully automate the documentation of KPI definitions and in particular the stipulation of target values, measures and areas of responsibility. In addition, simulation components are conceivable that could simulate (based on quantitatively assessed cause-and-effect relationships between the KPIs) how values will develop in the future in specific decision-making scenarios for the system as a whole. Supported in this way, IT performance management simplifies control processes and reduces the administrative effort required when designing, collecting data for and assessing KPIs.

3.2.4   Implementing IT performance management smoothly

When anchoring IT performance management in the company, the following sentence applies, which also holds true for IT projects: 'The world is complex, managing the complexity must be simple.' When introducing IT performance management, mathematically precise approaches such as quantitative weightings of goals and KPIs, and the correlations between them, should only be used if absolutely necessary. It is much more important to allow IT management to focus on the key strategic value drivers and thus to place the emphasis on goal achievement.

The introduction of an IT performance management system however presents a challenge to both IT management and the business units involved: IT strategy and IT goals must be addressed, prioritized and structured with those involved for all the business units. Further, meaningful KPIs for measuring goal achievement must be developed and prioritized. Both of these tasks are difficult to manage alongside day-to-day business. Therefore it is a good idea to set up a working group on IT performance management, which involves all of the areas working on the concept - for example, the relevant IT performance manager and other competent representatives from the business units and IT management. The working party functions as a 'standardization point' for defining new KPIs and developing the concept further. It also serves as a platform for exchanging experiences between the business units and presenting any measures taken and their impact on values to the other units, providing an opportunity for learning from each other's work.

The working group can also ensure that the input of all those involved in the process is heard and forms the basis for discussion. Furthermore, it also functions as a communications interface for company- or unit-wide IT performance management concepts. If the company already has a ratios-oriented perspective, for example as a result of data collection in the form of extensive monitoring and data processing center analyses, then it is difficult to get it to accept a broader indicator concept, for example, in terms of customers or employees. This can only be achieved by a superordinate committee.

Challenges to IT performance management

An International conglomerate with sub-groups in such widely differing sectors as chemicals, metals and real estate decided to introduce IT performance management to control and measure IT at group and sub-group level. The group CIO was responsible for group-wide IT strategy. Each sub-group had its own sub-group CIO and its own service providers. It also had varying levels of IT value creation scope, ranging from fully outsourced IT to IT services developed completely in-house.

The CIOs in all of the sub-groups were faced with the following challenges:

■   It was difficult to control and monitor the implementation of IT strategies.

- There was no common ground for group-wide benchmarking or systematically exchanging best practices.

- The CIOs were under pressure to justify their budgets, since they were not able to present and communicate IT performance with sufficient transparency.

As a consequence, an IT performance management concept was developed for the largest sub-groups, the IT service providers, the holding company and the combined group. The aim was to create a common control instrument for increasing efficiency and effectiveness and allowing best practices to be exchanged among the sub-groups. Furthermore, the IT services were to be communicated better to the business units and stakeholders.

An IT performance management team from the sub-groups, consisting of representatives from IT management and IT controllers or IT performance managers, developed the concept with the close involvement of the CIOs. At first, the corporate strategy and IT strategy for each sub-group was recorded and the IT goals and KPIs for each sub-group were then developed and prioritized on this basis (taking care to create standard KPI definitions for each sub-group). Based on this, the CIO balanced scorecard was set up and cascaded down into the business units or IT units. The common IT scorecard covered some 40 detailed, well-defined strategic KPIs, taken from a base of some 140 IT-related KPIs. The IT performance management was then integrated into the control process and group reporting. Furthermore, the roles required for control were then anchored in the IT organization. Goal achievement for the performance indicators was then measured at the sub-group level in the group portal using a data warehouse solution. Based on benchmarking values, target values were then agreed on for selective KPIs, such as workstation costs or ERP user costs.

With IT performance management, the group was able to measure and control IT performance better. Furthermore, it was able to identify potential for improving efficiency and effectiveness more easily, and to develop suitable measures for achieving this. In addition, each CIO from the subsidiaries had a sub-group-specific IT scorecard for implementing specific IT strategy. All the CIOs were able to rely on a common basis for continuous benchmarking and exchanging best practice initiatives: The scorecard perspectives, KPI definitions and the overall methodology of their IT performance management system were all the same, and made communication and sharing experiences a lot easier.

Directly after it was implemented, the IT performance management system ran without a hitch and was already beginning to support the company in increasing IT efficiency and effectiveness. Thanks to this positive experience and the openness and flexibility inherent in the system, they have since been able to integrate new, foreign subsidiaries into the system.

Checklist: Does the IT performance management system of your company enhance value through IT?	Yes
Is the implementation of the IT strategy given quantifiable support?	
Is there a systematic and structured basis for internal and external communication between business units and users?	
Are the measures for goal achievement stipulated and measured in terms of goals and KPIs?	
Do the business units swap experiences on best practices?	
Can services be easily compared with internal and external benchmarking to recognize areas where performance could be improved?	
In the IT projects, is there a clear distinction between the areas of responsibility for costs and services between project managers and those responsible for operations?	
Is there enough communication between those responsible for IT performance management, those responsible for operations and project managers?	

Part C: Reducing Costs – Increasing the Efficiency and Effectiveness through IT

There is a natural limit to how IT can generate economic benefits and increase corporate value: It's IT cost. Many value-oriented IT projects are discontinued, not because the resulting benefits cannot be quantified but because the company's focus has shifted. And this shift does not necessarily have to include changes in the long-term corporate strategy, as would be caused by external developments in market and competition: To produce less-than-positive effects, all a company needs to do is shift its focus from IT growth drivers to IT-driven cost reductions, as often happens in times of economic downturns or internal restructuring.

Companies taking this route lower their chances for future growth and value increase. Therefore new IT projects, as well current IT operations, should be benchmarked and prioritized as early as in the planning phase (*cf.* Part B, Chapter 2, 'IT Planning'). A continuous IT optimization on this basis – including everything from IT applications to IT infrastructure to strategic IT sourcing – offers numerous possibilities to lower IT cost without jeopardizing an optimal support to business processes.

In addition to these efforts to optimize the cost/benefit ratio of IT, companies can also obtain savings in IT procurement – either by establishing ('spinning-off') internal IT service providers or by outsourcing IT services. It will depend on the development stage of the company's IT landscape what needs to be done most urgently:

- *Stage 1: Fragmented IT.* The greatest optimization potential – and the most pressing need for action – will exist at companies operating without valid IT standards, and with IT departments that do not understand the need for IT architectures: The resulting diversity of IT applications and infrastructure will drive up IT costs and limit IT performance. At this stage, IT sourcing decisions are often triggered by requests from technical departments and justified with available budget reserves, and there is little flexibility for 'unplanned' IT purchases. As a result, the costs of IT procurement tend to be high. The IT and business departments have not agreed on target service levels or performance figures, so service quality is rather poor. There are no customer analyses, and users do not really expect to get effective IT support if problems occur in day-to-day business.

- *Stage 2: Cost oriented IT.* At this stage, standards have been established for individual business units, limiting at least the costs of IT applications. Some cost reduction opportunities are also exploited in IT procurement – provided it really adheres to those standards and do not tolerate a multitude of exceptions and individual solutions, as will often be the case at this stage. As far as IT service levels are concerned, some basic performance figures have been introduced which, however, are not used as a basis for service agreements between the IT and business departments; as a result the support is still inadequate. All user requests are accepted and dealt with in succession, without any prioritization, providing some degree of user support in day-to-day business. Cost reduction opportunities through IT outsourcing are seldom used at this stage.

- *Stage 3: Standardized IT.* At this stage, corporate standards have been introduced and architectures have been developed which are scalable in certain areas. IT, thus, is largely standardized. While procurement is based on the standards defined for IT architecture, there is no obligation for the divisions to adhere to these standards, resulting in additional costs through individual purchases. In some cases, IT is outsourced to external firms - not for cost reasons but to bridge resource gaps. IT support to the business processes is enhanced by exchanging selected staff members between the IT and business departments; its quality is, however, difficult to assess since most service agreements and performance figures – obtained through sporadic customer surveys – are rather informal. When dealing with requests, IT staff make sure to tackle core issues first, which is a major improvement to user support.

- *Stage 4: Optimized IT.* At this highest development stage, company-wide standards for hardware, software, and networks have been communicated and accepted, and architectures have been introduced which are expandable in certain parts. This way, excessive costs are largely avoided in both, IT applications and infrastructures. IT procurement actively exploits cost savings opportunities by adhering to the corporate standards and allowing very few exceptions only. In global procurement the company employs strategic sourcing techniques; all IT projects undergo rigorous make-or-buy analyses. A tight linkage of IT to the company's business activities is promoted by staff rotation, both within the IT department and between IT and the business units (and vice versa). It is further supported by incentive agreements and programs for proactive employee development and technology training. Service level commitments, quality and efficiency criteria have been introduced and are monitored on a regular basis. Internal customers' perception of internal service levels is regularly analyzed and measured. To ensure optimal support for users in day-to-day operations, quick-response teams have been installed which deal with incoming requests according to their business relevance.

At each of these four stages, there is considerable potential for IT optimization and a professional management of internal and external IT service providers. Its goal must always be to decrease cost in such a way that the value potential of IT for the company is never adversely affected. After all, the purpose of utilizing IT is to increase corporate value!

1.   IT Optimization – Reducing Costs without Diminishing Returns

IT today plays a major part in reaching business objectives. Many companies realize its importance when business processes don't run smoothly, or when IT projects run over budget or time. Difficulties like these often result from heterogeneous IT landscapes, characterized by different application systems in similar functional areas, several hardware platforms, decentralized IT departments without central coordination, or insufficient IT service levels. The consequences are severe: IT users are dissatisfied; top management perceives IT to incur high costs while delivering poor value.

To avoid this, CIOs need to install a process to permanently increase IT efficiency – just like any other corporate activity is regularly examined for its value contributions and cost savings potential. However, their degree of liberty is likely to depend on the current state of the business: In fat times they will be free to give high priority to the creation of a flexible IT landscape, even if it requires a great deal of time and investment, and to consider its costs in relation to the benefits expected; in thin times IT-driven cost savings will become a top priority, while the operational obstacles resulting from a lower IT ser-vice level will now rank second – the motto being 'So long as our IT is running, it serves the purpose.'

The objective of IT optimization is to ensure the best possible IT service for internal customers at lowest possible costs. Depending on the individual company, optimal IT sup-port for business processes can either consist in flexibility and responsiveness to changing external conditions, or in superior efficiency leading to minimal unit costs in mass processes. In order to allow for IT to unfold its positive effects on business processes, a best possible IT performance also includes optimal support for end-users whenever problems occur in day-to-day operations. All that, of course, while keeping the life-cycle costs of IT systems as low as possible.

Optimizing IT, therefore, does not equal cost reduction. Reducing the costs of IT can only refer to a cost block which, depending on the industry, comprises one to seven percent of a company's total cost. IT cost reductions reach their limits when further efforts would curtail the benefits of IT for the company's business. This might best be illustrated by a simple thought experiment: Companies' IT cost would be lowest (namely, zero) if they simply switched off their IT and closed down their IT departments. Of course, the benefit of IT would be reduced to zero as well. This exact scenario threatened to become reality in the context of Y2K. To avoid that risk, many companies invested enormous sums to ensure the availability of their IT. Company managers do know about the benefits and value contribution of IT. Encouraging them to reduce IT costs, there-fore, usually means asking them to make appropriate 'cuts' which will continue to en-sure IT functionality while leading to a clear cost alleviation.

IT cost reduction requires a meticulous evaluation of current and targeted IT costs. In most cases, traditional analytical tools will be too coarse for this purpose – cost structure analyses and IT-cost benchmarking may serve as starting points for a cost reduction de-bate in IT, helping to roughly assess whether IT costs are on an appropriate level, and define a target corridor for future IT costs. Based on these findings a more profound discussion will be necessary, comparing IT benefits against IT costs and analyzing the existing IT landscape – including existing IT-related dependencies, as well as the opportunities resulting from new developments.

1.1   Strategic IT Cost Analysis: Finding the Right Leverage Points

In order to avoid 'economizing' those IT applications and infrastructural components that are crucial to a value-added use of IT, the entire IT landscape – including infrastructure and applications – and its key components must be subject to a thorough value analysis. Three dimensions of value are examined (figure 33):

- *Contribution to corporate value:* This dimension reflects the importance of the respective IT component to the company. For instance, a company wishing to develop new markets will find flexible infrastructures, expandable applications, and sales support more important than sophisticated HR applications. Consequently, this part of the analysis will derive company-specific criteria from corporate goals, requirements to business processes, and performance figures – such as support for strategic goals, coverage of business processes and functionalities, importance of business processes and functions to company performance, or the prevention of process disruptions by integration.

- *Technological suitability of IT components:* This dimension of the analysis is included to avoid further upgrading of technologically outdated IT components, and to ensure that companies invest in the right IT applications and infrastructural components. Available capacities, utilization, life-cycle and age of the application or hardware component, its conformity with the state-of-the-art and its complexity are only some of the criteria that may enter into the technological evaluation.

- *Overall costs for the company:* This part of the analysis covers the costs of an application system or a hardware platform over its entire life cycle. Should these data not be present in the company, at least the annual costs of operation, licensing, and maintenance will be analyzed.

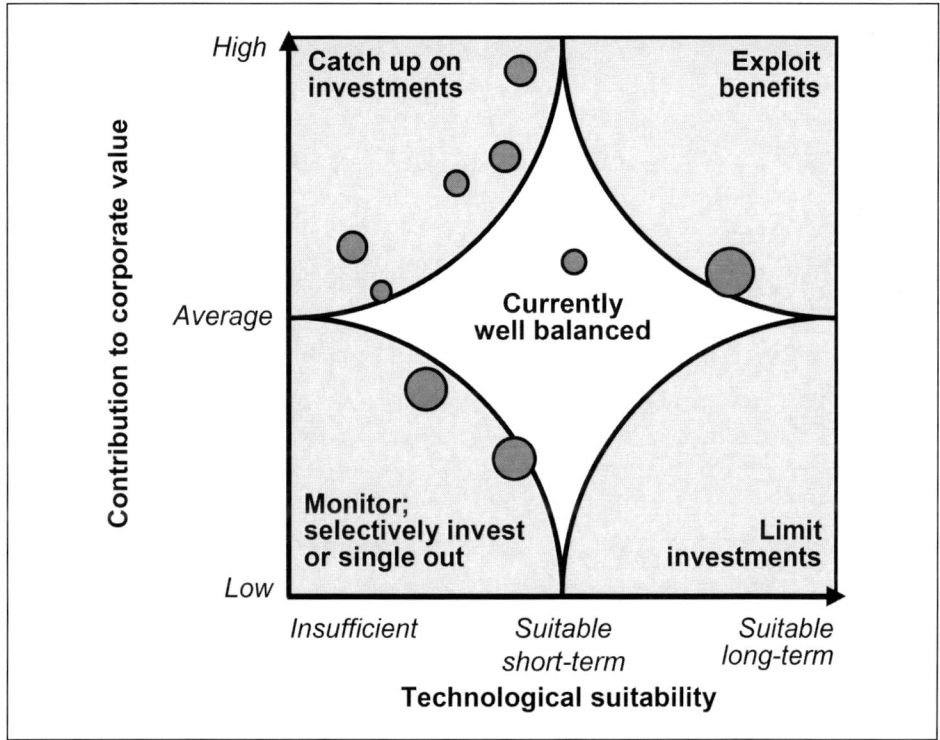

Figure 33:   *Strategic cost analysis (size of circles representing overall cost volume)*

Positions in the matrix indicate where IT cost reduction efforts would be appropriate and where they should better be avoided for the sake of a sustainable, future-oriented IT support.

■ *Catch up on investments:* IT components in the upper left corner are highly important to the company, yet current IT support is inadequate. It will therefore be advisable to intensify investments in order to diminish or eliminate existing shortcomings, so that the potential benefits of IT can be better exploited for the company. In the energy industry, for example, distribution systems rapidly gained importance once the liberalization of the market had set in. Existing systems for the 'administration' of 'purchasers' no longer represented a suitable technology. Huge investments were overdue and, in part, still are.

■ *Exploit benefits:* The upper right-hand field contains IT components that are well positioned from both, an entrepreneurial and a technological perspective. Instead of cutting costs here, companies should look for ways to use these applications and infra-structural components in more business areas in order to fully exploit their benefits. In addition, these IT components should continually be developed further, as their performance, utilization, or the requirements of business processes change over time. A highly diversified group in the construction and plant engineering business used a sophisticated project management system for its made-to-order plant production, while its construction business lacked a functional IT system for managing complex construction projects. As both divisions worked on similar business principles – such as made-to-order production – the company adapted the IT system from plant engineering and introduced it in construction. This way, the benefits of an existing application could be exploited much more effectively.

■ *Limit investments:* Companies should invest very selectively, if at all, in IT components which are state-of-the-art yet contribute little to corporate value. It is often due to changed business processes – or simply over-investment – that IT applications or infrastructural components have 'slipped' into this state. For instance, if customer orders were formerly accepted and recorded by a central department, whereas they are now largely entered locally via the Internet, a central order entry system will have lost all significance to the company, even if its technological platform is state-of-the-art.

■ *Currently well-balanced, continue:* The center field comprises IT components delivering an adequate contribution to corporate value. There is a sound balance between investments and IT benefits. This is often the case with IT systems for corporate support processes. For example, the financial accounting system of a manufacturer must work quickly and reliably but will not necessarily have to be top-notch. In such cases, standard business software will usually serve the purpose.

■ *Monitor; selectively invest or single out:* This refers to IT components which contribute only little to corporate value and are in a poor technological condition, which may, for instance, be reflected by poor reliability. Possible examples include IT components which have reached the end of their life-cycles, are no longer required, and might just as well be shut off, or IT components which must better be aligned with business unit requirements. Should the latter be the case, the company will need to check how focused investments could be used to improve the technological condition and increase the value contribution to the business. One example: Even today, some 10 years after the launch of SAP R/3, remainders of the precursor system SAP R/2 can still be found on companies' premises. In most cases the system is no longer in active use; rather, it sort of 'runs along' for information reasons, due to the fact that old data were not incorporated during the previous system integration. SAP R/2 is frequently the last mainframe application left in the company, with corresponding serious cost implications. The question here will be whether to completely terminate these applications – are the data really still needed? – or whether to invest in a suitable archiving system to replace the outdated one.

This systematic analysis and evaluation of the IT landscape provides a sound basis for IT cost reduction measures. We will take a closer look at two areas – IT applications and IT infrastructure – as these IT components are the main drivers of IT costs and any cost reduction efforts will have to start here.

1.2   Reducing Costs in IT Applications

Prior to cost reduction efforts in IT applications, most companies are in the same kind of situation: Their software landscape is a mix of proprietary developments and standard solutions which have proliferated over time. In the course of the years, business focuses have shifted, business units have been restructured, added, or sold, and business processes have changed. New applications have continually been added to meet changing requirements, and previous applications have become obsolete. If standard software is used at all, the different subsidiaries or divisions often use different systems tailored to their needs, and licensing and maintenance fees for these systems are a heavy burden on the budget.

This fragmented application landscape curtails the benefits of IT for the company – for example, because the logistics data required for supply chain optimization are 'hidden' in many different systems using incompatible definitions. In situations like these, the need for system harmonization is obvious. If the organization comprises several divisions, country operations, or subsidiaries, a systematic process to reduce IT application costs should begin with harmonizing business processes, thus preventing unnecessary IT expenses from the outset. Harmonizing the IT application portfolio will be the second step.

1.2.1   Harmonizing business processes

Companies with a history of M&A-driven growth often face a very heterogeneous business process landscape, even if business models are in part very similar. One example: A manufacturer had acquired several regional sales organizations which were managed as independent entities. All of them essentially had the same business model and were selling the same product to end-consumers. Each regional organization, however, had its own business processes for functions like procurement, payroll accounting, or controlling. This resulted in different requirements to IT support, covered by different ERP systems – which, however, served the same functions due to the similarities in business models. This is not a rare case: Many large companies simultaneously work with systems by SAP, Baan, JDEdwards, Oracle, proprietary developments, or several different systems by the same provider, resulting in multiplying costs for system launch, operation, maintenance, and licensing.

Moreover, different business processes for identical activities make it difficult to compare performance figures, as they are based on different data sources and calculated in different structures and methods. The same is true for logistics and financial data. Interfaces are often managed manually – or specifically programmed at great expense – and the business units keep to themselves, rather than working closely together. These situations call for a harmonization first of business processes, then of IT applications.

Harmonizing business processes is much more than a means to reduce IT costs: Many corporate strategies virtually depend on the availability of company-wide data and harmonized – in the case of service providers, even standardized – business processes. Purchasing, for instance, needs clear information on what materials or products have been purchased from what suppliers at what price, in order to determine for each material category whether the bundling of purchase volumes would be helpful to negotiate better prices with suppliers. By the same token, sales and marketing need comprehensive information on all customer interactions to design a consistent customer interaction strategy and build brand awareness. In an equipment-intensive manufacturing business, production scheduling and production controlling need up-to-date information from all sites, for instance on plant utilization and inventories, in order to permit the integrated optimization of production scheduling procedures.

Savings potentials from harmonizing business processes are enormous in both, IT and the business itself. Case examples suggest procurement cost savings in the order of over one hundred million Euros for a total procurement volume of approximately one billion Euros, achieved by bundling purchasing volumes across several business units, in addition to 50 to 70 percent cost reductions in IT systems, achieved by transferring the new, harmonized procurement process to one single system and switching off the previously used, redundant purchasing systems.

Tips for harmonizing business processes:

Involve business departments:
In harmonizing business processes, business departments and IT need to cooperate very closely – departments bringing in their knowledge regarding the business functions of the respective division or unit, IT contributing cross-functional know-how on the informational linkage between them, as well as on new IT design options.

Facilitate change through change management:
In the context of harmonizing business processes, traditional liberties of business units or subsidiaries will be curtailed to obtain a better cost or performance position for the overall company. Roles and responsibilities change. Top management support will help to facilitate this change.

On the other hand, harmonizing business processes requires enormous effort and expense, justifiable only through sufficient savings potentials in IT and business units. The necessary changes in IT (such as the introduction of a company-wide supplier portal to facilitate a harmonized purchasing process) usually trigger further changes in other units (such as tighter supply chain linkages with suppliers to reduce inventories).

One thing is certain: Reducing IT costs by replacing the existing heterogeneous IT landscape with a new one, based on harmonized business processes, initially costs money – sometimes enormous sums. However, as the economic benefit potential is usually much higher, it can easily 'pay' the required IT investments in new system introduction, data migration, and change management. And while the original motivation behind all these changes is to reduce IT costs, at the end of the day the overall economic benefit achieved by harmonizing business processes will include much more.

Optimization of business processes in a chemical company

A chemical products supplier had achieved domestic growth by acquiring several subsidiaries. Each of the new business units enjoyed great degrees of freedom with regard to the design and IT implementation of business processes. A harmonization of controlling and financial processes was initiated, starting with a search for cost reduction potentials.

Originally, the controlling and financial departments had comprised more than 500 people and used almost eight different IT systems. A thorough analysis of controlling and financial processes revealed that, while all of them were aligned towards the same process targets, they used very different working tools (such as account charts or costing sheets) and different processes (for example, for data entry).

Since process targets were identical and corporate guidelines called for identical procedures particularly in costing, business processes were harmonized: Account charts were adapted, costing sheets largely standardized, costing procedures coordinated, evaluation methods aligned, and the detailed processes within the controlling and finance departments, as well as the interfaces with up- and downstream IT systems were largely standardized.

Once this had been completed, an integrated IT landscape could be designed and implemented for all subsidiaries, based on the most up-to-date system among those already used. As a result, the number of IT systems – including those for controlling, general ledger, accounts receivable, accounts payable, and asset accounting – was reduced from eight to one. A new central organization unit entitled 'Shared Financial Services Center' was established and the staff of the previous units transferred.

These measures enabled the chemical company to achieve substantial savings in IT and process costs for controlling and finance. At the same time, the improved data transparency and higher speed of controlling and finance processes helped to reduce the total volume of receivables. The payback period for related IT implementation costs was less than two years.

1.2.2 Standardizing and consolidating IT applications

Standardize first, and then consolidate – this approach will help exploit the greatest savings potential. In many cases, the existing IT portfolio has very heterogeneous over time. This is true for both, shared applications for logistics and financial management (frequently referred to as 'commercial IT') and special IT systems for particular business requirements (such as CAD/CAx systems in engineering companies, bioinformatics systems in pharmaceutical companies, or process control systems in conventional and nuclear power plants). Even on users' PCs and workstations (as well as PDAs and other devices) we often find quite complex application landscapes: Microsoft worlds coexist with Macintosh worlds; in addition, Linux is currently making an entry into companies and government agencies and, needless to say, many users keep a regular potpourri of specialized applications on their PCs.

This diversity drives up the costs of applications in many ways:

- It there are several different IT applications for a given application purpose, costs for their implementation, operation, licenses and maintenance multiply

- Different IT applications usually require people with different qualifications and only limited possibilities of substituting for one another. If staffing levels are low this also results in a great degree of dependency on the know-how of individual persons.

- Different applications often lead to inconsistent and frequently intransparent data files which, in turn, require a variety of interfaces

The data from different applications remain uncoordinated. While it is basically possible for a data warehouse to solve resulting problems by making the data comparable in retrospect, this will further increase IT costs.

Multiple applications usually cause multiple interruptions to business processes, mostly involving media breaks and, on the users' part, a lack of information with resulting uncertainties in decision-making.

Different application landscapes on PCs require broader qualifications and more staff for user support at the call center; in addition, they raise the cost and complexity of data protection and data security.

Effective IT management in the applications area therefore calls for reducing complexity, as well as standardizing and consolidating the application landscape wherever possible. For large business applications (in particular those used in logistics and finance) this involves two major steps: One is to look for identical application areas across divisions or subsidiaries; the other is to identify cross-functional, integrated systems along the value chain. As far as PC applications are concerned, strict standards must be set for admissible applications. At times when budgets are tight, measures like these will help to make room for necessary IT investments.

Tip for standardizing IT applications:

Make sure your business case accounts for possible monopoly positions of software suppliers: Standardizing IT applications will intensify you dependency on one or few software suppliers. They will obtain a monopoly position vis-à-vis your company – and, changes of suppliers are always costly, this monopoly situation is often exploited via excessive licensing fees or poor service. Make sure to take account of these negative effects in your business case for the standardization of applications.

Implementation begins with the step-by-step migration of data, after which applications that have become obsolete are switched off. PC workstations need to be cleared in the context of the next upgrade, or as a special action carried out company-wide. For central business applications it should also be examined whether, on the occasion of this renewal initiative, outdated or 'exotic' hardware components should be 'cleared out' and switched off as well, which would help to further increase the effects of the IT cost reduction. For instance, once the last application has been migrated from the mainframe computer to the client/sever environment, switching off the mainframe will enable the company to save on operating expenses, as well as licensing and maintenance fees.

Standardization of application systems at a manufacturing company

At a large group operating in the manufacturing sector, the number of application systems had grown to over 3,000 in the course of the years. In production alone, more than 1,000 applications were in use, as well as almost 100 in accounting, and nearly 200 in HR. Most applications were no longer up-to-date, their average age being around 10 years. These outdated applications caused enormous costs: IT expenses for their operation were 50 percent higher than those of comparable companies, the complexity of the application landscape was hardly manageable.

By standardizing applications, the company managed to reduce the number of applications systems by more than 40 percent. IT costs were reduced by an even higher percentage, as one hardware platform became obsolete and the number of different database types could be reduced.

Such 'cleaning-up efforts' offer the most potential when performed in the context of a post-merger integration: In the case of a merger between two companies operating at the same stage of the value chain, over 60 percent of existing IT applications and almost 60 percent of the related costs could be saved (figure 34. Before, the companies had used different systems for virtually identical tasks – one of which was now simply dispensable.

The limit of all standardization and clearing efforts has been reached once IT-related changes clearly start affecting the business. Therefore close cooperation between IT and the business departments is indispensable, not only in harmonizing business processes but also in standardizing and consolidating IT applications. If, for instance, the IT department demands controlling systems to be 'cleared out', this change – and the resulting savings in IT costs – can be accepted or rejected by the business departments. By this we do not mean to say, however, that changes to IT systems should be the responsibility of the business departments. Rather, IT departments tend to be much too hesitant in using their right to suggestions: In many cases, they could have much more influence than they actually do.

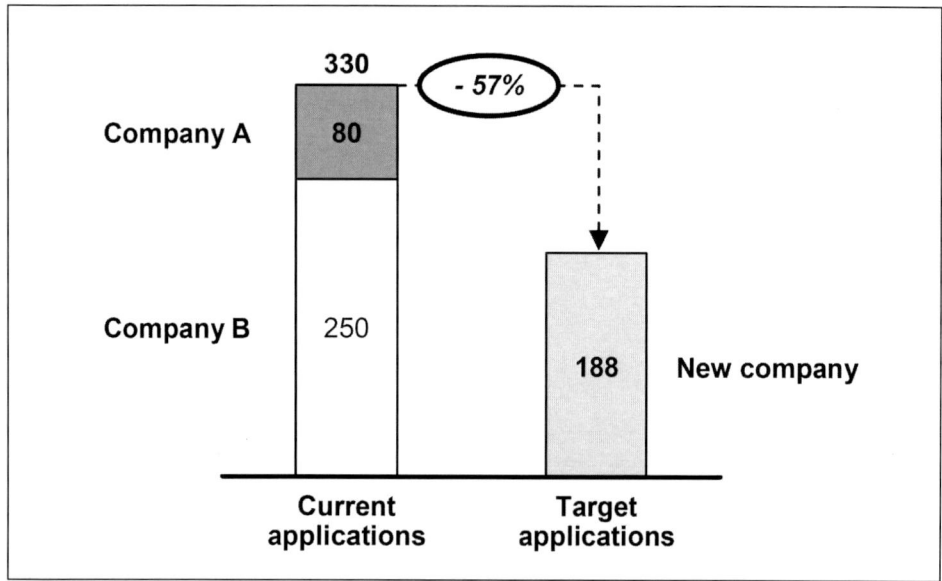

Figure 34:   *Strategic 'Cleaning up' in the context of a post-merger integration;*
            Source: A.T. Kearney

Another limit for the standardization and consolidation of IT application systems has been reached once any further action would start having negative effects on individual divisions or subsidiaries. Standardization is not an end in itself – its purpose must always be an improvement of costs and benefits to the company. In large groups we often find that headquarters, for many good reasons, wish to introduce one integrated ERP software which, however, would simply be over dimensioned for a medium-sized subsidiary. In this case a possible solution could be to equip the subsidiary with a suitable IT system for medium-sized organizations, and link it to the group's IT solution via standardized interfaces. Alternatively, if an integrated solution offers substantial benefits to the group – for instance, by enabling it to build an integrated supply chain – this might justify granting financial support to the subsidiary for implementing the group's standard system.

In short, standardizing application systems offers considerable potential for IT cost reductions and increases the benefits of IT by using fewer, better coordinated data files. Chances for a successful implementation are best if business processes have been harmonized beforehand. The standardization of IT applications can be immediately followed by a standardization of the IT infrastructure.

1.3 Reducing Costs for IT Infrastructure

When we talk about IT infrastructure we refer to all those IT components which, contrary to IT applications, are not visible to the user – such as database systems, operating systems, mainframe and client/server systems, LAN/WAN communication systems. To simplify matters, we are also including PCs, notebooks, and printers, as well as email systems and other systems of structural importance for the communication flow in an organization.

An analysis of companies' IT costs often reveals situations like this: All in all, more than 20 different types of PCs and printers from over 10 different suppliers are in use, as well as several database systems, development environments, and programming languages. Operating systems include several versions of Windows, as well as UNIX, AS/400, sometimes still OS/360, and more recently also Linux. Not surprisingly, large groups – especially those with a history of M&A-driven growth – are particularly prone to heterogeneous IT landscapes.

Uncontrolled growth of this kind costs time and money; during projects it also ties up scarce development resources in the IT department. Moreover, it is not advisable from a strategic point of view to maintain, for example, several different email systems in a company or group, as this will obstruct communication flows between the individual divisions and entities, and slow down the organization's speed of reaction.

1.3.1 Standardizing the IT infrastructure

There is one key principle for IT infrastructure: comprehensive standardization. It enables companies to reduce IT costs for all those IT components which users are not even aware of (such as client/server systems) and/or which, due to their overriding structural importance to corporate communications, must be standardized at any rate (such as email). In the case of PCs, notebooks, and printers, standardization leads to better replaceability, better service, and lower cost, which is why it usually makes sense to standardize these components as well. In exceptional cases, the business case will have to compare the costs of complexity against the benefits expected.

Among other things, standardization best practice calls for one single email system for the entire organization, standardized PC and printer configurations for all users – limiting the number of suppliers to between one and three, depending on the current procurement situation – and the elimination of old systems with specific programming languages and special, expensive runtime environments (hardware, operating systems, networks). The rule of thumb is: The more standardized the better. Rather than trying to cover each and every IT requirement of each individual IT user or user group, the overriding goal must be to determine adequate, overall reasonable workplace equipment which will be standard for the majority of all IT users.

Category	Original situation (2000)			Target architecture (2002)		
	Examples		No. of variants	Examples		No. of variants
Hardware	Terminals PCs: IBM, Compaq, Siemens	Midrange: IBM, Sun Compaq	IBM 9272 R45 Siemens	9	IBM PCs RS/6000 IBM G6	IBM 9672 AS400	3
Network	Novell 5.1 X.25, X.400 X.21, G703	Ethernet Token-Ring CISCO	PCM ISDN FDDI	21	Novell Ethernet	X.25, X.400 X.21 PCM	12
System software	Windows 3.1, NT 4.0 Solaris, AIX OS/390,OS/D1	ADABAS DB/2 Small-world	TIVOLI Manage Wise Openview	24	Windows 2000 AIX OS/390	TIVOLI Oracle DB/2	16
Standard software	SAP R/2 SAP R/3 PAISY PT-Com	GIS Smallw. Valex MS Office M/Mail	ABB-EMAD BKK GroupWise Visio, ABC	144	SAP R/3 Edifax Valex FAME	CCR DWH MS Office Outlook	39

Operating costs of IT infrastructure (p.a.):	35 mil. Euro ⟶ -23% ⟶ 33 mil. Euro

Figure 35:   Areas of standardization and potentials

Standardizing the IT infrastructure enables companies to reduce the number of variants by 50 percent on average, and to reduce IT costs by 20 to 30 percent within a year or two (figure 35. In addition, it is a prerequisite for reducing IT costs by establishing Shared Services centers, or by centralizing or outsourcing computing centers. Companies with a high degree of external growth, or striving for internationalization, should standardize their IT infrastructure.

In addition to cost reductions, standardization offers plenty more advantages – such as a more consistent IT infrastructure: It enables employees on business travel to link themselves into the corporate network with their notebooks from any of the company's offices, and exchange documents with colleagues worldwide, based on a standard IT application package and email system. In this case, standardization will greatly improve the benefits of IT for both, individual users and the company as a whole, at limited extra cost.

Standardization and consolidation of IT application systems at a manufacturing company

A manufacturer of heat and air conditioning equipment operates several production sites across Europe, as well as sales organizations in every European country. In 1997, the company's IT – like that of many large group – was highly fragmented: Decentralized IT responsibilities over the years had resulted in a heterogeneous infrastructure at all levels – from workplace systems to server and even mainframe platforms.

In the course of a company-wide efficiency program, the IT infrastructure was examined for cost reduction potential and radically standardized. This effort placed particular emphasis on workplace systems: While users had formerly worked with PCs configured to their preferences, the company now introduced three types of standard workplaces: One type, which was entitled 'Common', comprised Office components for text, graphics, and spreadsheet analysis, as well as the SAP front-end SAP GUI and the standard mailing system. It was introduced for almost 90 percent of users. Another workplace type, entitled 'Advanced', was additionally equipped with organizer software. The third type, which could be configured quite flexibly, contained special components such as development tools for IT personnel.

1.3.2 Centralizing IT infrastructure and consolidating computing centers

Standardization efforts in companies' IT landscapes are often a first step towards centralizing the IT infrastructure and additional IT services. Once hardware and network components, applications, and IT services in the different locations have been standardized, a logical next step will be to centralize selected topics, thus ensuring a better use of under-utilized resources, the bundling of know-how, and an increase in service quality.

Typical candidates for IT centralization are companies with numerous small locations worldwide or numerous remote users. In these companies, individual IT infrastructures and internal support organizations cause considerable costs for each location, as well as skill deficits in the local IT staff – for example, if each location has its own email and file/print server(s) and each server houses additional capacities for individual data back-ups. Local and regional application servers are usually not coordinated, housing only few applications which are only centralized locally. Many application servers are not archived; frequently there is only marginal protection against unauthorized access and viruses. These are just a few examples.

In addition to an increased service level, resulting from a more efficient IT infrastructure and IT support organization, standardizing and centralizing the IT landscape will also lead to considerable cost reductions. Resources maintained to cover utilization peaks can be bundled, thus better tailored to existing capacity needs, and used more effectively. This applies to server, back-up, and network capacity, as well as IT expert know-how. A decentralized IT unit usually cannot afford to employ IT experts for everything, from the entire spectrum of security issues to data warehouse concepts. If this know-how is bundled centrally, employees at local organizations can dedicate their capacity to value-added IT tasks. This bundling of know-how does not necessarily have to imply physical centralization – rather, the concept of the virtual organization provides local entities with the flexibility to assign both, central and local projects to their IT staff.

Tips for the centralization of computing centers:

Retain control rights:
Business units giving up their computing center will probably fear a deterioration of service quality; they should therefore be given certain control rights over the corporate computing center.

Avoid loss of "customer proximity":
At the previous computing center locations, "internal customers" will no longer find local contact persons to approach with their concerns. To close this gap, a centralized support structure with long service hours and agreed service levels should be established.

Prevent staff fluctuation: To avoid a know-how loss caused by IT staff leaving the company, relocation plans should be communicated proactively and employees should be involved at an early stage of the decision process.

Ensure system stability:
Concentrating IT computing in one place will result in higher demands to server and network reliability. Hardware and network architectures with redundant systems and varied back-up solutions are usually helpful.

Centralization, however, first of all means investments – for it will include the relocation of hardware and computing centers, as well as the restructuring of the entire IT architecture. New requirements will result with regard to hardware dimensioning, network capacity, performance, and system stability. Savings achieved through centralization must therefore be offset against potentially increased communication costs.

To quote an example from practice: The decentralized infrastructure of a large service provider, which had comprised 125 servers worldwide in 1999, was restructured to a total of 12 centralized servers within three years. Results were impressive: Due to improved server availability, employees now had much better access to central data files and applications; in addition, network performance – which was crucial for field service staff – was greatly improved; systems were equipped with much better back-up functions and highly redundant structures. In IT operations, many processes could be simplified, and the reduction in complexity was reflected in substantial cost savings.

There can be two types of limits to the centralization of IT infrastructures: One lies in the existing geographic conditions (for instance, if a country's communication infrastructure is inadequate); the other follows from the overriding corporate strategy: If, for instance, a company plans to spin off a certain division, it would be a mistake to centralize the IT infrastructure of that division, as this would lead to unfavorable dependencies which would later have to be eliminated in the context of an IT disintegration.

One type of IT centralization practiced quite frequently is the consolidation of computing centers. In one case, integrating four computing centers, who had previously been in different locations within the same country, led to cost savings of over 30 percent. In our experience, savings potentials for ongoing computing center operations will amount to between 15 and 40 percent, depending on the number, size infrastructure, and existing capacities. Additional advantages result from the creation of one single platform, as well as improved support and shorter project launch periods.

Centralization of computing centers at four financial service providers

Four companies from the financial services industry decided in 2000 to cooperate in the IT area. At the time, the companies were using different banking systems, as well as expensive customized solutions for sales, integrated bank management, and other purposes; they also operated four independent computing centers.

The companies started their cooperation by focusing on the computing centers – on the one hand because they seemed to offer enormous potentials to be quickly exploited, on the other hand because business processes would remain untouched and therefore the risk involved would remain calculable. In parallel with the computing center consolidation, several comprehensive optimization measures were taken:

- System architectures were strictly standardized to create a basis for efficient production.

- Redundant tasks, such as infrastructure stability, system and network design, network operation and management were consolidated.

- Licensing and maintenance costs for hardware and software were optimized promptly.

- Previously separate tasks such as release management, change management, system and network stability were selectively merged.

- The working hours required for servicing the standardized hardware – including hardware and software support, communication software, back-up/disaster management – were reduced.

Within a year, these measures enabled the banks to save around 15 percent on their computing center costs. Benefits consisted in a consistent and high service level, a broader know-how base for the systems used and, as a result, noticeable quality improvements in production. New requirements could be met faster, due to the effective management of interfaces with the units in charge of new applications. Both, the release and change management were optimized through consistent project control.

1.4   Exploiting Cost Savings Potential through Strategic IT Sourcing

Information technology – hardware, software, services – is an asset like any other, in that its procurement can be optimized. However, this opportunity is often neglected. In many cases, the IT department does not involve purchasing when making new acquisitions; subsidiaries buy whatever they feel like buying, without bundling purchasing volumes to negotiate better prices; often purchasing is simply not qualified and therefore unwilling to take responsibility for the procurement of a complex and heterogeneous asset like IT. In contrast to the mostly sophisticated procurement procedures in other categories, cost savings potentials resulting from strategic IT sourcing are, in our experience, seldom exploited.

At a European service provider which had enjoyed considerable external growth, the formerly separate business units procured IT services from numerous suppliers and manufacturers. An analysis of procurement and supplier portfolios revealed large overlaps in the types of systems and services purchased. Consolidating the supplier portfolio helped reduce procurement costs by more than 20 percent. Savings potentials in this order of magnitude – between 15 and 20 percent – are possible for companies in almost any industry.

In parallel with the optimization of procurement procedures, every company should regularly verify whether certain goods and services should really be produced in-house or, for good strategic reasons, rather be outsourced to external suppliers. These same make-or-buy questions are also relevant for IT managers: What are strategic core areas of IT, to be provided internally and exclusively by the IT department – and what other services are not critical to the company's competitiveness and can therefore be outsourced? Finding clear answers to these questions should be part of any IT strategy.

IT category	Savings potential – percent –	Sourcing approach
PCs, notebooks, printers		Standardization, bundling, e-auction, leasing
Midrange servers, routers, etc.	Reduction of remaining licensing costs; up to 70% if number of variants is reduced	Standardization, bundling, bid invitation, leasing
Application software (ERP, CRM, PDM, etc.)		Standardization and consolidation, negotiation with supplier
Workplace software		Standardization, bundling, negotiation
Development and system software		Reducing number of variants, negotiation
IT consulting and software development		Preferred supplier, competitive bidding, fixed price/total cost approach, quality management
Software development		Offshoring
Desktop management and computing center operation		Competitive outsourcing
Outsourcing contracts		Renegotiation

Figure 36:   Effective approaches to IT sourcing

In most cases, however, the optimization of IT sourcing is triggered by high cost-saving expectations, rather than strategic considerations. Experience shows that projects to optimize IT sourcing, just like projects to optimize other procurement categories, quickly take effect. Interestingly, the percentage value of procurement cost reductions is almost unrelated to the absolute procurement volume. In individual IT categories, up to 40 percent cost savings can be achieved; usually 15 to 20 percent are possible across the entire IT procurement portfolio (figure 36).

Prior to IT sourcing, a consistent demand management must be established to ensure coordinated activities. The first question here will be, what needs to be outsourced and what needs to be produced in-house. Rule number one is: Less is more. Rather than trying to negotiate lower licensing fees with the different ERP suppliers, it will often be preferable to change to one single ERP platform and prevent multiple licensing fees. Corresponding strategies begin with the harmonization of business processes, continue with the standardization and sorting out of IT applications, and end in the standardization of the company's IT infrastructure (see previous subchapters). Based on these measures, the key questions of strategic IT sourcing can be tackled:

- *Make or buy:* Which IT services – both, critical to competitiveness and on a competitive level – should the IT department focus on?

- *Bundling:* What IT services should be bundled for either the 'make' or the 'buy' case?

Both questions can only be solved in conjunction with the corporate strategy. As any other strategic decision, the answers cannot be determined once and for all, but need to be revised at regular intervals in the context of the company's medium- and long-term planning.

1.4.1   Examining the degree of vertical integration in IT

Experience has shown that the key question is not whether all IT services should be provided internally or externally, or whether they should always be sourced centrally or individually. While the coordinated sourcing of computing center services usually makes sense due to their homogeneity and economies of scale, in other cases – such as the maintenance of company-specific aged applications – the coordination effort often exceeds possible synergies. It is therefore preferable to determine for each of the company's key IT services which approach will be more suitable.

On the other hand, IT resources are scarce and expensive. The general rule should therefore be to focus in-house development capacities on those areas where proprietary developments can help achieve major competitive advantages. Above all, this applies to IT services through which companies differentiate themselves from competitors, and which therefore increase corporate value. A possible example would be an energy supplier's decision support systems used in energy trade, which are based on company-specific algorithms and therefore provide a competitive edge. This company would be best advised to bundle its internal IT resources in order to maintain and expand its competitive advantage, an approach often facilitated by the outsourcing of standard IT services.

It will depend on the industry and company-specific situation which IT services need to be categorized as 'Make'. Some examples from our consulting practice:

- In *telecommunications*, low-cost systems and CRM systems are often specialized applications. They are frequently developed in-house or tailored to the specific needs of the organization or product (customized) based on packages. In the wireless sector, for example, new topics emerge in GPRS/UMTS data communication (including i-mode as a special form) – such as data driven service products, event-based billing, etc. – for which no standard solutions are available as yet.

- In the *energy sector*, specialized systems that are frequently developed in-house include industry-specific control systems for optimizing capacity utilization at the different stages of the value chain.

- *Large trade groups* usually operate proprietary systems in enterprise resource planning and sales because so far, there is no standard software available for these key areas.

- *Service providers in tourism and logistics* (such as airlines, hotels, railway, car rentals; logistic providers for land/air/sea freight) tend to focus on reservation, tracking and tracing systems.

In *all industries*, the following standard services are suited for outsourcing or strategic sourcing, since they are either uncritical to competitiveness, or cannot be provided in-house at competitive terms:

- Standard business functions including finance and account, purchasing, logistics, HR

- Workplace software

- Operation of PCs/desktop computers, and LAN/WAN (= end-user computing)

- Operation of computing centers.

Only in very exceptional cases will companies have an IT procurement volume large enough to justify the in-house production of these services.

1.4.2   Bundling IT services

The harmonization of business processes, the consolidation of IT applications, and the standardization of the IT infrastructure all result in a clear need to bundle the sourcing of services. In this context, even IT services outsourced for only one division or subsidiary should be checked for possibilities to have them covered by one of the company's existing providers, possibly at lower costs. In the end there will be only few specific, 'exotic' IT services which must be outsourced separately. According to our experience, more than 90 percent of any IT procurement portfolio will be suited for the bundling of purchasing volumes.

What distinguishes strategic sourcing projects in IT from those in other areas is the composition of the project team, since users need to be closely involved. Individual persons, business units, or subsidiaries usually have very diverse interests, as well as different preferences with regard to workplace systems, application software, and service providers –which, in turn, often prevents companies from making use of the most important and effective IT sourcing lever: standardization. This is why demand management plays such an important part in such projects: If the organization can be committed to only one standard software or one type of terminal, bundling purchasing volumes and achieving sustainable major savings in procurement costs will be a breeze. Likewise, if these efforts are not successful, all sourcing approaches based on extensive bid procedures and supplier selection will be doomed to fail, due to small volumes and a fragmented supplier portfolio.

Introduction of strategic sourcing at a global IT service provider

At a large, globalized group with an IT procurement volume of 1,300 million Euros, the sourcing process for hardware, software and IT services was quite intransparent, due to a high degree of complexity and a very international business. Hardware was procured from a number of different suppliers which were frequently changed. The company's application landscape was very heterogeneous as a result of several acquisitions and a large share of customer-specific projects. What complicated matter was that the company had to make high demands on quality and delivery times to avoid competitive disadvantages. Last but not least, it had to meet specific requirements in many countries, for instance with regard to accounting systems.

The company started its improvement efforts by establishing clarity on the different divisions' requirements, capacities needed, supplier relationships, and other cost drivers of IT sourcing. On this basis the IT infrastructure and workplace software were standardized. Next, a target portfolio for business software was determined and a migration plan set up; in addition, a standardized award procedure for IT projects was defined and agreed upon. For the IT infrastructure, competitive bids were invited using e-auctions; for workplace and standard business software the company conducted supplier negotiations which turned out to be very effective thanks to the larger volumes. Together these measures enabled the company to reduce its IT procurement volume by 15 percent.

To ensure that this success would be sustained long-term, processes and responsibilities for IT sourcing were clearly defined. This included the centralization of responsibilities where IT procurement categories would in future be bundled across the organization.

Checklist: Should your company optimize its IT?	Yes
Does your software comprise numerous proprietary developments and redundant standard solutions?	
Does the heterogeneity of IT constrain business processes, rather than supporting them optimally?	
Has your company recently undergone a period of considerable external growth, without integrating the newly added IT applications and infrastructures?	
Do your employees use several database and/or email systems, or numerous PCs and notebooks in different configurations?	
Are hardware and network components distributed over several locations?	
Do individual departments or divisions purchase IT services at their discretion and from different suppliers?	

2. In-House IT Service Providers – Exploiting Efficiency Potentials

In the 1990ies, many companies integrated their internal IT functions, spinning off IT service providers as separate corporate entities. There was a regular wave of start-ups across all industries, seizing manufacturing companies, energy suppliers, airlines, and banks alike. While this trend has subsided over the past years, there is still a great number of companies facing the decision whether or not to spin off their internal service units.

Key motives for spinning off internal IT service providers are cost reductions and quality increases in IT performance:

- *Cost reductions:* The company wishes to reduce IT costs by integrating IT departments and staff under one management and exploiting economies of scale (for example, by consolidating applications and computing centers – see chapter 1 of this section, 'IT Optimization'). In particular when companies have several similar divisions, each with its own IT department, there are usually considerable synergy potentials in the different areas of IT. The same is true for companies which have passed through phases of strong external growth: They can usually exploit substantial cost and market synergies by spinning off internal IT service units. The objective must be to procure IT services at market prices, which are usually lower than internal transfer prices.

- *Quality improvements:* The integration of IT systems and staff helps consolidate the existing know-how and thus to improve IT performance. Service levels can be raised, simply due to 'more mass', IT solutions can be transferred between business units, launch times can be reduced if more people are involved, and many more optimization measures can be taken. Transforming the in-house IT unit into an independent IT service provider leads to a clear distinction between the role of the client – played by the company – and that of the contractor, which is the IT provider's part. It should result in a constructive service mentality in the provider's organization, while enhancing transparency on the IT services purchased and the related costs. Finally, companies might seek quality improvements by establishing an external IT service provider if they face substantial IT investments which, contrary to historical practice, will be introduced and used across the organization.

In the second half of the 1990s, when qualified IT resources were scarce and sought-after in the market, many companies also hoped that spinning off their internal IT service units would help them market their IT services to external customers. A positive side-effect of establishing an internal IT service provider is the support for the company's IT governance: If, for instance, the IT provider becomes aware that several uncoordinated orders for identical IT requirements or system solutions are placed by the business units or subsidiaries, and if the company's IT governance calls for integrated IT solutions, the provider can bundle these requests and implement standardized IT systems based, for example, on template solutions

– which incur much lower costs for implementation, operation, and maintenance than would customized solutions for individual business units or subsidiaries.

The question that remains is: Why should a company go through the trouble of spinning off an internal IT service unit, instead of simply outsourcing IT services from an established external provider? The answer is that in many companies, outsourcing is unacceptable for one or several of the following reasons:

- The company has critical know-how in IT systems and business processes, which may not under any circumstances be passed on to third parties (example: merchandise management in trade).

- The company is highly specialized or innovative, or present in exotic locations, or it requires very specific IT services which external service providers can only deliver as 'special customer requests' at excessive extra cost (example: market launch of data communication products in telecommunication).

- The company faces major change with substantial consequences for IT, and therefore wants to retain IT in its own control.

- Corporate tradition or explicit agreements with the employees' representatives prevent outsourcing.

Prior to the spin-off of an internal IT service provider, the company should be clear about its objectives, taking them into account when deciding on the service provider's design configuration. Similar to the outsourcing of IT services to external IT service providers (see chapter 3 of this section, 'IT outsourcing and offshoring'), working with internal IT service providers requires strategic lifecycle management – spanning from the spin-off itself to professional cooperation to an exit strategy that works for both parties.

2.1   Strategically Aligning and Spinning-off the IT Provider

With regard to technical and commercial details, the cooperation between the internal IT provider and its customers – the divisions of the parent company – is set up in the same way as is customary between third-party providers and their clients. Mutual service relations are based on a service level agreement, with service levels tied to prices and a system of incentives (bonuses/maluses), and the cooperation is continually adjusted to the changing requirements of the company or the potential for technological innovation in the provider's operations.

However, since IT providers are created from the centralization and spin-off of existing IT departments, there is a certain risk that previous inefficiencies and shortcomings will live on. Therefore, a series of stipulations is required covering everything from the IT provider's organization structure, to staff competencies and responsibilities, to the redesign of business processes. The aim must be to ensure the transition form a mere organizational unit to an independent corporate entity.

This is where spinning off an internal IT provider differs from IT outsourcing. Determining the configuration of the internal IT provider and defining the rules for cooperation will involve opportunities and new challenges for the company. Even prior to the spin-off, the company must be aware of the goals it is pursuing with this move, and integrate them in the design effort.

The first question in this context is: What parts of IT should be spun-off at all? There are three basic answers which, in practice, will vary in several ways:

- *Everything:* The entire IT including all systems, computing center locations, and IT executives and staff will be transferred to the internal IT provider. Only demand management will remain in the company, to be taken care of by a CIO Office.

- *Only central IT systems and staff:* In this case, the CIO Office and decentralized IT remain in the company

- *Only shared IT systems and staff:* In addition to the CIO Office, division-specific IT systems and staff remain in the company

Other varieties include spinning off the entire IT (with the exception of the CIO Office) and leaving certain IT components in individual divisions. To simplify matters, we will base the following on the assumption that a company's entire IT is spun off, while the CIO Office controls IT demand and determines the IT governance rules relevant to the cooperation with the internal IT provider.

2.1.1   Determining 'strategic parameters' for the IT provider

For a successful later cooperation it is crucial to determine the 'strategic parameters' of the IT provider's business model from the very start (figure 37): Should it operate only from the company's primary locations, or should it be present internationally to support the company's growth strategy? Should its focus rather be on service quality or competitive prices? The clearer the answers, the easier it will be for the IT provider to support the company's goals.

Strategic parameters	Design options		
Regional presence	Focus on primary locations	←——→	International presence
Service portfolio	Focused	←——→	Broad
Service strategy	Cost-driven	←——→	Performance-driven
Financial targets	Profit center	←——→	Cost center
Focus of orders	Individual customer	←——→	Cross-divisional
Sales activities	Key Account Management	←——→	"Real" sales operations
Vertical integration	100 %	←——→	An optimized 50 to 70 %
External market	Yes (5 to 10 %)	←——→	No

Figure 37:   Strategic parameters for the business model of the IT provider (examples)

The IT provider's position in each parameter will determine its further actions, development, and cooperation with the company. Some of them enhance, some constrain the entity's growth potential or its ability to meet the company's cost and performance requirements. Most important from the company's point of view are those parameters concerning the interface between both parties, as well as those affecting the IT provider's technical and financial performance.

■ *Regional presence:* After existing IT functions are spun off, the new IT provider will immediately be present at all company locations. What should be clarified in addition is whether the IT provider will focus on supporting the primary locations of the company, or cover all existing and future locations. The latter may require establishing new international operations, for instance if the company intends to go to China. If the international focus of the IT provider is to be expanded, it will be crucial to ensure that executives and employees are gradually introduced to working on intercultural teams, and that they build the necessary language skills (most importantly in English).

■ *Breadth of service offering:* As far as this parameter is concerned, less is more: Due its specialization, the industry and company-specific know-how, and the physical proximity to its customers, the internal IT provider is likely to be better positioned than external providers when it comes to application development and maintenance, on-site support in small, dispersed locations, and the management of infrastructure projects. On the other hand, where standard services like the operation of computing centers or help-desks are concerned an internal entity will usually not be able to compete with the prices of external providers which, due to their size and the standardization and centralization of their services, will benefit from fixed-cost degression and other economies of scale. The internal IT provider should therefore focus on those services where it can offer the company a price, performance, and quality level superior to that of external vendors. Likewise, it should give up those services where it cannot be competitive in the medium or long term, seeking alliances with external providers which are able to render these services at better terms.

■ *Service strategy:* The service offerings and qualities requested by the parent company will differ from one division to the other: Some attach more importance to quality, others emphasize costs. Particularly large differences exist between the United States, Europe, and Asia: The high labor costs in Europe and the U.S. have resulted in higher penetration rates for automation and IT, which in turn calls for higher quality standards in user support and application development. The homogeneity of languages between the U.S. and U.K. facilitates the bundling of telephonic user support, as would be provided by a user help desk. The high qualification level found in some Asian regions, along with comparatively low labor costs, provide an excellent basis for location and language-independent services delivered on a worldwide scale. They include server and network management and certain parts of application development (*cf.* chapter 3 of this section, 'IT outsourcing and offshoring'). The company should therefore consider carefully whether the internal IT provider should offer high-quality services based on a broad presence in all corporate locations, or cut down on local presence and transfer some of its IT operations to other countries, thus benefiting from factor cost advantages which it can pass on to the company.

■ *Financial targets:* If an internal IT provider is set up as a profit center with fixed financial targets in terms of ROCE or EBIT, conflicts of interest with the divisions are virtually unavoidable, which can seriously hamper an effective cooperation. Divisions will argue that the provider's profits result from a simple transfer of their own profits, rather than representing 'real' business results. This accusation seems justified in those cases where the IT provider – at least in the divisions' perception – does not charge market prices but cost-covering internal transfer prices which are above market level. Corporate divisions will therefore often demand that the IT provider be operated as a cost center. This, of course, contradicts the intended market orientation and other strategic goals which have been set for the IT provider. The provider's prices should be such that it can achieve an adequate profitability level while preventing the divisions from outsourcing to external providers for cost reasons. In short, it is imperative to use sound judgment in setting financial targets.

■ *Focus of orders:* The IT provider can either work by order of each individual customer (i.e., division) or it can be given the mandate to seek cross-divisional synergy potentials, for instance by transferring IT solutions. In the latter case it will bundle similar requests from individual customers and strive for joint, cost-optimized and benefit-increasing IT solutions, using parameterized IT systems and template models.

■ *Sales activities:* The need of the IT provider to build up own sales activities will depend on whether it will be closely involved in the parent company's IT planning processes – or treated as a third party, competing for bids with external IT service providers. In the former case, all the IT provider will need is a key account management staffed with knowledgeable IT specialists with problem-solving skills, and closely cooperating with IT users and CIOs at the divisions and subsidiaries. This solution is optimal in terms of costs because it provides planning certainty; it requires, however, the divisions' confidence in the quality and price competitiveness of the IT provider. If such confidence is lacking, a sales team must be set up at the IT provider at considerable extra cost, since the staff from the company's previous IT departments will usually not include any sales professionals.

■ *Degree of vertical integration:* Many IT providers, particularly at the beginning, tend to cover most of their value creation in-house. From the perspective of the parent company, this only makes sense it the IT service rendered is crucial to competitiveness and cannot be outsourced. In most other cases companies will demand their IT providers to focus on core activities at competitive prices. This means for providers that they must outsource certain parts of the value chain to external vendors, and assume a management and integration function for these parts. Services suitable for (partial) outsourcing usually include those related to infrastructure, an area where specialized or large external IT providers enjoy scale advantages. A similar, project-based strategy suggests itself in application development. Outsourcing these types of services will enable internal IT providers to counterbalance the high volatility in staff utilization; in addition, it offers opportunities to selectively buy in innovative know-how which they expect to become critical in the future, and which they can then develop, step by step, in-house.

■ *External market:* Many companies count on external sales potentials when spinning off internal IT providers. In individual cases, they can contribute up to 50 percent to the provider's overall sales. This, however, is another point which – just like the setting of financial targets – requires a good deal of discretion: The new IT provider will initially suffer from considerable competitive disadvantages against established providers, which can be eliminated only through substantial and ongoing investments on the company's part. In addition, the high quality demands of most external customer will force the IT provider to assign its 'best people' to external projects, which means that these experts will not be available for services to the parent company. In this scenario, unrealistic sales targets for the IT provider can easily fall back on the company. At least in the starting phase, companies should therefore expect their IT providers to achieve a maximum of five to ten percent of their sales in the external market.

In order to fulfill the strategic parameters of its parent company, the IT provider will have to develop corresponding capabilities: At the beginning of its existence, it will be nothing more nor less than the sum of the IT departments it was formed from, with all the strengths which the company has built and fostered over the years, and all the weaknesses it has been tolerating. This will include the usual, industry-specific compromises in HR policies (for example, where regulations for the protection against unfair dismissal must be observed) which, in the case of an external IT provider, would result in the cancellation of orders.

The quality of human resources is a key success factor for an IT provider. Consequently, the staff of the former IT departments will need to shift their focus from IT technology to customer orientation and service-mindedness. While they are usually highly motivated at the time of the spin-off, they will probably need some time to really adopt and live a true service culture. Suitable measures in HR leadership and management systems, as well as organization changes (such as introducing key account management or establishing cross-functional 'solution teams') can help accelerate this cultural change. Supporting tools like project evaluations, performance evaluations, performance-related compensation systems, trainings, and organizational transparency between the IT provider's individual departments will provide the necessary incentives.

In many countries the need to be fluent in English can be a major issue. And it goes without saying that employees of an independent IT provider will additionally need brilliant IT expertise, broad business management knowledge, excellent problem-solving skills, and long-standing experience from numerous projects. The new IT provider's staff will need to build and develop these capabilities and skills over time – 'from zero to hero' in no time will always be an exception.

Nevertheless, in many cases the divisions of the parent company – now customers of the new IT provider – will immediately tend to apply the same standards they use when dealing with other providers. If the parent company (which will have to cover the new entity's losses, just as it will benefit from its profits) now exerted too much pressure, demanding immediate competitiveness on the external market or setting excessively high targets, the failure of the IT provider would be inevitable. It is therefore imperative to determine clear rules for the starting phase.

2.1.2   Allowing for a start-up phase to set up and professionalize the IT provider

During the first two years after the spin-off, the newly established IT provider will need to get organized as an independent entity, and develop professional structures and processes. The transition must be made from the sum of IT systems, IT executives and staff, computing centers, etc. that were spun off, to a high-performing organization. During this period mutual tolerance is a top priority, along with swift advances in professionali¬zing the cooperation – on both sides.

During the start-up phase there is much to be done. Existing staff must be trained, new personnel may have to hired to build the customer interface, and this very interface must be set up depending on the desired type of customer relations – either as an IT-driven key account management (operating 'closer' to the customer) or as a sales organization (keeping a greater distance from customers). The core processes of IT service provision must be built up, efficiency potentials exploited.

In one case example, several computing centers were transferred to the newly established IT provider, which immediately consolidated them from formerly over 10 to only three centers in optimal locations, thus achieving a substantial cost reduction. The IT provider's own value creation must be contrasted with market-level performance and cost data, and its structure must be effectively aligned – in particular by outsourcing IT services which in the long run cannot be rendered at market-level quality or prices. Simultaneously, as performance increases are achieved in IT core processes, administrative services with respective commercial processes must be set up, in particular order processing with concurrent cost/revenue accounting and calculation, as well as bookkeeping, controlling, procurement, and HR.

While management will be busy initiating the transformation of the company, customers will expect continuity in IT operations. At the same time, the services rendered will not be on a competitive level – nor will the cost structure, and thus the prices for these services. Therefore some temporary relieving arrangements should be made to give the new IT provider a decent starting chance.

- *Cost allocation guarantee:* Up to a predefined point in time, which should be no later than in two years, the IT provider charges its actual costs to its customers – just like the IT departments did prior to the spin-off. To ensure that the divisions – the provider's customers – register some positive development before that point, efficiency gains achieved should be passed on to the customers in the form of across-the-board cost reductions, such as '3 to 5 percent IT cost reduction per year'. At the same time, the services rendered should be recorded, a cost/price calculation should be set up and the prices should be determined based on criteria customary in the market. Cost allocations should gradually be replaced by service level agreements, thus building up a price mechanism which will be valid for all services no later than in two years' time

- *Order placement guarantee:* The newly established IT provider could hardly survive intense competition with long established external providers; after all, the previous IT departments of the company did not have to compete in the market. Therefore, it makes sense to guarantee order placement for the duration of the start-up period. Whether this guarantee will be maintained or gradually redrawn, remains to be clarified in the context of the subsequent strategic rules of cooperation (see following subchapter, 'Defining the strategic rules of cooperation').

- *Gratuitous use of infrastructure:* The offices and infrastructure of the newly established IT provider will be on the premises of the parent company, at the locations of the previous IT departments – which means that they will draw benefits from the parent. These are usually provided at no cost, at least in the beginning, then sometimes charged to the provider (e.g., as rental fees). In that case the IT provider will need to consider these costs in its cost calculations and prices.

Granting the new provider a start-up phase has shown to be useful in particular with regard to fulfilling two strategic parameters – financial targets and sales targets for the external market:

- For meeting *financial targets* a gradual transition has proven effective. On principle, the IT provider will be managed as a profit center. Profitability targets for the first two years will be based on market prices, plus an overhead charge to compensate for an initial lack in competitiveness, or for any cost-intensive internal agreements with employee representatives that may not be customary among competitors (for example, if the IT provider has originated from the collective labor agreement of a manufacturing company). In these cases, profitability targets need to be introduced successively, oriented by the profitability targets of other divisions. This must be done with substantial discretion, as in many cases the parent company's profitability figures will not 'fit' the IT provider – for instance if the parent runs an equipment-intensive manufacturing business where profitability targets must reflect the high capital lockup – which is usually not the case with IT providers.

- If the parent company wants the IT provider to work the *external market*, a low-key start might be an interesting option – for instance, by winning a few associated or friendly companies as customers before actually entering the external market. As the IT provider continues to build critical capabilities, sales targets can gradually be increased.

Even if the management, executives, and staff of the newly established IT provider do everything possible and necessary for a speedy professionalization of their organization, according to all experience there will be complaints from the customers – the divisions – during the start-up phase. Previously internal IT departments are turning into a legally independent service provider: a change like this is bound to affect the relationship between users and IT and often causes multiple grievances. Severe disturbances in the relationship, however, will manifest themselves in very concrete ways:

- IT orders from the parent company's divisions or subsidiaries will increasingly be placed with external vendors, without checking back with the internal IT provider, thereby dodging the order placement guarantee.

- Divisions will gradually (and in part secretly) build up in-house resources, stating reasons such as higher quality, lower costs, and better controllability.

- The IT provider's internal customers will demand that, for quality reasons, certain projects or user support be given to subcontractors they have selected.

Unless the causes for such disturbances are identified, analyzed objectively, and resolved in a constructive manner, a downward spiral will set in which has led to the failure of many IT providers. A suitable tool for this cause analysis is a customer survey, in particular one focusing on strengths and weaknesses: It helps identify the areas to be addressed most urgently, also in comparison to external providers. Such surveys should generally be conducted by 'neutral' institutions (such as consultants or market research firms) to prevent accusations of instrumentalizing it for political purposes. In many cases, such surveys reveal a need for action in the following areas:

■ Enhance customer orientation in key account management or sales, as applicable (typical complaints: 'order generation takes too long', 'contact persons keep changing' 'incompetent contacts').

■ Improve coordination and cooperation between sales and delivery (typical complaints: 'if customers don't keep calling back about their orders, nothing will get done', 'sales people sell services which are impossible to deliver').

■ Improve delivery quality (typical complaints: 'project got out of control', 'service levels were not maintained').

■ Improve administrative support processes, in particular invoicing and knowledge management (typical complaints: 'external providers accomplish more', 'invoices are intransparent' 'the left hand doesn't know what the right hand is doing').

In almost every case, the internal provider's 'market share' in the parent company's IT budget will gradually decrease and external providers will take over. This development threatens the IT provider's existence in two ways: First, the decrease of critical mass in sales will resulting in an increasing fixed-cost share (as resource utilization goes down); secondly, there will be a lack of projects on innovative topics to safeguard the future of the business. This is why disturbances in the cooperation, particularly during the start-up phase, require top management attention and possibly a change management program, in order to enable the IT provider to take proactive measures. Apart from serving the provider's own interests, this will also help the parent company to meet the original goals of the spin-off.

2.2   Stipulating Strategic Rules for Cooperation

Soon the start-up phase will be over. In almost all cases the customers of the IT provider – the parent company's divisions and subsidiaries – will now demand that full competition with established external providers be opened. At the same time, the parent company will increasingly expect the IT provider to form an 'IT bracket' around divisions and subsidiaries, actively contributing to IT cost reduction at consistent – or even improved – IT performance quality by developing shared solutions. On top of that, the IT provider will be expected to be highly innovative, providing the parent company with current know-how and latest-generation IT systems to strengthen its competitive position and optimize its costs, thereby rendering a clear contribution to corporate value increase. In short: The IT provider will be caught between conflicting goals.

To increase the benefits from IT and from the in-house provider, and to reduce overall IT costs, the company will need to determine strategic rules for the cooperation between the provider and the divisions. In practice there are three variants, each with its own specific consequences:

▦ *'Arms Length' – full competition, no involvement:* In this scenario, the IT provider is in full competition with established external IT providers, and is not given any guarantees in terms of order placement. The only way for it to obtain an order is by winning the parent company's bidding process through superior prices, services, or delivery quality. Rather than being involved in the planning processes of the parent and its divisions, it receives the same information as any other IT provider.

This approach is only advisable if the IT provider's performance has reached market level and if a sufficient share of its business (30 to 50 percent) comes from the external market, enabling it to buffer fluctuations in demand. Another essential prerequisite is that divisions and subsidiaries maintain a neutral relationship with the IT provider, neither discriminating against it nor giving it preferential treatment.

In reality these criteria are impossible to fulfill: Almost all IT providers start by achieving only limited sales and experiencing losses. Usually there is no or only very little external business and it cannot be expended quickly, least of all with 'real' customers which are not associated with and independent from the parent company. Moreover, customer relationships are mostly burdened, as all the 'sins of the past' – when the provider was still an IT department at the customers' organization – will come back into play. Full competition will, in all probability, result in a rapid sales decline and high losses, which the parent company's divisions and subsidiaries will ultimately have to compensate for. Therefore this option is not advisable. Rather than establishing an internal IT provider, the company should look into outsourcing its IT services or – if the internal provider has already been established – selling it to an external provider.

▦ *'Preferred supplier' – some competition, some involvement:* In this scenario, the IT provider is involved somewhat in the company's IT planning processes, enabling it to better prepare for its customers' short, medium, and long-term requirements. While the divisions may invite external bids, the internal IT provider can be sure to win the bid if terms are at least comparable. This, in turn, enables the IT provider to invest in building innovative IT know-how, helping the company to achieve higher increases in corporate value. This approach is quite common in practice: It combines competitive elements (bid invitation) with corporate control and planning mechanisms, which in the long run will be beneficial to both, the company and the IT provider, while divisions can be sure to obtain market-level prices and services.

▦ *General provider – no competition, tight involvement:* This approach entails a very tight, possibly even full involvement of the IT provider in the company's IT-related planning and decision processes. There is no competition with other IT providers in the external market; instead, there is an IT monopoly with an obligation for the provider to submit proposals, and an obligation for divisions and subsidiaries to accept them. The result is a tight and stable relationship with full mutual transparency on the customers' IT needs and the IT provider's cost and services structure.

This scenario guarantees long-term survival for the IT provider, but not necessarily optimal or even market-level IT services and prices for the company. In fact, this type of involvement does not even correspond to the idea of an independently managed IT provider – rather to that of a Shared Services center with an IT focus, in particular because it lacks the element of entrepreneurial risk that would legitimate the profits obtained. All in all, this option is only advisable if, due to special circumstances or very specific requirements, there is no alternative offering in the market (a conceivable scenario for instance in the defense sector or in highly specialized or very low-revenue industries) or if the performance of the internal IT provider is so far below market level that even in the longer run – that is, after the start-up phase – it is not likely to become competitive. This is another case where the company should consider IT outsourcing, or selling the internal IT provider to an external vendor to restore its competitiveness.

In any case, a monopoly situation with purchase obligations for the divisions will not be sustainable long-term – in particular if these divisions operate in very competitive industries: Their willingness to tolerate non-competitive services and prices will quickly subside since, after all, they are evaluated based on their own results, not their merits in subsidizing a sister company.

For all these reasons, it will be advisable after the start-up phase to strive for a 'Preferred Supplier' solution: It requires the IT provider to keep its costs and services at or above market level – permanently and structurally. If not explicitly demanded by management, this is usually fostered by customers' demands for more transparency on IT costs and services, including comparisons with external IT providers. Benchmarking its own services and prices against the market will help the IT provider to identify levers for improvement. In practice they usually include the following:

■ *Extensive consolidation:* For standard services – in particular infrastructure services – consolidation across locations or regions can help achieve substantial cost reductions (see chapter 1 of this section, 'IT optimization'). Examples are provided by external IT providers following an outsourcing effort (consolidation of computing centers and help-desks, integration of service teams for user/PC support, centralization of central functions like sourcing, sales, and others).

■ *Optimization of the product portfolio and of vertical integration:* IT services or individual components of IT services, which the IT provider cannot offer at market-level terms due to insufficient volumes, are outsourced to external subcontractors.

■ *Optimization of key and cross-divisional functions:* In case of shortcomings in bid preparation and invoicing, external providers' best practice can be used as a reference in optimizing the efficiency of service delivery processes, and adjusting service quality to market standard.

■ *Aligning qualification, leadership, and management systems of the internal IT provider with customer requirements:* Common approaches include intensive staff training with particular emphasis on service-mindedness, introduction of customer-oriented performance evaluation and incentive systems, adjustment of tariff structures and career paths, and finally systematic recruiting of lateral hires from external IT providers and IT consultants for leadership positions.

Choosing a suitable business model for the internal IT provider and striving to professionalize the cooperation are both crucial to reaching the original goals of the spin-off. They are also key factors for the success of the company's exit strategy.

Spin-off and professionalization of an internal IT provider at a manufacturing group

A group of companies in the manufacturing sector had completed several large-scale mergers, and was now looking for synergies. Management's attention was drawn to the regionally dispersed and hardly consolidated IT organization, which had largely remained the same as before. An agreement was reached to consolidate all IT activities in one IT service company, in order to exploit synergies in IT costs and improve the allocation of resources (for example, by increasing utilization rates in application development) with corresponding advances in professionalization.

After a twelve-month start-up phase the organization structure was complete. After another twelve months, key IT cost synergies had been realized. There was, however, a series of strategic and quality-related factors raising doubts in the sustainable success of the new entity: With roughly 1,000 employees, the IT provider covered almost the entire service portfolio of the group, with a particular focus on Europe and smaller marginal activities in the U.S. and Asia. The group's divisions placed their orders directly with the IT provider, with very limited central coordination.

After approximately three years, there were increasing signs of problems in the cooperation:

■ The IT provider's market share in the group was declining

■ External providers won numerous bids for new application projects

■ The IT provider was perceived by its internal customers as being bureaucratic, expensive, inflexible, and not in line with corporate strategic goals

■ The IT provider had made only small entries into the external market

■ A newly established IT sales organization met with limited acceptance.

These problems went all the way back to the start-up phase: The substructure of a classical IT department had been left unchanged, and transferred to the organization of the new IT provider. Employees did not perceive themselves to be service providers, and the entity's regional presence did not match the requirements of a group operating on a global level.

The IT provider started a quality initiative in delivery: The status quo was verified through internal customer surveys, and compared against the parent company's requirements. Likewise, the group compared the IT provider's services and costs with the experiences gained with external providers on similar projects, and derived strategic guidelines for the IT provider's future positioning. Resulting measures were detailed in business plans and a change management process was set up to eliminate the deficits in the cooperation. In addition, standard services were outsourced to external, lower-cost providers; for selected regions, a strategic alliance was established with an external IT provider present in those regions.

These measures helped to turn the cooperation between the group and its IT provider into a win-win situation: The IT provider's position within the group was secured long-term by means of permanent benchmarking with external providers, continuous customer surveys, and concentration on its particular strengths. This way the group ensured that critical know-how would remain in the company, safeguarding its strategic independence from external IT providers. At the same time, the IT provider was able to reduce the costs of IT operations by 15 percent in the first two years, increasing the bundling of specific IT functions (such as computing centers and call centers), with additional structural cost reduction potentials in the entity's further development.

2.3   Expanding, Insourcing, or Divesting the IT Provider

Despite all efforts made by management, executives, and employees, long-term prospects for corporate IT providers tend to be poor – the wave of consolidation is rolling. Even very successful spin-offs are divested by their parent companies. A prominent example is debis Systemhaus: Despite its rapid and profitable growth, a large share of third-market business, and an excellent market position, DaimlerCrysler decided to divest – another indicator that groups are increasingly focusing on their core business again. The exit happens even sooner if the original goals of the spin-off are not fulfilled, or if the parent company's need for cash has increased. In this case the IT provider is sold, most likely to one of the leading international providers.

'Survivors' have so far included those IT providers which have enjoyed a stable order in-take, due to very tight links with the parent company, and which have used external benchmarks to continually optimize their processes and structures. By contrast, those IT providers that emerged during the 'New Economy' boom specializing on Internet, e-business, and CRM services have mostly failed or been taken over by a large-scale IT provider. Those hat remained include mainly IT providers offering a broad service portfolio and focusing on a customer segment so far neglected by large providers (such as small and medium-sized companies).

The generally weak IT market of recent years has even affected IT providers with an established position in the market and highly competitive services. Price competition and the resulting pressure on margins, to be compensated only through increasing scale effects, require globally active service providers with large computing centers, consistent standards, and high service quality. Regional providers face increasing pressure, as customer tends to prefer providers that operate on the same global level. Corporate providers are at a disadvantage her because the majority of them is only present in the group's primary locations.

The competitive situation of IT providers is additionally influenced by changes in demand. Rather than purchasing their entire IT from an external provider, more and more companies start to outsource only services unrelated to their core competences. Almost all customers keep process and application-related, strategic, and controlling services in-house. What remains is basically services standardized to such an extent that they can be outsourced to several providers, thus intensifying price competition among them.

Together, these factors have led to a profound, and still ongoing, consolidation in the IT market. Large, international IT providers take over smaller corporate IT providers, mostly after five to ten years of existence when it has become apparent that the possibilities for internal growth are limited. Figure 38 illustrates some of the important changes in the IT market.

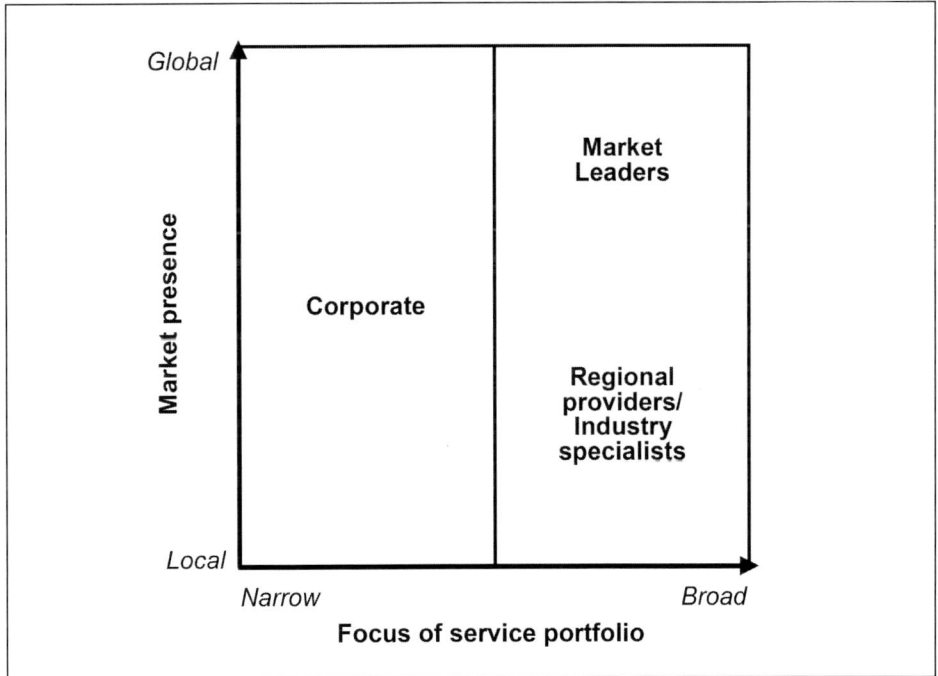

Figure 38:   *Consolidation of IT providers in the market*

Many companies have realized that they will not be able to exploit the cost and in particular benefit potentials they have hoped for when spinning off an external IT provider – despite all efforts to professionalize the cooperation. They have come to a crossroads where they must choose between two options: divesting the IT provider, or separating its services into strategically relevant ones to be returned into the company (insourced) and non-critical services to be outsourced to external providers.

The first option, disinvestment, will be relevant for companies which, in the long run, do not consider IT a core competence and which, faced with a make-or-buy decision, would rather opt for outsourcing. The decisive factor is the IT provider's critical size: If it is not able to offer professional processes (from new-business acquisition to project management and invoicing) at fair prices, it will be a candidate for sale, as small and medium-sized IT providers have survival chances only in certain market niches – based either on industry-specific know-how, or on strongly segmented IT services such as SAP development.

Once the company has decided to divest, potential buyers must be identified. Main motives for them to take over a corporate IT provider will usually include non-organic sales growth, procurement of industry specific IT know-how from the parent-company's industry, or simply access as Preferred Supplier to the IT provider's previous customers, the parent company's divisions. Depending on the competences of the internal IT provider, several potential buyer groups may come into question:

- Software firms for IT providers which have developed marketable and competitive software products

- IT consultancies for IT providers which have built up strong development and consulting skills

- IT outsourcers wishing to enter into existing contracts of the internal IT provider.

The price achievable will depend on the existing (industry) competence of the IT provider, as well as its future sales potential with its previous parent company. In individual cases, restructuring the IT provider might further enhance its attractiveness to potential buyers. This may include dividing it up in several segments, each of which may be even more attractive to the target groups mentioned than their combination would. The result may be partial insourcing, or negotiations with several target groups. If no buyer can be found, the only remaining option is to outsource the services so far rendered by the IT provider, and close down its operations step by step.

Insourcing can be an interesting option if the IT services have strategic relevance for the parent company. It can be accomplished either by closing down the internal IT provider, transferring its operations to the parent company, or by integrating it with the parent company and focusing on in-house production (de-facto insourcing). Based on the parent company's strategic requirements, it will be necessary to professionalize the IT provider, build up market-oriented activities, eliminate redundant administrative functions, and reduce the product portfolio to what is needed by the group. In this case the IT provider, together with the corporate CIO organization, will assume responsibility for a strategy-conform, market-oriented and efficient IT supply. Regions and IT services where there are internal know-how deficits, or lack of critical mass, can be developed based on alliances or selective outsourcing.

Even if the spin-off of internal IT providers, as a general rule, will not be a long-standing solution but mostly a more or less temporary state of affairs, cost and benefit increases in the context of the spin-off can contribute to IT optimization, and to exploiting the savings potentials of IT outsourcing and offshoring.

Checklist: Does your company's cooperation with its internal IT provider rest on a solid basis?	Yes
Have appropriate targets been defined for the IT provider in terms of sales, cost reductions, quality improvements, and financial results (ROCE, EBIT)?	
Has the design of the IT provider been guided by the structures and business processes of external IT providers, and have services and prices been aligned with the market?	
Are executives and staff being developed with regard to customer and service orientation?	
Have the scope and depth of the IT service portfolio for individual regions and customers been derived from a business case, ensuring that only economical activities will remain with the IT provider?	
Have the parent company's divisions and the internal IT provider established formal, market-oriented service level agreements in line with technological state of the art?	
Have temporary arrangements been made for a transitional period of about two years, allowing the previously internal IT departments to grow into one professional IT provider?	

3.   IT Outsourcing and IT Offshoring – Cost Advantages from Contracting Out Services

If you want to drive a car, do you have to be able to build and repair it? If you need electricity, do you have to operate your own wind, water or coal-fired power plant? Well, for most people the answer will be No. Cars can be bought or leased from a variety of manufacturers, electricity comes 'out of the wall' – as long as you have a power supply contract and regularly pay the bills.

The principle of division of labor implies that companies specialize in certain products and services which they can deliver better and cheaper than other companies, so that ultimately they will become suppliers to others. From the perspective of the overall economy, this is a very positive phenomenon as it generates jobs at the specialist and prevents a waste of resources at the non-specialist. The same applies for IT: Information technology is complex and subject to continuous change. The management of IT, therefore, binds precious corporate resources: highly qualified staff, capital for hardware and software investments, office space, and others. Most companies, however, are 'only' users of IT: Yes, they need the performance – but why should they obtain or retain an 'IT production'?

As early as in the 1960s, innovative entrepreneurs in the U.S. started specializing in 'IT production – either as IT service provider, without their own hard- and software, or as a value chain extension of hard- and software producers. Today, the first approach is pursued by globalized companies like CapGemini Ernest & Young, EDS, SBS, or T-Systems. Outstanding examples of the second approach include IBM, Hewlett Packard, and more recently also SAP.

IT outsourcers are plenty today. The IT outsourcing sector has become an established industry with numerous professional suppliers. In every industry there are prominent examples of extensive outsourcing relationships – including areas where IT sourcing had previously been considered to be difficult or even impossible: Nowadays, even banks, telecom suppliers, and governments outsource large parts of their IT to external vendors. In other sectors which are less IT-driven – such as manufacturing – IT outsourcing has long prevailed. This raises a question for every company still retaining an in-house 'IT production': What do we need this for? Is it a real necessity or a luxury?

The advantages consisting in a sharper business focus, obtained through IT outsourcing, can be further expanded through IT offshoring – a rather young approach which is currently finding its way into European business practice. Pioneers in this field include the global automotive industry and the financial sector, where the share of IT is particularly high and the prevailing proprietary systems are hard to replace with standard software. The positive experiences they have gained with IT offshoring provide excellent learning examples for other industries.

3.1   Reducing Vertical Integration with IT Outsourcing

The motive for outsourcing is the same in most cases: Companies want to cut IT costs. Reduction targets are defined, specifying a 20, 30, or even 40 percent cut in IT production cost. Other crucial factors can be higher performance requirements with regard to IT service availability or shorter project durations.

A highly successful mechanical engineering company, for example, which so far had its main focus of operations in Germany and Western Europe, expanded into the U.S. market by acquiring a local company. As a result, its IT was now expected to run global systems, establish transcontinental networks, consolidate a number of locations, and introduce a standardized IT landscape. Moreover, support to U.S. users would require the computing center to go from a two-shift to a three-shift operation. A critical self-evaluation led the company to realize that all those IT activities could not reasonably be in the focus of an engineering company. A powerful outsourcing partner was identified and the IT outsourced. The new partner's competences, capabilities, and local presence enabled the engineering company to obtain the improved and broader IT qualities required, quickly and at moderate cost, without having to make any major investments.

Such situations mostly happen in companies where IT performance and the speed in implementing innovative IT products are critical to competitiveness. For instance, at banks and insurances, telecom providers, and airlines, value creation massively relies on IT (in telecommunications, for example, on rating and billing systems and on data communication products for GPRS/UMTS; in airlines, on reservation and check-in systems). Above all, they seek outsourcing partners helping them enhance their IT capabilities, for instance by bringing in the additional know-how needed to meet specific market challenges, or by providing the critical mass and capabilities required to carry out large-scale projects or manage the technical complexity of global IT operations.

In many cases, the company will expect its IT outsourcer to bring additional business in-to the cooperation, for instance by actively offering the company's services to the outsourcer's other customers or by integrating its services into its own portfolio. Let us take, for example, a cooperation between an IT outsourcer and a telecom provider: The IT outsourcer will need telecom services to globally network the 'IT productions' it is running for other companies, so it can either use the telecom provider's services or recommend them to other corporate customers. Another example would be an IT outsourcer assisting in the establishment of a new financial services provider by adapting an existing IT platform to the new company's needs. The financial services provider could pay back this service by granting the IT outsourcer a fixed percentage of its sales, which it could not have achieved at the same extent and speed without the IT outsourcer's help.

One way or another, IT outsourcing offers economic benefit potential to companies of all industries:

- *Reduction of complexity:* For many companies, certain services provided by their in-house 'IT production' (such as the operation of the infrastructure) have become an essential part of their IT which, however, does not belong to their core competences and therefore adds little to their competitive differentiation. For these companies, IT outsourcing will have the advantage of reducing the scope of services rendered in-house – known as 'vertical integration' – and focusing their 'IT production' on strategically relevant, value-added IT activities.

- *Consolidation:* For companies running several IT landscapes in their different divisions, outsourcing is often the only way to break through particular interests, enforce the consolidation of the IT landscape from an integrated point of view, and speed up necessary restructuring efforts. By setting ambitious cost-saving and service improvement targets, the

IT outsourcer can be encouraged to follow a tough consolidation course, and will usually have the experience needed for a complete redesign of the IT landscape. In many cases the outsourcer will be prepared to make the necessary initial investments, in return for a fixed share in the savings obtained by the company (depending on the duration and terms of contract).

■ *Fixed-cost variabilization:* Once the IT landscape has been consolidated – usually after the so-called transfer phase – the IT outsourcer can jointly run several customers' IT. These economies of scale will enable the outsourcer to offer flexible pricing models and to charge for IT services based on the quantities delivered (pay-per-use) – for instance, per MIPS (Million Instructions Per Second, a measuring unit for processor capacity or storage space in a computing center), per workstation, or even per business transaction. This way, the previously fixed resource IT becomes a variable that can be adjusted to changes in the business activity.

■ *Improvements in reliability and innovation:* IT is highly complex and volatile. Companies are forced to continuously follow the latest technological trends, while maintaining a standardized environment that will guarantee high availability. This is only possible with high-level IT staff specialization – which, in turn, requires substantial critical mass. Benefiting from the specialization and innovativeness of an IT outsourcer is often the better alternative.

■ *Reduction of staff levels and achieving of cash effects:* Outsourcing, as a general rule, involves a transfer of IT assets (computing centers, all hardware licenses, possibly some software licenses) which means that previously fixed assets turn into current assets. For the company in question this can be a means to improve its short-term cash position, as the IT outsourcer will purchase its IT assets at market prices – often based on their residual book value – so that the company will obtain corresponding sales revenue. The outsourcer, however, will need to earn back this purchase price in the course of the service contract in order to be profitable, and will therefore integrate it in the service prices to that customer. Consequently, it will not be advisable for most companies to maximize the sales price for their IT assets.

Initially, the value-creation potential of IT outsourcing will lead to increasing IT costs (figure 39): In many cases the reason is that companies, instead of systematically optimizing their IT, hope that IT outsourcing will 'automatically' lead to optimization effects. Winners will be those who have positioned their IT as a value driver, separated demand management from supply management in the context of IT governance and continually pursued optimization measures, such as standardizing PC workplaces or switching off outdated or redundant IT applications. Even in those cases, however, the transfer of IT to the outsourcer's business system will initially cost money. This temporary cost increase, typically for a period of one or two years, will affect both parties involved.

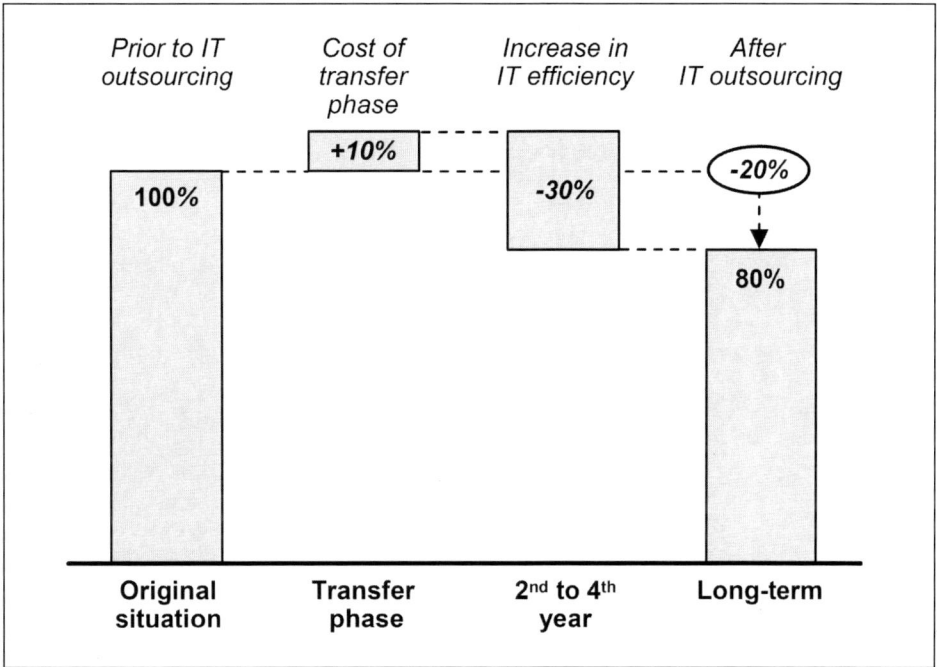

Figure 39:   Typical results curve of IT outsourcing;
Source: A.T. Kearney

For the company, IT costs will temporarily increase due to the transfer of the previously in-house 'IT production' to the IT outsourcer, as well as the resulting need to set up a CIO func-tion for demand management (unless it already exists) and to make any 'hidden' IT costs visible.

▦ *Costs for setting up demand management:* The IT outsourcer will need a competent con-tact person in the client company to prepare IT-related decisions and carry them through. The company will need a person in charge of managing the IT provider. Both requirements can be met by a CIO Office: In addition to managing and monitorring the IT provider, its task will be to manage the interface with the business departments and IT users, jointly identifying innovative IT topics that might contribute to the value increase of the com-pany. Consequently, the CIO Office will bundle demand vis-à-vis the IT outsourcer, and strive to prevent any increases in IT costs as would result from uncoordinated IT requests.

▦ *Transfer costs:* The IT outsourcer receives the company's IT technology (hardware sys-tems, communication networks, software systems, computing center locations, and others) and IT staff. In order to be able to achieve the targeted cost reductions and performance improvements, the IT outsourcer will integrate the IT technology and staff into its own business system (for example, by connecting the computing center to a central control sta-tion, or by ensuring better utilization of the IT staff, dedicating their spare capacities to projects for other customers). In many cases, the outsourcer will also obtain better purchase terms for PCs, notebooks, and printers, as well as software licenses. To be integrated into the business system, the IT usually needs to be 'rebuilt' and optimized – which requires IT investments. The extent of the integration into the outsourcer's business system will be ruled in the outsourcing contract. Likewise, the contract should stipulate who will bear the one-off costs for rebuilding the IT, and the possible severance payments for, and/or training of, the IT staff.

■ *Making 'hidden' IT costs visible:* In the course of the transfer of IT technology and staff to the IT outsourcer, the actual extent of IT services rendered will become transparent for the first time: While the IT staff will continue to deliver extensive services to the divisions and other IT users at the company, these services will now be recorded and billed.

The costs of establishing a demand management function at the CIO Office, as well as transfer costs and the new visibility of the previously 'hidden' IT costs will add up to a temporary increase in IT costs by roughly 10 percent (possibly more in individual cases, depending on the expenditure for 'IT consolidation'). 'Temporary' here means one to two years at maximum. From the second year, a steady state of affairs should have been reached, including performance improvements and 30 percent cost savings – which, in absolute terms, will translate into a total improvement of 20 percent. It is due to the expenditure and time required to reach the targeted improvements, that such outsourcing contracts are usually laid out for several years. At present five- to seven-year contracts are common, with optional extensions – but also the possibility of a premature cancellation, if mutual expectations are not fulfilled.

It is up to the company to strive for value increases through IT outsourcing at any time – including options to insource certain parts of IT, or outsource additional processes. And even if the company opts for insourcing at some later point, this does not necessarily mean that its original decision was wrong – rather, that either the corporate strategy, or the market, or the significance of IT to the company have changed.

To exploit the value increase potential targeted, companies should consider the entire life-cycle of an outsourcing effort from the beginning, so they can set the right course at any stage (table 2). From entering into an outsourcing partnership, to actively developing it, to the decision to outsource further activities or insource certain parts of IT, the company will need to resolve crucial issues at every life-cycle stage.

Table 2: Important issues in the outsourcing life-cycle

Life-cycle stage	Issues
Make-or-buy decision	Do we want to outsource IT? If yes: What are the IT services we want to outsource?
Entering into an outsourcing partnership	Which partner will be a good strategic and cultural match for our company, and can offer the best service, greatest flexibility, and lowest prices in the long run? How can we motivate the partner to continually support our goals? How can we motivate our divisions to cooperate and deal with IT in a cost-efficient manner? How can we manage the cooperation?
Active development of the partnership and renewed make-or-buy decision	How can we, as a company, stay in control? What will we do if service problems occur? What will we do if costs rise? What will we do if there is a lack of innovativeness? What are the incentives for renegotiating the partnership? Do we want to continue or expand outsourcing, change the IT provider, or insource?

There are plenty of good reasons for outsourcing. The decisive factor will be that ambitious expectations are fulfilled. Companies must be prepared to take massive consequences, including the transfer of staff, changed roles between IT and the business departments, as well as new leadership and control mechanisms. Not surprisingly, a study by Dun & Bradstreet in 2000 revealed that 20 to 25 of all outsourcing efforts fail within the first two years; after five years the failure rate exceeds 50 percent. Outsourcing, then, offers exciting opportunities but also involves high risks. Minimizing these risks while exploiting the opportunities – that is the art of IT outsourcing.

3.1.1 Defining the objectives of IT outsourcing and identifying suitable IT services

Many of the causes for the later failure of outsourcing partnerships can be prevented if the company is clear on its motives. It will make a great difference, for instance, whether the goal is simply cost-cutting, or achieving an optimal economic benefit for the company. If the company aims for IT cost reduction, a sensible measure may be to transfer the existing IT staff to other parts of the company and give them other tasks (or let them go) and to outsource only the IT task itself, expecting the outsourcer to cover it with own resources (for example, desktop support). While resulting in the lowest annual fee for the IT outsourcer's services, this option will increase the costs to the company during the transfer phase, due to the retraining of or severance payments to the previous IT staff. In addition, the interface between the company and the outsourcer will be quite anonymous since the previous staff, which are familiar with the company's requirements and peculiarities, will not be available for the outsourcer's task.

When determining the objectives of an outsourcing partnership, it will be important to consider the company's strategic, economic, and personnel-related goals:

- The *strategic goals* of the company are usually focused somewhere between cost reduction and performance improvement. They provide the basis for considering whether the IT staff should be transferred to the outsourcer, what part of IT should remain in the company (and why), and how the company's demand for IT services will be managed in the future. Another crucial factor is how IT outsourcing will affect the company's long-term strategic coals, such as focusing on core competences or external growth via mergers and acquisitions. These and many other questions must be clarified beforehand, even if they can partly be adjusted or detailed in the course of the outsourcing partnership.

- *Economic goals* comprise both, the costs and quality of the IT services required. Necessary decisions include what service level will be required at what price, and what the scope will be for possible later price negotiations with the potential outsourcing partner. This includes the option to pay higher prices in the initial phase, which is more capital-intensive for the outsourcer, and to pay less in the later, steady-state phases – or vice versa, depending on the company's financial state (and opportunities for optimization through financial engineering). An important question in this context is how business units will be involved in the bidding process and the outsourcing contract negotiations, as well as the later fulfillment of the contract.

- *Personnel-related goals* are particularly important if the company intends to transfer staff to the IT outsourcer. For many employees, outsourcing – when considered from a neutral perspective – will be an attractive opportunity since they will proceed from a company's marginal activity to the IT outsourcer's core business. In addition to attractive career and compensation prospects, this will also involve higher-level performance standards. By contrast, what the IT staff really feels in most cases is that they are unwanted and therefore 'pushed out'. However, as the previous IT staff will be required to run the company's IT business from the outsourcer's organization, early and clear communication will be imperative to help people explore the opportunities involved in the outsourcing move – and, of course, to ensure that these opportunities really exist.

Along with the company's objectives, its current situation will have to be considered as well: It will make a lot of difference, for instance, whether the company has already taken measures for IT optimization, and exploited cost savings potentials in IT, or whether "clearing out" is an essential motive for outsourcing.

A European company in the service sector had already outsourced large parts of its IT. When the question came up whether country organizations should do the same, analysis revealed that cost savings would only range between 15 and 20 percent – a disappointing figure in view of the fact that the majority of divisions delivered the same service products and business processes were largely identical. Based on harmonized business processes and standardized IT systems, cost savings through outsourcing could have reached an estimated 60 percent. In cases like this, it will be worth the effort first to explore efficiency potentials by clearing out the IT landscape, thus achieving 60 percent cost savings, and to reduce the remaining cost base by another 20 percent, benefiting from an outsourcer's economies of scale – in other words, to save 70 percent on IT costs and while achieving simultaneous IT performance improvements.

Tips for selecting IT services suitable for outsourcing:

Do not outsource "problems":
While internal shortcomings such as insufficient IT performance or unsatisfactory service levels can be eliminated through outsourcing, the resulting cost savings will be close to zero. Rather, internal potentials should be exploited and the company should be prepared for the outsourcing effort before it is actually taken into consideration.

Do not outsource all IT services to one IT provider:
In accepting a company's IT, the outsourcer will strive for profitability and growth. Profitability is achievable through appropriate prices and a fast integration of the company's IT landscape into the outsourcer's business system. Growth potentials, however, mainly result from the chance to be award further parts of the company's IT. The outsourcer will reach both objectives through good performance and fair prices, leading to a high degree of customer satisfaction. Retaining some IT parts or distributing the services outsourced over several IT providers will constitute permanent incentives for the IT outsourcer's good conduct.

Not all of the IT services that could potentially be outsourced are really suitable for that. In addition to company specifics, mainly strategic and economic factors will have to be considered in evaluating the outsourcing potential.

Strategic IT services contributing to company's competitive differentiation had better be retained in-house. Examples include billing systems at telecom providers: The continuos change of products, processes, and tariffs calls for proprietary development, as these systems need to be tightly linked to the corporate strategy.

Another lesson learnt from practice is that, while outsourcers are usually capable of eliminating operational inefficiencies, they often have difficulties coping with the rapid change and strategic development of IT systems. Above all, strategic IT systems in industries with strong competitive or regulatory dynamics will require permanent, speedy development with a careful eye on the competition and/or regulation.

In less dynamic industries even strategic systems can be outsourced. Banks, for instance, are very dependent on their IT systems; nevertheless, the stability of the industry makes it possible to outsource even strategic IT, as external IT providers are likely to be able to develop these systems in a tightly managed process.

As for the question whether non-strategic IT systems and 'basic IT supply' services should be outsourced, the answer is a clear Yes. These are mostly commodities and therefore highly standardized, and their prices in the IT outsourcing market will be transparent. In general they include infrastructural services like computing centers, networks (LAN and WAN), personal computers (desktop and laptop) and back-office applications (such as SAP/ERP in financial accounting). Just like electricity or gas, such commodities are usually highly suitable for outsourcing.

In practice we will find the following design options for IT outsourcing – each of which will require a CIO function for managing both, internal demand and the external provider:

■ Outsourcing of the entire IT

■ Partial outsourcing

   – only of computing centers
   – only of application development
   – only of end-user computing (PCs, LANs, user help-desks)

■ Outsourcing of parts of IT tasks ('outtasking')

The greatest opportunities exist in complete outsourcing to only one IT provider. At the same time, this will require the strongest control: The transfer of all IT tasks will enable the outsourcer to optimize the company's entire IT landscape with regard to both, costs and benefits. However, this option also requires a maximum of control since, for the duration of the contract, the company will be dependent on one monopoly supplier. In most cases it will therefore be preferable to opt for partial outsourcing (see box on page 183).

An economic factor of great significance for any decision on IT outsourcing is the pricing of IT tasks. Companies will need to objectively analyze their 'in-house production costs' in comparison to the IT outsourcer's prices. This comparison needs to be based on the 'total costs of ownership' – which, beyond the actual costs of the central IT department, also include the local IT costs in the divisions, the 'hidden' IT costs, the IT costs of local IT departments, and opportunity costs in the business departments (for example, for losses in HR capacity due to insufficient system availability, or for the manual reworking required due to missing interfaces between IT systems). Other factors to be considered include the capital tied up in the corporate IT, and the labor costs for internal IT specialists. Only if all relevant IT costs of the company are considered, taking into account the organizational allocation to divisions or departments, the result will be a 'true' cost comparison sustainable long-term.

Weighting the relevant strategic, economic, and company-specific factors against corporate goals will provide management with a sound basis for decision. The ultimate make-or-buy decision for IT tasks should always be made by top management, for IT outsourcing involves a long-term, structural linkage to an outsourcing partner who will make an important value-added contribution to the company's economic success – and who cannot easily be changed for another if the partnership runs into rough waters.

Outsourcing IT by selling an internal IT provider (disinvestment)

A large German group had established an internal IT provider to consolidate its in-house IT and place industry software and IT services on the external market. After a few successful years, the IT subsidiary started making losses and prices started getting out of control; in addition, the expected international expansion could not be achieved in parallel with the parent company. The group therefore decided to give up on the 'IT adventure' and refocus on its core competences.

The plan was to sell the internal IT provider to an international IT outsourcer who would be able to ensure the group's IT supply at lower costs. De facto, this would involve two contracts between the outsourcer and the group: one ruling the sale of the internal IT provider, and one ruling the group's outsourcing of IT services.

In this constellation of outsourcing and disinvestment, the outsourcing contract between the external IT provider and the group constituted an essential share of the IT subsidiary's corporate value: The higher the savings expected from the outsourcing contract, the lower the value at which the outsourcer would assess the subsidiary. The company thus had to find and negotiate an optimal balance between the selling price and the service costs, which turned out to be a particularly challenge.

This special situation was pointed out clearly in the bidding process, to be taken into explicit account by the bidders. The selection of the future IT outsourcing partner was based primarily on the usual key criteria which would influence the cooperation in the coming years (such as scope of services, references, international presence, market prices, cultural fit). Maximizing the selling price only ranked second, as the company was aware that it constituted a pleasant financial one-off effect that would not be sustainable; nevertheless it was an important topic in the negotiations.

At the end of the day, the IT subsidiary was sold to the IT outsourcer at an attractive price, while the prices set for the future IT services were considered appropriate by the company. All staff were transferred to the IT outsourcer, and the majority of them was still there after three years. Today, the relationship between the group and the IT outsourcer is stable, the contract is 'lived' in mutual respect, service levels are maintained. In addition, the group has achieved 15 percent in annual cost savings. An evaluation of the outsourcing strategy after three years has led the group to consider the outsourcing of further IT tasks.

3.1.2   Developing the outsourcing partnership

The foundation for a successful outsourcing partnership is laid by selecting a suitable IT outsourcer and actively developing the cooperation with that provider. In view of the strategic importance and duration of this contractual relationship (typically, five to seven years) there will obviously be changes in the course of time – either because the company's requirements to the outsourcer change or because technological or market developments on the outsourcer's part call for adjustments to the relationship. Such milestones, which are decisive for an active management of the partnership, need to be considered in the design of the partnership in order to prevent later conflicts and ensure that the economic potentials from outsourcing are fully exploited. To facilitate straightforward decisions the company should make sure that, in addition to top management, key executives are involved as well:

- IT managers and staff, because they are immediately affected

- Business departments / business units, because they are the outsourcer's future customers and will depend on its services

- Purchasing, legal department, and HR, because they will be involved in the selection of, and transactions with, the outsourcer

- PR, because they will need to be able to defend the 'logic' of outsourcing vis-à-vis external stakeholders, such as customers or suppliers.

An early involvement of representatives of these areas of responsibility will ensure that all corporate interests and perspectives on outsourcing are considered in the process. A frequent mistake, for instance, is the late involvement of functions perceived to be 'only supporting', such as purchasing, legal, and HR: Companies often realize too late that essential legal requirements in the transfer of staff or important agreements with employee representatives have been 'overlooked'. Mistakes like these can cause the bidding process to be prolonged or even called off. Therefore, all the individuals listed above should get together at the very start of an outsourcing effort and jointly set up a permanent team to manage the bidding process.

3.1.3   Selecting a suitable outsourcing partner

The selection of a suitable IT outsourcing partner is a complex process for which companies need to make sufficient time (in simpler cases three to six months, for global out-sourcing contracts even six to twelve months). After the objectives of outsourcing have been clarified, there will be a bidding process comprising several phases, in the course of which the long-list of potential outsourcers is gradually cut down to a short list, from which the company finally selects a favorite and an alternative candidate (figure 40).

Bid phase 1		Bid phase 2		
Request for Information	**Evaluation of first bidder contacts**	**Request for Proposal**	**Evaluation of bidders and bids**	**Transfer phase**
Define objectives of bidding process Develop communication plan Draw up long-list of IT providers Request confidentiality agreement, references, and confirmation of interest	Evaluate IT providers and references based on strategic fit Draw up short-list of qualified IT providers Send out RfP with detailed information on IT tasks	Receive detailed bids Make reference visits to bidders' customers Invite bidders to present bids Receive revised bids based on discussion during presentations	Evaluate detailed bids and reach agreement on preferred IT provider Negotiate Letter of Intent for service contract with future IT provider	Negotiate contracts with future IT provider Transfer IT tasks to future IT provider

Figure 40:   Bidding procedure for IT outsourcing

The first task for the outsourcing team will be to draw up a reasonable long-list of all IT outsourcers capable of delivering the services required. For instance, if a global company wishes to outsource its IT, the long-list should only comprise IT outsourcers which are also present on a global scale.

The market for outsourcers can roughly be structured into the following segments (names are only examples, lists are not exhaustive):

■ Global providers with a broad presence and portfolio, such as Accenture, CapGemini Ernest & Young, CSC, EDS, HP, IBM, and others

■ Predominantly European providers present in several EU states and with a comprehensive range of services, such as Atos Origin, Siemens SBS, T-Systems, and others

■ Predominantly national providers including Datev, HVB Info, is:energy, ITERGO, its.on, Lufthansa Systems, RWE Systems, Triaton, and many others

■ Local providers.

To identify the 'right' outsourcer, the first step of the bidding procedure will be to obtain information on services and prices from potentially interesting providers. For this purpose, a *first Request for Proposal (RfP 1)* is drawn up. It should be detailed enough to allow IT providers to write a qualified proposal. In comprehensive bids, the RfP 1 may well comprise several hundred pages. On the one hand, its clarity and quality will facilitate discussions in the company, helping to synchronize the different user interests; on the other hand, the document will signal to providers that the company is seriously interested, and allows them to draw up meaningful and robust first proposals.

Tips for bid phase 1:

Give prior notice of RfP:
It has been proven practice to call the management of the providers selected in the long-list, informing them about the intended dispatch of the RfP, and asking them to confirm their interest in writing to speed up the bidding process

Communicate frequently: It will be advisable early on to point out the advantages of outsourcing to the relevant constituencies, such as the works council / union representatives, the board of directors or other boards and committees, and – last but not least – the employees concerned, in order to prevent rumor mill effects, calm down fears, and motivate staff for the changes to come.

The IT providers' replies to the RfP are then compared and evaluated. Based on this evaluation, the company will be able to make a realistic estimate as to whether its out-sourcing objectives (IT services and costs, personnel transfer, and others) can be fulfilled; in addition, the number of bidders can be cut down to a short-list of interesting candidates.

The responses of the different outsourcers will permit first conclusions on their interest and commitment: Bids submitted with substantial delay or in poor quality (for instance, containing a standard proposal rather than addressing the company's specific concerns) should lead to the immediate exclusion of the bidder.

In bid phase 2 the company will intensify its contacts with providers on the short-list. A *second Request for Proposal (RfP 2)* is drawn up, informing bidders in detail on the IT services required. In addition, selected providers are invited to present and discuss their bids, permitting the company to obtain a detailed picture of the respective outsourcing concept (in particular with regard to staff transfer), outsourcing services and costs, and other terms of the proposed cooperation.

The company will want (and have) to 'live' with its IT outsourcing partner for many years. It is therefore imperative to establish through thorough discussions whether potential partners will really be a good match for the company in the long run. This also includes 'soft factors' like management philosophy, employee conduct, communication style, and many others which could turn out to be serious obstacles to the cooperation.

Reference visits to customers of the IT provider will help to round off the 'familiarization phase'. Many things can be made to appear in a positive light in the context of a proposal; companies should therefore take the opportunity to pay visits to existing customers of the IT outsourcer's – both, visits arranged by the outsourcer itself and visits arranged directly with the respective customer (and without prior notice to the provider). Following discussion with the company, IT outsourcing providers will further detail their proposals, possibly revising the services and prices offered.

Tips for the internal evaluation of final proposals:

Evaluate in several dimensions:
The final evaluation of outsourcing proposals should always be carried out by the entire team in charge of the bid procedure. In particular HR, the legal department, and purchasing should play a major role.

Ensure neutrality of IT staff:
In the majority of cases, the company's current IT staff will be transferred to the IT outsourcer. In the course of the process there will be increasingly frequent contacts between IT staff and the provider, and it is only natural that IT people will think about which of the providers they would prefer to be their future employer. In order to keep control over the different options, management should make sure that IT staff remain neutral.

The detailed and revised proposals are finally evaluated in the second round. At this point in time, the company's specific concerns have been clarified in several discussions and presentations with the remaining bidders, so that the services and costs specified in the updated bids will be clear and comparable. While in this phase economic criteria will usually be given highest priority, the company should make sure to take proper account of its strategic requirements as well, to ensure that the future outsourcing partnership will provide optimal and long-term support. If, for instance, an expansion to China is intended in the near future, the IT outsourcer should be present there or, at least, be able to present a conclusive concept.

On this basis, the company will select a preferred IT provider from the remaining candidates. Both parties then sign a *Letter of Intent (LoI),* thus initiating a limited Due Diligence and negotiation phase. Since it will be in the company's interest to keep control of the negotiation progress, the results of each negotiation round should be recorded in-house. Likewise, the company should insist on drawing up the outsourcing contract and scheduling the negotiation dates, and refuse to give up the helm at any time.

At the end of the second bid phase the company will have selected its preferred IT provider. However, as long as a contract has not been concluded it will be advisable to keep the second-priority candidate 'on the back-burner' – and to let the preferred candidate know about it. This will strengthen the company's negotiation position, and offer a realistic alternative in the event that, contrary to expectations, negotiations with the preferred supplier fail

3.1.4   Using the outsourcing contract to constitute a long-term partnership

In the course of the contract negotiations, the course will be set for either a long-term partnership or a dead end. There is a series of typical causes for later failure, all due to contracts negotiated insufficiently:

■ *Tasks have not been defined clearly enough:* Often, the company's targets and respective service levels are not clearly defined at the beginning of the partnership. As a result, the services rendered by the IT provider either do not meet the company's needs or are not duly acknowledged by the company. To provide a sound basis for resolving such conflicts, the contract should stipulate in detail the reporting procedures for services rendered.

■ *The outsourcing partnership is too rigid:* Companies change; outsourcing partnerships must be adjustable. For instance, the number of IT systems and desktop work-stations may increase due to mergers and acquisitions, or decrease due to restructuring. In these cases, corporate reality will soon no longer match the outsourcing contract. Even if the company 'only' grows organically, consequences for the planning data must be clarified in the course of negotiations, or discussed early in the cooperation, in order to be taken account of in the design and development of the outsourcing partnership.

■ *Prices are considered too high by payers:* In large groups, outsourcing contracts are often concluded centrally, while the costs incurred by the respective services are allocated to the divisions and must be borne by them (or gained through their economic performance). Not surprisingly, costs are often closely monitored in these cases. Allocation ratios which have not been made sufficiently clear, or prices that were originally considered appropriate but have not been adjusted to recent economic trends (such as overcapacities and resulting price drops) will then be a constant source of annoyance. To avoid such nuisances, prices can either be tied to economic indexes, or regularly (every one or two years) benchmarked by external experts.

A European service company facing illiquidity sold a number of assets, including several IT subsidiaries. The acquirer was chosen based on its price offer, which by far exceeded the usual level. While this helped the company temporarily to overcome its cash shortage, the IT provider was forced to earn back the purchase price, and consequently set the prices for its IT services – to be paid by the divisions – well above market level. From the very start, the outsourcing relationships suffered from the fact that all advantages from the high selling price remained at headquarters, while the divisions, which were engaged in fierce brand competition, had to pay excessive IT prices. Since they were also the ones to deal with the IT outsourcer in day-to-day business, the relationship was programmed for permanent conflict – which soon led to the renegotiation of the out-sourcing contract, as this was the only way to 'rescue' the partnership.

In order to place the outsourcing partnership on a sound basis from the beginning, the company and its IT provider need to agree on a series of details in negotiating both, the master agreement and the individual Service Level Agreements (SLAs).

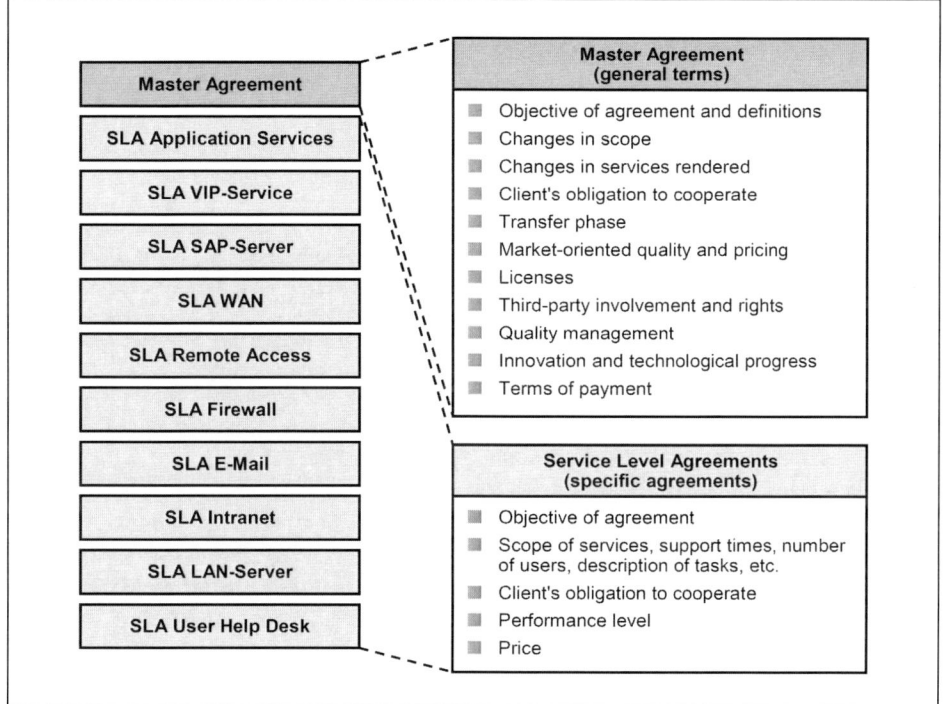

Figure 41:   Master Agreement and SLAs;
Source: A.T. Kearney

The Master Agreement will contain all general stipulations regarding the duration and scope of the contract, price conditions, rights of cancellation, property rights, and others (figure 41). Further stipulations will concern compliance monitoring and the continual adjustment of the contract to possible changes in requirements – for instance, how to deal with changes in the types of services rendered, and how they will affect prices. In addition – similar to the spin-off of an internal IT provider – arrangements must be made for a six- to nine-month transitional phase during which all IT tasks are transferred from the status quo to the future operations model. Last but not least, the company should ensure that the IT provider will treat all information obtained confidentially, strictly adhering to data protection laws and industry-specific regulations.

If the company decides to outsource its entire IT, the congruence of interests should be safeguarded by corresponding incentives incorporated in the payment model, as well as cancellation clauses in the contract. In one case, the outsourcer's compensation was not based on service prices stipulated in the SLAs but simply on the changes in certain items on the client company's balance sheet, which were highly influenceable through IT. This constituted a clear incentive for the outsourcer to contribute to balance sheet improvements and align all IT optimization and upgrading efforts to this single goal. Such incentive and compensation systems are possible; however, they require mathematic precision to be set up prior to the signing of the contract: Both, the client company and the IT outsourcer will be required to understand the cause-and-effect relationships between IT systems, business processes, and balance sheet figures, and to agree on a corresponding calculation formula – which also needs to cover the simulation of possible scenarios in the company's development (such as market share gains or losses) as well as possible effects on IT and balance sheet figure.

Even during contract negotiation, the company should also think about the time after its expiration. To maintain flexibility, arrangements should be made with regard to a possible insourcing of IT, or outsourcing to another IT provider, covering aspects like the obligation to cooperate, periods to be observed, and the coverage of costs. For if the company really decides not to renew the contract, this will usually be preceded by a period of conflict between both parties, resulting in a very unfavorable basis for further discussion if no arrangements have been made beforehand.

While the Master Agreement will contain the general terms valid for all SLAs, the latter will rule the details on individual services to be delivered, such as scope and availability, unit prices, obligations of the client to cooperate in the provision of services, and others. In negotiating the SLAs, the company should be sure to define its requirements very clearly so that the outsourcer's services can objectively be measured against them. In particular, this will include the definition of parameters, times, and responsibilities for measuring, as well as of a mathematic formula to point out the correlation with bonus/malus components of the IT provider's compensation.

Table 3.2: Typical measuring parameters for the service level stipulated in an SLA

Requirements of the company	Measuring parameters for service level
Services must be available (hardware must be functional; software must be usable, etc.)	Average availability (may be between 95 and 99.9 percent, with clear price discounts for every percentage point)
The IT provider should deal with emerging questions according to priority, and within an acceptable period of time	Response rate (generally, 80 to 90 percent of replies should be received within a given time frame)
The IT provider should solve emerging problems according to priority, and within an acceptable period of time	Problem-solving rate (generally, 70 to 80 percent of problems should be solved within a given time frame)
System performance (speed) should be acceptable	System response times (generally, 80 to 90 percent of responses should be given within less than a second)

At first glance, drawing up detailed service level agreements may seem like avoidable extra work. Nevertheless they are highly recommendable, for without them there will be ambiguities with regard to services and prices which, in the course of outsourcing relationships, have often been the cause of complaints on both sides.

3.1.5   Actively managing the outsourcing partnership

An active management of the outsourcing partnership – including how changes are dealt with – is the most important and difficult tasks in the outsourcing process. There is a risk of immense losses if the partnership fails, while both the company and its IT provider can benefit from a harmonious and productive cooperation.

Both partners should be aware that an IT outsourcing partnership designed to last several years will hardly ever remain unchanged for the duration of the contract. Time and again there will be modifications – mostly initiated by the client company, but sometimes also from the provider. The company, for instance, might wish to include new requirements to locations, services, or other factors, or 'readjust' individual SLAs, typically including details such as user help-desk service times. On the IT provider's part, innovation leaps in IT might trigger a rapid upgrading of the IT infrastructure or application landscape which, subject to agreement, can be passed on to the company in the form of effectiveness and efficiency increases (examples: Computing on Demand/Grid Computing). A new topic for both parties is the transfer of labor-intensive tasks to low-cost countries in Eastern Europe or to India. Due to the resulting structural changes in the IT outsourcer's performance, companies and provides should evaluate the risks and opportunities of off-shoring jointly.

Whatever the cause of changes in the outsourcing partnership, the fact of the matter is that they are likely to happen. The challenge lies in recognizing them early on and managing them in a professional manner. Throughout the lifetime of an outsourcing partnership there will be early signals of an emerging need for change. In most cases, alarming signals will prevail and should be taken very seriously. Typically, everything will start with users in the divisions complaining about the IT provider's staff, which they perceive to be lacking in customer friendliness, too expensive, and too slow in their response times. Subsequent discussions with the IT provider will reveal that there are also causes for complaint, for example because the client company's requirements are not specified clearly enough, communicated too late, and targets are in part unrealistic.

According to analyses of failed outsourcing partnerships, the failure is hardly ever the fault of one partner only; rather, complaints on both sides tend to add up to a severe lack of mutual understanding, finally culminating in a total communication breakdown. Both partners are dissatisfied with how the outsourcing partnership has turned out, or fail to reach their individual objectives. Since contractual sums are usually substantial – in comprehensive outsourcing situations, several hundred million or even several billion Euros are not uncommon – these disagreements often end up in court. This, however, represents a worst-case scenario, for an outsourcing partnership is not that easy to dissolve.

It has been a proven practice to take precautions right at the beginning of the partnership ensuring that necessary changes will not cause the partnership to fail. An important prerequisite is continuous communication between the company's IT organization and the IT provider. It is institutionalized at three levels:

■ At the highest level, members of a *Review Board* – representatives of top management and the corporate CIO as well as of the IT provider's management board and key account management – meet once or twice per year to determine the long-term strategic direction of the cooperation – such as, what areas will need new IT systems or how technology leaps can be used to the mutual benefit of both partners

■ The *Steering Board* – comprising the corporate CIO and representatives of business departments/divisions, as well as key account managers and industry/functional specialists from the IT provider – meet three or four times a year to take important single-case decisions on new developments in the context of the strategic overall plan, or major changes in SLAs (services and prices).

■ At the operating level, a *Service Management Board* – consisting of corporate CIO and one person specializing in the management of the outsourcing contract, as well as key account managers and service specialists from the IT provider – meet once a month to decide on details of the cooperation, as well as smaller adjustments to SLAs, and to generate current reports on the cooperation.

On the company's part, important change requests will usually refer to the IT services agreed upon – which the company will want to expand or reduce – or the prices of existing services. While changes in the services outsourced are usually uncritical, demands for price changes often lead to disagreements, possibly even to the premature termination of the partnership. It has therefore proven useful in practice to define a set of mechanisms which will prevent the company's expectations and the IT provider's services and prices from drifting apart.

Quality monitoring carried out at regular intervals will help to measure service quality and customer satisfaction in day-to-day cooperation. In addition to quality analyses and customer surveys, some IT providers have begun to establish online quality data bases where appointed representatives of the company (such as the CIO and major users in the divisions) are free to give current evaluations of the IT provider's services at any time they please, for instance by entering them in a 'traffic light' system with additional room for feedback. Such procedures are very useful to quickly recognize, diagnose, and eliminate emerging problems. At the same time they improve the IT provider's negotiation position when it comes to bidding for further outsourcing services, since the – hopefully high – service quality it has been delivering can now be measured objectively.

An institutionalized *improvement program* helps to continually adapt the partnership to both parties' changing requirements throughout its lifetime (figure 42). This is necessary because it will only be after the transfer of IT staff to the IT provider, and the subsequent implementation of the partnership, that the company starts gaining concrete experiences with what the SALs actually mean in day-to-day business. This is often the point where the user helpdesks's contractual service and/or response times turn out to be insufficient, or prices for the services rendered are perceived as being too high compared to the situation pre-outsourcing.

When closing the contract with its IT provider, a manufacturing company had agreed to user help-desk service hours from 6 a.m. to 8 p.m. The IT provider had established two service shifts which were billed to the client company. When this service level was evaluated in the context of a continuous improvement program, it turned out that far more than 90 percent of staff were present between 9 a.m. and 5 p.m., so that one shift at the user help-desk would be sufficient. By adjusting this service level to actual demand, the company was able to achieve substantial cost savings without any noticeable negative consequences for users.

Like the changes in services, demands for price changes are usually foreseeable: Customers are entitled to expect prices to decrease in the course of an outsourcing partnership, as the outsourcer will also keep optimizing its internal prices. Additional factors giving cause for price adjustments will include changes in the market. During the e-business/IT hype in the late 1990ies, for example, prices for IT services were very high due to a lack of qualified specialists. These times have changed since the stock market crashed. If a company has con-cluded one or several outsourcing contracts during the high-price phase, it stands to reason that it will be able to obtain much better financial terms by adjusting or renegotiating them.

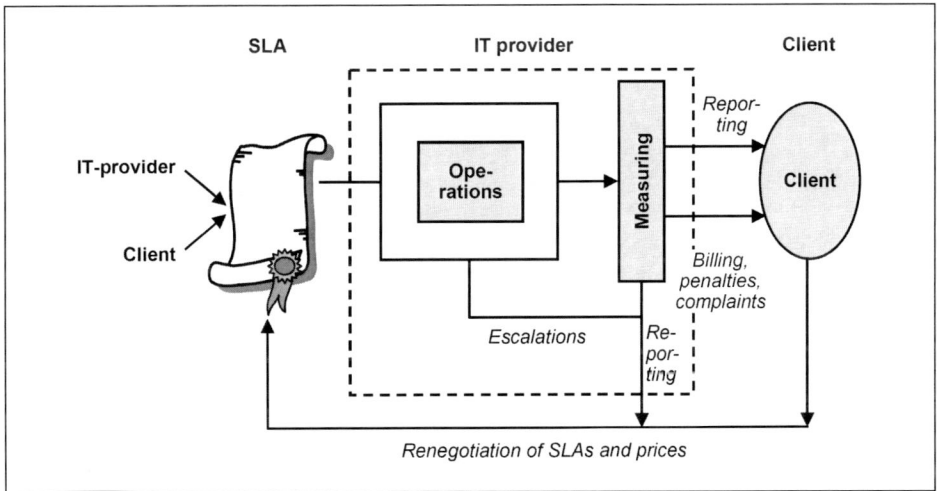

Figure 42:   Continuous improvement program

Another important mechanism is the systematic cost management of IT operations, in the context of which both parties should – ideally jointly – continue evaluating and actively managing the ratio of IT performance and prices. This implies, however, that a regular evaluation and adjustment of IT services and prices, based on transparent costs, has been included in the outsourcing contract. In practice, a systematic cost management will rarely have been agreed upon at the very beginning of a partnership; therefore the company should at least attempt to introduce annual performance and price benchmarking after one or two years, in order to obtain an objective and broad basis for negotiating any adjustments that may become necessary at a later point.

For other sourcing categories, purchasing would simply set up a bid procedure and use the results as a basis for negotiation. For IT outsourcing this is not feasible: First of all, the very subject matter is so complex that it would take too much time and effort to issue a new bid invitation. In addition, all other IT providers would be aware that the company has been having contractual ties with one outsourcer for several years. And in view of the fact that it takes plenty of time and resources to seriously deal with an outsourcing request, requests clearly meant to serve as a benchmarking tool would promptly be sorted out. It is therefore preferable to use a benchmarking firm to be selected jointly by the company and the IT provider, commissioning it to conduct a comparison of market prices at least for key services. If market prices are within a predefined corridor (such as +/- 5 percent) adjustments will be made automatically. If price benchmarks are outside the agreed corridor, the *Steering Board* will have to find a solution, which in many cases will be renegotiation. If the outsourcing contract covers a very large scope of services, it may be advisable also to reevaluate the company's IT demand, providing management with a clear view on the IT outsourcing partnership and its goals.

Price negotiations – whether they refer to adjustments within a given contract or complete renegotiations – need to be prepared thoroughly. Just like the initial bid invitation and conclusion of the outsourcing contract, they require a negotiation team consisting of the corporate CIO, representatives of IT controlling, the legal and purchasing departments, and IT users. It goes without saying that the IT provider will be less interested in renegotiating than the company, in particular since the client company is bound to the contract and, for its duration, will hardly have a legal handle to enforce any changes (temporary monopoly). Canceling the contract, on the other hand, will be very difficult due to the complexity of IT, the negative effects on business resulting from temporary non-availability of the IT services outsourced, and the – often very drastic – contractual penalties.

The IT provider's willingness to adjust prices will depend on the answers to a series of questions, which the company can influence in part:

- *What is the balance of power in the outsourcing partnership?* If it is a large-scale outsourcing contract with a leading company, the IT provider will hardly be in a position to risk losing the contract. Rather, the provider will be interested in a solution avoiding negative publicity, in particular as it is likely to be in negotiations for further contracts in the same industry.

- *What are the incentives?* The company's negotiation position will be best if it has not entirely outsourced its IT. Additional potential for the IT provider will be a powerful incentive for demonstrating flexibility

- *How great is the price difference compared to market prices?* The provider will, of course, be aware of the margins obtained with the client company. More than 10 percent above market price are not feasible in the long run.

A company and an IT provider had concluded a 10-year outsourcing contract amounting to nearly two million Euros. When prices where compared for selected services it turned out that they were clearly above market level, leading the company to assume that this was also true for the remaining services. A detailed benchmarking was conducted, revealing substantial opportunities for cost reduction in the computing center as well as in end-user computing (desktops and software, LAN/WAN, user help-desk). Renegotiating the existing contract enabled the company to reduce its annual costs by 20 percent; in addition, contractual penalties for purchase quantities below agreed levels (the company's demand was declining) were 'negotiated out'.

In some cases, the need to renegotiate and modify the outsourcing contract will be recognized not only by the company but also by the IT provider. Under some contracts, for

instance, the IT provider is responsible for managing and developing the IT while the company retains the right to choose the software or select a hardware supplier. Stipulations like these limit the outsourcer's possibilities to bundle quantities and negotiate better prices with suppliers. If IT infrastructure technologies are concerned, they can also make it difficult, if not impossible; to integrate the company's IT into the outsourcer's business system. To give an example: The IT outsourcer might want to connect the company's computing center to a central control station to ensure cost efficient operations at night, on weekends, and on holidays. This will, however, be impossible if the company insists on using incompatible software. In such a case the outsourcer will be justified in demanding modifications to the contract, to be able to better achieve the efficiency targets specified for the partnership.

Even if a company has originally had good reasons to opt for outsourcing, this does not necessarily mean they will remain valid forever. Therefore, the make-or-buy decision should be revised periodically in the context of strategic planning. Changes in the market, a realignment of the company, new IT developments, or changes in the IT provider's operations can be a cause for either expanding or reducing the scope of the outsourcing relationship. In any case, the company should decide no later than twelve months prior to expiration, whether to renew the contract or look for another outsourcing partner. A new bid invitation will take at least six months, and so will usually the transfer to a new outsourcer and/or the (partial) insourcing of IT.

Checklist: Is your company ready for outsourcing?	Yes
Have the objectives of outsourcing been clearly defined?	
Is the company prepared to go through the necessary change process – including both, the IT staff to be transferred and the IT users who will have to deal with new contacts?	
Has the 'right' outsourcing partner been selected – taking into account both, economic and long-term strategic and cultural aspects?	
Have contractual conditions been clearly agreed on between both parties, taking into account possible future changes in the company?	
Have possible scenarios for 'the time after' been discussed, prior to the conclusion of the contract, and corresponding stipulations been included?	

3.2   Using Factor Cost Advantages by IT Offshoring

When, in view of the Y2K threat, Indian software firms started taking over programming tasks at low prices, a new market had emerged: IT offshoring. Meanwhile, a series of other countries have positioned themselves as offshoring suppliers – from China, Malaysia and the Philippines, Australia and New Zealand, to Russia, Mexico and Brazil, Canada, Ireland, and finally Eastern European countries like the Czech Republic and Hungary. The outsourcing of IT services to geographically distant regions is now considered a growth market with exciting future potential (figure 43).

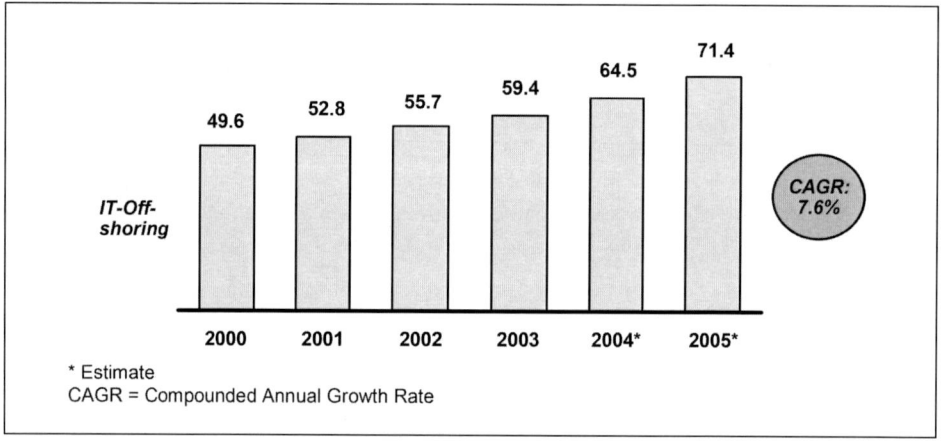

Figure 43:   *Growth of the IT offshoring market; Source: A.T. Kearney*

At first glance, IT offshoring does not seem very different from IT outsourcing. Consequently, recommendations will be similar with regard to the selecting and maintaining of provider relationships. There are, however, essential differences in the services suitable for IT offshoring, and the cost advantages to be obtained. At the same time, IT offshoring requires different risks to be evaluated than would apply for most globalized IT outsourcers. Companies looking into IT offshoring should start by identifying the services which, according to their IT strategy, are suitable for offshoring – then choose an IT offshoring model, and lay out the life-cycle of the offshoring relationship as they would in the case of IT outsourcing.

3.2.1   Developing a corporate IT offshoring strategy

IT offshoring is interesting for both, client companies and IT providers. Companies relying on the strategic sourcing of IT will be able to exploit factor cost advantages and/or reduce the degree of vertical integration. IT providers can use IT offshoring as a means to reduce IT costs and improve competitiveness. Offshoring, then, adds to the selection process in the context of companies' sourcing decisions; at the same time, it plays a vital role in the decision for a certain IT provider: Providers using offshoring to reduce their own costs will be able to pass on the resulting cost advantages to their customers.

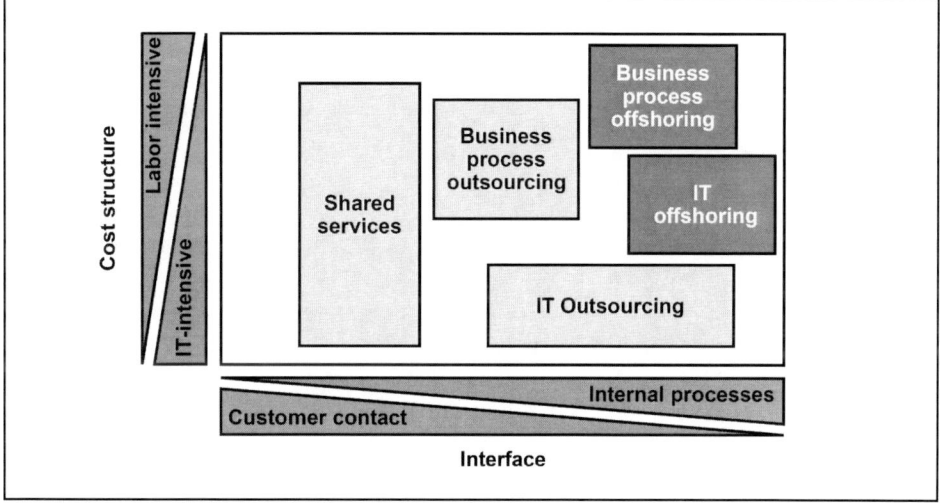

Figure 44:   Optimization strategies for business processes; Source: A.T. Kearney

IT offshoring fills a gap in the previous approaches for business process optimization (figure 44):

- *Shared services* – The internal bundling of business processes – are used primarily for labor-intensive processes with customer contacts (for example, call centers). Companies can achieve substantial cost advantages through the shared use of certain tasks; however, since these processes can comprise critical internal know-how in some industries, the pros and cons of outsourcing them must be carefully evaluated with regard to the risk of a know-how loss.

- *Business process outsourcing* – Subcontracting business processes to an external provider in one's home market – is possible for internal processes, including those with customer contact (such as call centers and user help-desks).

- *Business process offshoring* – Transferring business processes to lower-cost locations – is suitable in particular for labor-intensive internal processes which are highly standardized and not very critical in terms of corporate know-how (such as HR administration, accounting, transportation). Cost reductions will mainly result from factor-cost advantages.

- *IT outsourcing* – Transferring (predominantly) IT infrastructural services to external providers in one's home market – is suitable primarily for standardized processes, such as the

operation of computing centers or communication networks, with cost advantages resulting primarily from the IT processes

■ *IT offshoring* – Transferring labor-intensive IT services to lower-cost locations – has established itself for standardized, clearly definable processes requiring limited coordination
but a substantial degree of project work (such as software development and maintenance,
as well as user help-desks). Topics less suitable for IT offshoring include those requiring
proximity to the market or customer, such as CRM applications or customer portals providing access to corporate information and processes, as well as IT consulting, developing
professional concepts, and training. Cost advantages will result, above all, from lower labor costs at offshore locations.

The 'new' concept meets with lively interest in the U.S. and Europe, particularly in industries
with a substantial share of highly standardized, labor-intensive processes with limited strategic relevance to the respective company (such as banks and insurances). An A.T. Kearney
survey of 120 financial service providers in the U.S. and Europe in 2003 revealed that so far,
companies' experiences with offshoring (mainly IT offshoring, only in some cases also business process offshoring) have been positive: Almost every second company has achieved
over 30 percent savings, 17 percent of companies even more than 50 percent. Among other
things, this also reflects the high degree of professionalism which offshore suppliers have
managed to built in the past years – although at different degrees of maturity. While business
process offshoring is currently still in its infancy, IT offshoring has already reached a medium
to high level of maturity:

■ The initial service offerings have reached an advanced stage of maturity. They include
(Y2K) debugging, the development and maintenance of mainframe systems, migration and
upgrading of application systems, release changes as well as code conversion.

■ A lesser degree of maturity applies for IT services in the context of the introduction and
modification of standard software (such as ERP systems) as well as upgrades programmed
in-house.

■ The new development of application systems has reached a medium stage of maturity

■ Offerings on EAI (Enterprise Application Integration) or business intelligence (such as
data warehousing) are still at an early stage of development

■ Service offerings like help-desk, call centers, business process outsourcing are at the beginning of their market development. They are, however, gaining importance for offshoring, and some offshore suppliers have already gained experience with these services.

Companies opting for offshoring their IT services should take account of these conditions,
and compare them to their strategic goals to arrive at a sound offshoring strategy. IT services
that could be essential to competitive differentiation in the medium or long term should defi-
nitely be excluded. By contrast, the offshoring of standardized IT services can help free up
substantial financial and personnel resources for value-added IT projects.

Tips for selecting services suitable for offshoring:

Develop migration strategy:
Make sure that local IT staff are involved early in your offshoring plans, and prepare them for deployment at offshore providers

Optimize first, then go offshore:
Consolidate your IT processes in shared-service organizations or internal IT providers before outsourcing them to an offshore IT supplier

Go for early wins:
Begin by selecting IT services for offshoring, which can reach a steady state in less than six months. Make sure you select closed processes only.

Even more than IT outsourcing, IT offshoring strategies need to take account of the company's current situation: Companies which still have deficits in IT optimization should eliminate them before thinking about outsourcing to offshore IT providers. Likewise, transparency on the IT costs and tasks – company-wide – will be an essential prerequisite for evaluating the risks and opportunities involved.

Uncoordinated IT offshoring projects in individual division involve a major risk, in that the value gained through IT offshoring could be destroyed by enormous migration costs. When the offshoring potential is evaluated from an integrated point of view, it will be advisable to involve all stakeholders on both, the IT and the users' part, in order to make transparent the benefits of IT offshoring for the company and eliminate fears and uncertainty in the IT staff.

Systematic development of an offshoring strategy for a U.S. based group

In a U.S. based group, several divisions had initiated offshoring to test out the possibilities it offered. These individual efforts were now to be integrated in a corporate offshoring strategy, in order to limit the number of offshore suppliers and reduce the amount of time and effort required for all those individual decisions.

A key factor for success of the offshoring effort was its systematic preparation: First, the objectives of offshoring and the restrictions following from the corporate strategy were determined, and the future requirements to IT derived. On this basis, suitable topics for offshoring were identified organization-wide, and a value proposition developed. Totals costs were determined for each application system and IT service, compared to the costs at different offshore locations, and prioritized. As a result, the user help-desk and the development of individual application systems emerged as priority themes. Next, suitable locations and offshore suppliers were selected. For the help-desk, Canada turned out to be a slightly better location than India; in the field of application development it was vice versa.

Once this was established, a corporate offshoring strategy was developed, including the requirements to the offshore suppliers (type of suppliers, global, company-wide contracts and service levels). This strategy was broken down to division level, and the detailed off-shoring issues and time frames for implementation were agreed on with the departments concerned. A key element for success was the integrated implementation plan, based on agreed sub-plans per division, which was carried out successively.

3.2.2   Evaluating risks and opportunities of a location

Whether companies will be able to fulfill their cost and benefit expectations, and whether they will build a successful and long-standing cooperation with their IT provider, largely depends on their selection from the numerous offshoring locations available. The systematic selection of a suitable IT offshoring location should be based on three key criteria: resources, location factors, and the offshore country's cost position. A.T. Kearney has evaluated key outsourcing countries against these three criteria, based on our project experience, market surveys, and expert interviews (figure 45). This evaluation confirmed India's dominant role: The country received best values in both, costs and HR resources.

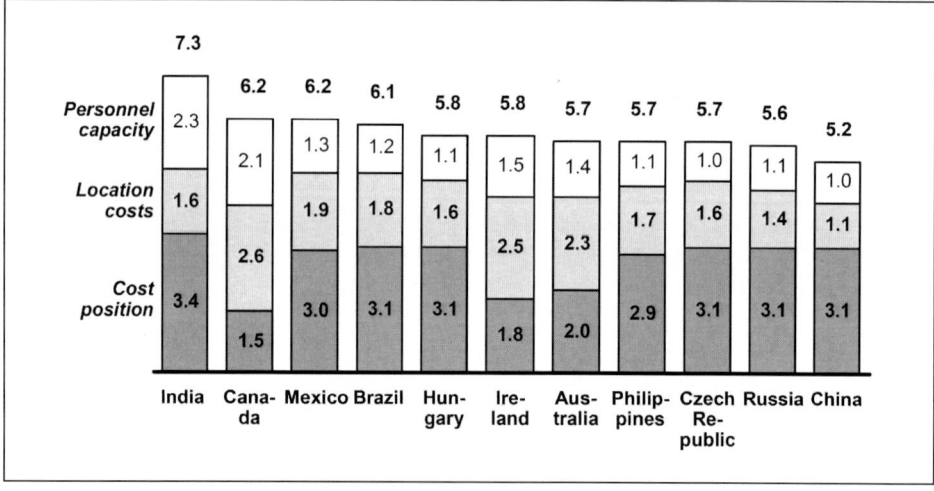

Figure 45:   Evaluation of offshore locations;
                 Source: A.T. Kearney

An essential criterion for the success of an IT offshoring initiative, frequently emphasized by companies, is the availability of qualified local personnel. Many companies foster staff rotation between onshore and offshore, which is not easy to do on a large scale with IT providers in faraway countries. Time changes are another factor that makes the management of the IT partnership highly challenging. In view of twelve hours' difference between India and the

U.S., and six hours between Europe and the Philippines, office times in the regionally dispersed project teams will have only minor overlaps. Moreover, complex matters and business processes will be harder to communicate long-distance, in particular if the business environment in the countries concerned is very different from one's own. Last but not least, the protection of intellectual property, such as program codes, and the observance of licensing laws must be ascertained – for instance, through respective regulatory measures in the suppliers' countries.

Cultural differences are another crucial factor for the offshore provider's ability to fulfill the customer's requirements: If two people speak to each other in English this does not necessarily mean they understand one another. German companies accustomed to working with qualified IT experts have often experienced that their specifications, which are in part highly complex, are perceived to be imprecise by the IT offshore supplier, and fail to be fulfilled in a satisfactory manner. In an IT offshoring partnership there is no sense in expecting that the provider will understand the context of one's request and align its execution with the user's goals, possibly even make own suggestions for its execution. U.S. based companies, used to issuing clearly structured and precise instructions without any 'irritating' contextual comments frequently get better results.

It is mainly due to culture and language factors that companies in the U.S. and central Europe differ in their choice of IT offshoring locations: In the U.S., 90 percent of all companies prefer India (figure 46), with China at Philippines following at some distance (20 percent each).

Quite different were the results of an A.T. Kearney survey among companies in German-speaking countries: Only 50 percent quoted India as their preferred location. Again, the reasons are obvious: Even in the globalization age, language barriers vis-à-vis India is still higher for a German company than they are for a U.S. company. And while it is true that there are also language barriers vis-à-vis Eastern European countries, they are much 'closer' to Germany not only geographically, but also politically and culturally – in particular after the European Union's recent expansion to the East. In addition, the higher degree of vertical integration in German companies is also reflected in a higher share of in-house IT. It comes as no surprise, then, that IT offshoring has long been popular in the U.S., whereas in Europe (with the exception of the U.K.) it is still in its beginnings.

All of the countries listed have made considerable efforts over the past years to build a stable infrastructure and extensive data networks, and they offer highly qualified, English-speaking It specialists. Their long-term success in the offshoring market, however, depends not only on economic factors but also on political trends and global influences.

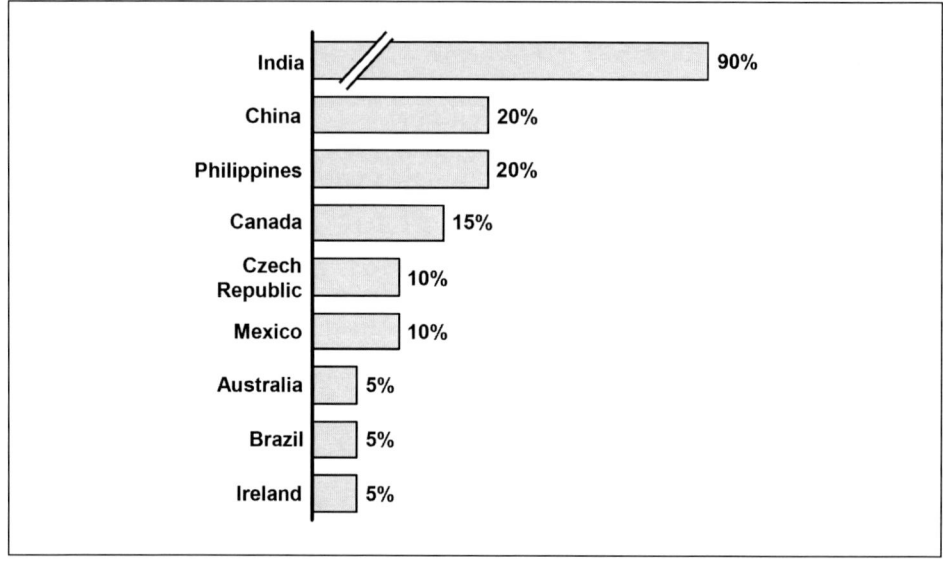

Figure 46:   *Offshore locations preferred by U.S. companies;*
            Source: A.T. Kearney

Above all, these include terrorism and military conflicts: They can prevent companies from transferring their business processes to the regions concerned, such as the Middle East, China, Taiwan, or Corea. In addition, there are risk factors for traveling, such as diseases or epidemics: In the case of SARS, for instance, the IT offshoring regions Asia and Canada were affected the most. Another risk for the development of the IT offshoring market consists in (hacker) attacks on data networks: AS IT offshoring depends on the possibility to exchange data across long distances using a variety of networks, any attack on these data transmissions would have disastrous effects on the IT offshoring market. Finally, protectionist measures taken by the customer countries can play a major role, if they are used with the aim of preventing the migration of jobs to 'low-income countries'. The supplier countries, on the other hand, must be able to offer not only a qualified workforce, but also adequate incentives to prevent a migration of these specialists, who will be sought after in the international labor market. According to our surveys, leading companies do no longer rely on one IT offshoring location only, but pursue multi-country strategies. This way, should there be a natural disaster in, say, New Delhi, they can use Manila as a back-up.

In the past years, the attractiveness of IT offshoring was mainly based on the cost savings potentials which, depending on the location, could be anywhere between 10 and 70 percent. Cost advantages from IT offshoring mainly result from the lower labor cost level in offshore countries. This is a major issue for the customer countries where labor costs are high: After deduction of hardware and software costs (40 to 45 percent on average) the remaining 55 to 60 percent of TI costs go to internal labor or external providers. This cost block can be considerably reduced with offshore locations (figure 47).

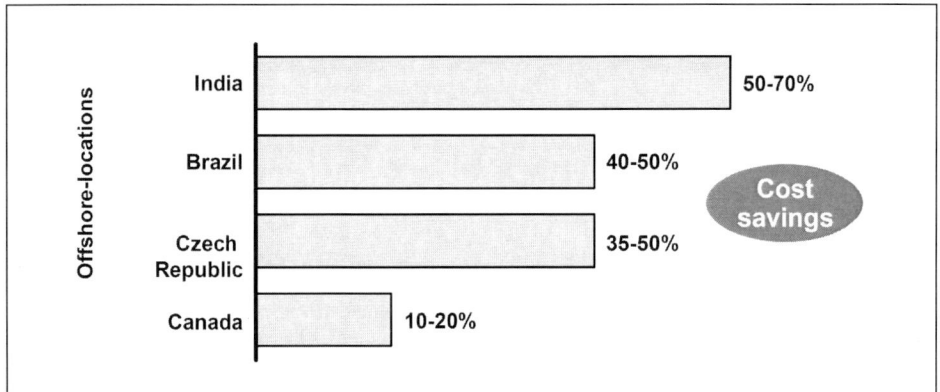

Figure 47:   *Total cost savings (labor costs, infrastructure, taxes) compared to the U.S.;*
                 Source: A.T. Kearney

Labor costs strongly depend on the cost of living in the particular country, the wage level, and the educational level of employees. Costs of IT programmers, for instance, are 60 to 70 percent lower in India than they are in the U.S. While labor costs are currently rising in India – partly at a faster rate than in the industrialized countries – they are not expected to reach comparable levels any time soon. This may, however, change along with the increasing consolidation of IT offshore suppliers: Even today, the Indian offshoring market is dominated by five suppliers which have made first efforts to expand to other offshoring countries and Europe. 'Globalization' of the industry, however, will inevitably lead to 'globalization' of labor cost.

The situation is similar in the locations preferred by European companies. At present there are still considerable differences in labor costs, making 'nearshoring' to Eastern European countries very attractive: While average labor costs in the 'old' EU (prior to expansion) amounted to 22.7 Euros per hour, it is only 2.9 Euros per hour in countries like Poland, the Czech Republic, Hungary, and the Slovak Republic. However, wage levels will clearly rise in those countries in the process of their integration into the EU: In Hungary, for example, wage levels are expected to double between 2000 and 2006 according to corresponding analyses.

For all these reasons, the cost issue should be considered with great caution – as in the case of IT outsourcing: Current labor cost advantages are partly offset by higher transaction costs, additional expenses for documentation (due to the geographic distance and time differences) as well as travel costs. Experiences in the U.S. and U.K. – where the outsourcing of complete services and partnering with other companies are common practice – have shown, however, that economic benefits to companies from offshoring go far beyond the cost savings expected:

■ *Higher productivity:* As IT offshore suppliers annually improve their internal processes by 10 to 15 percent, their productivity is often superior to that of European competitors

■ *Better service quality:* A major share of IT offshore suppliers has achieved a very high level of international certification, such as SEI CMM Level 5 (the highest level) while most IT providers only fulfill CMM levels 2 or 3. This involves considerable quality advantages, such as lower error rates

■ *Flexible resource quantities and capacities:* IT offshoring was begun in 1999, at a time of scarce IT resources. Meanwhile, in particular India has established itself as a new and, above all, flexible labor market (comprising more than 400,000 IT specialists).

■ *7x24 capacities:* Internationally leading IT providers with corresponding capacities in all continents and, as a result, regionally dispersed project teams, are able to guarantee 7x24-hour capacities. (Upon closer scrutiny, these theoretical 7x24 hours will be cut down to a very short time period, as on a typical 8- to 12-hour day within a given time zone, around 10 to 15 percent of labor will be spent on documentation and handing over tasks to other parts of the worldwide project team. In view of labor cost advantages, the 7x24 benefits should be weighed against alternative solutions, such as two-shift models in another offshore location.)

For each individual IT task, the strengths and weaknesses of each offshore location, as well as the opportunities and risks in three dimensions – cost position, location factors, and resources – should be analyzed in detail.

The IT task itself should be evaluated against two criteria: its potential value to the company (number of IT staff, and costs per IT staff member) and the possible savings. Only if IT tasks involve substantial value to the company while incurring limited migration cost – for instance, if existing IT staff can be put in charge of managing the IT offshore supplier – will the company draw maximum benefits from this optimization process.

3.2.3   Selecting a suitable offshoring model

Once an adequate offshoring location has been chosen, a suitable IT provider must be selected. IT offshoring services can either be delivered in-house, or outsourced to an offshoring partner or an external provider (figure 48). In either case, the division of tasks between the company and the provider needs to be clarified.

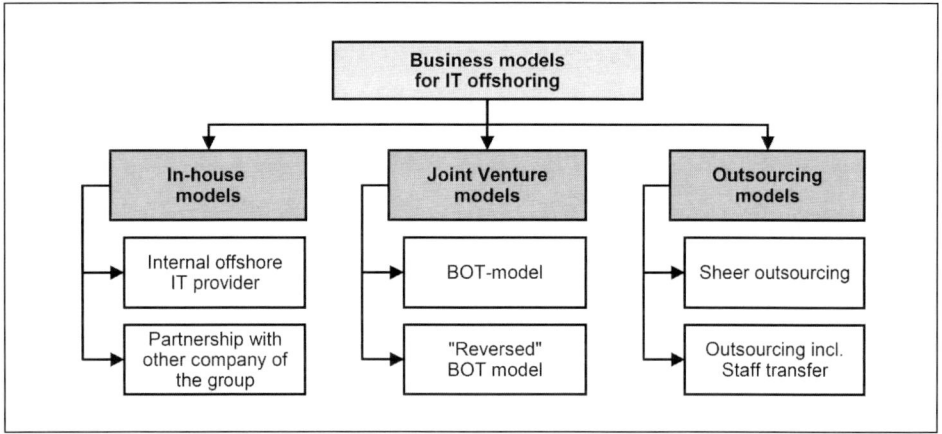

Figure 48:   Variants of IT offshoring;
Source: A.T. Kearney

In-house models imply that the company establishes its own location in an offshore country. This will be an option only for large groups present worldwide, which consider IT a core competence while involving IT offshoring providers to exploit labor cost advantages. These companies will retain control of the entire project, which will require them to have the necessary capabilities and experiences. Examples of companies which have opted for this solution early on include General Electric, with 15,000 employees in eight offshore locations, as well as HSBC with 2,000, and American Express, also with 2,000 employees in India. Intel, Boeing, and Motorola have established locations in Russia.

This option is suited in particular for longer-term tasks, such as IT processes in IT operations, or large-scale application development projects where IT resources are scarce and there is a substantial need for resources to meet project milestones. It is also chosen by most global IT providers who improve their cost structures (and prices) by transferring tasks to offshore countries.

Outsourcing models represent the other extreme: Companies outsource IT services to an IT offshoring partner who will execute the entire project or service offshore. This solution is suited for simple, clearly defined tasks, and is often chosen for the operation of application systems and hardware, user support, and self-explanatory mass processes like data consolidation. Possible outsourcing partners for the 'sheer outsourcing' model are the large IT offshoring providers, such as TCS, Infosys, Wipro, Satyam, HCL Technologies, and Cognizant. The disadvantage of this solution, which involves no exchange of resources between the company and the provider, is the considerable management and control effort required from the company. Some companies resolve this by sending individual members of their IT staff to the offshore location to manage the provider relationships at least during the initial phase, and facilitate the know-how transfer. Outsourcing cum staff transfer is also used in the cooperation with smaller offshoring providers which do not have sufficient resources to build an international presence and operate from the company's local premises.

For many companies which have included offshoring in their longer-term strategy, the best solution will be joint venture models with an IT offshoring partner. The provider's staffs, together with the company's IT staff, carry out the design phase on the company's premises while the later implementation will happen off-shore. This way, there will be no 'start-up' phase for hiring suitable candidates, and for selecting and leasing suitable infrastructure. Likewise, the company will not have to go through the initial, often painful learning phase. In particular companies with little outsourcing experience, or with reservations against offshoring, will find this option attractive since it permits them to manage the know-how transfer while the IT offshoring provider will monitor the off-shore activities. Language or cultural differences will be mitigated as the regional distance is overcome.

In joint venture models, the BOT approach can be used when the IT offshore supplier returns the IT tasks to the company after a predefined period of time. In this case the staff of the offshore supplier will be deployed both, on-site and off-shore. On-site topics will be strategic issues, architecture, design, implementation, while off-shore activities will include development and maintenance/upgrading: It is obvious that this model will be particular suitable for complex projects. An example is the joint venture between British Telecom and the Indian IT-offshoring provider Mahindra. The BOT model can also be reversed, in that the IT offshoring provider initially focuses on implementation support, successively taking over the location as predefined milestones are reached. This model has been chosen by the insurance company AIG with Polaris, as well as British Airways with WNS.

The future will show which of these models will ultimately turn out to be the dominating one. It is, however, becoming more and more apparent that in the case of IT offshoring – as opposed to IT outsourcing – the geographic and cultural distances speak for a very fine definition of service relationships. IT offshoring is therefore ideally suited for covering the 'basic IT needs' of a company in terms of IT commodities (such as the operation of computing centers and user help-desks), helping them to quickly achieve sustainable cost savings of 20 to 40 percent. By contrast, company-specific and differentiating IT tasks will be kept in-house. As a result, the role of the IT department will change, and with it the IT staff's qualification profile: Instead of application programmers with extensive IT-system know-how, solution oriented business shapers will drive value-added IT contents with competitive relevance and a clear business focus.

Checklist: Is your offshoring strategy promising?	Yes
Have the objectives of your IT offshoring strategy been defined clearly and with a careful eye on corporate strategy (for example, growth targets)?	
Have all stakeholders been involved in your offshoring plans?	
Have IT processes been optimized prior to transfer to an offshore supplier?	
Have conclusive IT services been chosen for offshoring – labor-intensive, with limited customer contact and non-critical to competitiveness?	
Have the opportunities and risks of IT locations been evaluated with regard to your long-term goals – not only cost aspects?	
Does your offshoring partner maintain the key capabilities you will require? In case of doubt, did you engage several offshoring providers to spread the risk?	

Outlook

The role of IT and the tasks of those working in the IT sector will be subject to major change in the next decade. The most prominent trend will be the drifting apart of *basic IT supply* and *strategic IT demand.*

■ *Basic IT supply* will comprise, in addition to infrastructure, the development and operation of all applications not necessarily company-specific

■ *Strategic IT demand* refers to those IT components by which companies can differentiate themselves from their competitors.

There are substantial differences in the objectives, methods, competences, and organization models for these two areas.

Providing basic IT supply at moderate cost

The significance of IT for the business activity of companies will increase dramatically. The more companies of an industry build competitive advantages through IT, the greater the pressure on competitors to follow their example and obtain cost efficiency, as well as innovative, customer-oriented products and services through value-added use of IT. Next, up- and downstream stages of the value chain will get sucked into the wake of this development: 'IT won't work without IT!'

Just like staple foods, energy, air, and water, the quality of IT products and services will no longer be a pleasant surprise but an essential prerequisite for acceptance by consumers and users. To safeguard the basic supply with IT on a constant high quality level, development and production procedures for IT will be further industrialized. In parallel, the demand for basic IT supply will be standardized by harmonizing non-differentiating business processes.

This development, in turn, will permit the basic IT supply to be managed purely from a cost perspective. Cost savings potentials from scale effects and location advantages will clearly reinforce the already visible trend towards IT outsourcing, IT offshoring, and the consolidation of IT providers. In view of eroding margins, cost optimization in basic IT supply will continue to be a central management task. In most cases this will mainly refer to request management, procurement, and supplier management. Following the same logic, companies will not stop there: In addition to IT, they will increasingly outsource standardized, non-differentiating processes – ideally to the same outsourcer providing the company's basic IT supply. The development into a Business Process Outsourcing (BPO) provider will, in turn, result in new requirements to these providers. In short: As in IT outsourcing, customers and providers have a steep learning curve ahead of them.

Using strategic IT demand for value increases

The burst of the Internet bubble and the general disappointment about broken promises by the IT industry have given rise to the general belief that IT is vastly overestimated ('IT does not matter') and should be reduced to basic supply functions. We would like to caution against such premature conclusions: In the next decade, too, IT will continue to be a major source of competitive advantages – more so than nanotechnology, the fuel cell, or genetic engineering.

Almost every company has a chance to obtain competitive advantages through specific combinations of IT and process or product qualities. Areas where innovation leaps will be possible include the following:

- ▣ Much more than before, the value chain will be penetrated and interlinked by IT ('digitalized'). A *digitalized supply chain* integrating suppliers and customers has often been promised but never implemented. Even today, there is no technically and economically viable solution so far. Other, equally high barriers to this next advance in streamlining consist in organizational problems. The lesson learnt from past failures is that automation is not always the best solution.

  A first mover in this field, establishing a wholly digitalized value chain, will gain a significant competitive edge in terms of speed, quality, and customer focus. Commoditization ('supply chain from the shelf') is not likely to happen anytime soon.

- ▣ Products are increasingly coupled to services (finance, warehousing/transportation, maintenance, disposal, and others) to increase sales and enhance customer retention. An essential prerequisite for that is the *higher information intensity of products.* Even today, the continuous price decrease for hardware products permits more and more industrial and consumer products to be equipped with data technology. The bottle-neck for gaining competitive advantages through these new possibilities consists in companies' processing capacity, which is much too low at present. In addition to new processes, also high-performance architectures, algorithms, and applications will need to be developed.

  The automotive industry, which had a pioneer role in this development, had to learn from painful experiences that processes for complex products (such as airplanes, elevators, and others), after having been handled well by plant engineers on an industrial scale, can present a mystery when transferred to large-scale serial production.

- ▣ The third area where companies will be able to differentiate themselves based on IT is the *better use of corporate intelligence:* The idea is as old as data processing itself: Business intelligence, knowledge management, document management systems, and collaborative planning are only a few examples of IT-based approaches to improved planning and decision-making. These approaches have only been successful in well-structured sub-areas, and have not been able to deliver on their far-reaching promises.

In parallel to these approaches – and independent of them – the workplace of the average employee (now: 'knowledge worker') has changed completely over the past years. Email, voice mail, PDA has become everyday tools. This development has proceeded powerfully – almost as if it was a law of nature – and seems to continue at undiminished speed. According to a recent study, 80 percent of companies' documented knowledge is contained in e-mail files. It is obvious, though, those companies' organizational capabilities are not keeping up with technological progress: 'Arming' the workplace with new IT tools has not accelerated or improved corporate decision-making – on the contrary, the cost-benefit ratio of these activities has continually declined.

Using IT to better exploit corporate intelligence has not worked out so far, as the respective processes are not sufficiently understood. Input/output models used for modeling supply chain processes do not suffice to describe the processes of developing, deciding, and reaching agreements. Without a deep understanding of the process, however, technology cannot be put to best use, and without clear targets there will be no satisfactory RoI. The task is clear, the solution is not obvious – but the reward will be enormous: A first-class challenge to management, science, and consulting.

To ensure that IT can cover a company's strategic IT demand, corresponding conditions must be created with regard to workforce and technology. The *working environment of IT people* – including the CIO, IT managers, software engineers, Java programmers, computing center operators, and others – will change even more drastically than in the 1990ies:

- The majority of operative IT staff will migrate to spin-off system vendors, increasingly also to large IT outsourcing providers

- The development and operation of IT – in particular in basic IT supply – will be further industrialized: Division of tasks, process disciplines, standardization, quality assurance, automation. Requirements to IT staff will be higher in this environment; their performance will be more transparent and comparable, jobs will be less secure.

- The difference between commercial and technical IT will disappear. Competitive differentiation through IT will increasingly be possible where technical, commercial, and planning processes are integrated.

- IT procurement will be professionalized and be autonomous in purchasing large parts of the IT services needed.

- Strategic IT management tasks will be increasingly re-centralized, and integrated in the management of value creation processes.

- Individuals in charge of IT will have to assume responsibility for the results of using IT for the benefit of the business.

IT people will be evaluated based on their ability to fulfill the role of business shapers. By the same token, the role of the IT department – and with it the qualification profile of staff – will change: Rather than application programmers with extensive IT system know-how, it will be solution-oriented business shapers promoting value-added IT contents with competitive relevance and a clear business focus. This direction will enable companies to exploit targeted IT benefits, and in the long run safeguard IT's right of existence.

Glossary

On the Internet in particular there are already a number of useful dictionaries which explain the wide range of specialist terms to both layperson and insider alike. The following terms provide an introduction into each theme and include the most important terms used in this book.

Application Service Provision (ASP): The operation of applications from a central computing centre without decentralized components. The provider aims to offer the same application and operating resources for several companies simultaneously. The crux of this model is that it allows pay-per-use billing of operating costs including license costs. To date this model has not been very successful as it appears that the needs of different companies are difficult to harmonize.

Budget cap: A measure by company executives to limit IT budgets in corporate budgeting. It is often an expression of a lack of transparency in IT costs and the loss of IT cost controlling at senior executive level. If not well managed and as operating costs increase, this can lead to ever smaller innovation budgets and thus to a complete standstill in IT development within the company.

Computer Aided Design (CAD): A collective term for all activities in which IT is used for development and design work for example in plant engineering. A CAD system is a stand-alone IT application that is installed on workstations or put on a network of several users for joint design projects. CAD systems have a great deal of potential for savings as they allow components to be reused in manufacturing and CAD systems also offer flexible adjustability and adaptivity.

Customer Relationship Management (CRM): Methods which place the customers at the centre of all considerations within a company. CRM is not only call-centre-automation, 1:1 marketing, sales force automation or database marketing, but a complete approach which encompasses strategy, operations and technology. CRM is a holistic concept which individualises the way customers are addressed and ensures that customers and their needs are analysed in depth and their needs are met above and beyond product and company division level.

Data warehouse (DWH): Central instrument for storing, consolidating, evaluating and presenting information on corporate strategy. DWHs are used in particular when data from several applications needs to be consolidated for reporting purposes or if external data for example need to be integrated by market research institutes. Companies with large databases such as telecoms companies use DWH to carry out evaluations separately from operational systems and thus avoiding blocking these systems with lengthy evaluations.

Enabler: A device that allows users to exploit a particular potential. In IT we refer to an enabler if IT enables the primary business of a company to improve efficiency in the form of cost savings or efficiency such as sales increases.

Enterprise Resource Planning (ERP): Software that controls the information and material flows within a company. Although these systems are process-oriented and company-specific, they are often referred to as standard software. Users are often torn between the desire for standards and their specific requirements, which demand a high degree of customisation, and thus become more and more non-standard.

Groupware: An application for supporting communication and interaction between various users. Typical groupware applications are email functions for exchanging information, calendar functions for example for coordinating meetings and deadlines, joint forums and data directories or workflow functionalities. Commonly used groupware products are Microsoft Outlook, Lotus Notes or Novell GroupWise.

IT applications: Applications software for supporting an operational functionality. An example of an IT application is cost accounting software which covers the operational functionalities of cost centres, cost items and cost unit invoicing.

IT asset management: The content (not purely accounting) administration of IT assets is the basis for increasing transparency in IT costs. Often part of a total cost of ownership assessment and thus of a user pays principle where IT costs are charged back to the consumers within a company.

IT costs: IT costs result directly from the introduction of IT and operating and maintaining already installed IT solutions. Launch costs encompass investment in software or hardware and one-off costs for adapting, programming or training. Operating and maintenance costs contain cost items resulting from version changes, corrections or regular, elementary activities such as loading or shutting down the systems or data securing activities.

IT infrastructure: Technical platform essential for using IT applications. Servers, workstation systems and networks are all part of infrastructure.

IT services: Services provided by IT. Examples could be PC support, operating computer centres or user help desks. Unlike one-off project services, IT services are provided on a continual basis.

Legacy applications: Since IT has been introduced into companies, a series of individual applications have arisen in many companies, which often fulfil functionalities that are essential for the company. Many of these applications today are technologically obsolete and disproportionately expensive to maintain and development. Most legacy applications were replaced by ERP systems in the course of the Y2K conversions, but the next generation of legacy applications is due out soon.

Product Lifecycle Management (PLM): Comprehensive method for integrating all product-related processes and information in companies and also among suppliers and clients in order to enable a holistic management throughout the lifecycle of a product. The benefits to be gained from this result in shorter times for development, production and shipment, a reduction in complexity, lower development, production, sales and after-sales costs and an increased faithfulness to deadlines.

Service Level Agreement (SLA): Service level agreements are an agreement between a service provider (internally or externally) and client (normally the divisions of a company) and they describe the service relationship. This includes the obligations of the service providers, the extent to which the client must cooperate, the level/quality of the services required and if necessary the prices per service unit. It is important to design these documents as pragmatically as possible, despite the fact that they are part of a contract, i.e. specialist legal terms should not be used. It is more important that the service level agreement represents a set of clear and easy-to-understand instructions for the service provider and users. These documents should 'work' in practice in the service relationship.

Shared services: Linking and centralizing cross-sectional processes, in particular accounting, finances, personnel and others. Usually this kind of centralization can only be realized with a high degree of IT deployment, for example an ERP launch. The basis is the simplification of basic processes across all of the organizational units involved. This can create considerable process efficiencies of up to 30 percent.

Total Cost of Ownership (TCO): The total costs of an IT service that not only includes the costs of any direct IT service, but also the costs indirectly linked to this service. Therefore the total cost of ownership of a network PC is not only the (immediate) hardware and software costs, but also the proportional network and support costs.

Workstation: A computer for workstation-related applications. This is usually a PC on which the most common communication and office applications are installed. Alternatively, a workstation can also be a 'thin client' workstation that allows users to access centrally stored applications and data via a local network.

Acknowledgements

This book was only made possible as a result of close collaboration with our clients on many strategic IT projects across all sectors of industry and on almost any kind of IT problem imaginable. We would like to thank them all for their confidence and cooperation. Within A.T. Kearney, we would like to thank our colleagues from Industry Practices for their incredible collegial teaming which made the strategic IT projects so successful in the first place. Many of the writers in this book are key players at the Strategic Information Technology Practice (SITP) of A.T. Kearney Central Europe. The following persons have particularly distinguished themselves and deserve a special mention here: Dr. Wolfgang Beck, Christian Beekes, Bernd Eulitz, Cay-Bernhard Frank, Heiner Himmelreich, Matthias Kannegiesser, Dr. Heinz Linß, Alexander Martin, Holger Röder, Patrick Schneckenburger, Günther Schneider, Jens Tischendorf and Robert Ziegler. Our highly dedicated editor, Dr. Julia Kormann, whipped the book into shape. Petra Werner, Lutz Ettrich and Axel Lönnendonker also supported us in many different ways. All of the above-mentioned, as well as many colleagues whose names are not mentioned here, brought their collective consulting dedication and years of know-how to bear on this book and we thank them most warmly for their contributions.

The Authors

Dr.-Ing. Dirk Buchta

is Vice President of A.T. Kearney and has been working in strategic consulting at A.T. Kearney for over 12 years. He is responsible for the consulting field of strategic information technology in Central Europe and heads the Strategic Information Technology Practice. His consulting work focuses on IT strategies, IT in merger/demerger situations, cutting the cost of IT, outsourcing strategies and comprehensive corporate transformations on the basis of IT.

Dr. Marcus Eul

has been supporting companies in various sectors with strategic IT issues for three years as a member of the Strategic Information Technology Practice. Before he became a consultant, he worked in industry for 10 years, latterly as CIO of a business unit of the Thyssen Krupp Group, prior to that he was an IT executive at E-Plus.

Dr. Helmut Schulte-Croonenberg

has been working for 20 years now as a management consultant. Following careers at ABB, Accenture und Booz and Allen & Hamilton, today he is Vice President at A.T. Kearney and a member of the Strategic Information Technology Practice. He has worked on numerous consulting projects for leading industrial companies with a focus on IT strategy.

Unternehmen global erfolgreich führen
↗

Was Sie wissen müssen, um auf dem indischen Markt erfolgreich zu sein

Hier bieten zwei Experten praxisnah und kompakt alles Wissenswerte für ein erfolgreiches Engagement im Indiengeschäft. Neben den wirtschaftlichen Rahmenbedingungen und dem kulturellen Hintergrund stellen sie konkret vor, wo Chancen und Risiken einer Investition liegen und worauf es beim Markteinstieg ankommt. Know-how bezüglich Personalmanagement und Verhandlungsführung wird ebenso vermittelt wie ein Leitfaden für die konkrete Gestaltung und Pflege von Geschäftsbeziehungen.

Manuel Vermeer / Clas Neumann
Praxishandbuch Indien
Wie Sie Ihr Indiengeschäft erfolgreich managen
2008. 244 S.
Geb. EUR 39,90
ISBN 978-3-8349-0535-2

Erfolgreiches Personalmanagement in China: Die besten Mitarbeiter finden und binden

Das Angebot des Arbeitsmarktes kann die rasante Nachfrage nach geeigneten China-Managern nicht befriedigen. Wie gelingt es Unternehmen, die besten Manager für ihr China-Engagement zu finden und zu binden? Karl Waldkirch, erfahrener China-Experte, klärt auf, welche Unterschiede es zwischen Expatriates und lokalen chinesischen Managern gibt und was bei der Personaleinstellung zu beachten ist.

Karl Waldkirch
Erfolgreiches Personalmanagement in China
Rekrutierung, Mitarbeiterführung, Verhandlung
2009. 208 S.
Br. EUR 36,90
ISBN 978-3-8349-0782-0

Chancen im globalen Wettbewerb gestalten

Dieses Buch vermittelt dem Management eine Fülle von Anregungen, wie Führungsverantwortung wahrzunehmen ist und wie kreative Mitunternehmer zu entfesseln sind. Viele ausführliche Praxisbeispiele weisen den Weg zu nachhaltigen und schwer imitierbaren Wettbewerbsvorteilen.

André Papmehl / Peter Gastberger / Zoltan Budai (Hrsg.)
Die kreative Organisation
Führungsverantwortung wahrnehmen, kreative Mitunternehmer entfesseln, Chancen im globalen Wettbewerb gestalten
2009. 296 S.
Geb. EUR 44,90
ISBN 978-3-8349-0647-2

Änderungen vorbehalten. Stand: Juli 2009.
Erhältlich im Buchhandel oder beim Verlag
Gabler Verlag . Abraham-Lincoln Str. 46 . 65189 Wiesbaden . www.gabler.de

GABLER

Wissen für die Unternehmensführung

↗

Die drei entscheidenden Kompetenzen für Führungskräfte

Führungskräfte sind für ihren Führungsjob nicht ausgebildet und lernen diesen, während sie ihn betreiben. Adolf Lorenz definiert die wirklichen Anforderungen und zeigt, dass es drei entscheidende Kompetenzbereiche gibt, die entwickelt werden müssen: die Orientierung in der Rolle, die persönliche Selbstreflexion und die Empathiefähigkeit. So weist das Buch den Weg zur kompetent und authentisch handelnden Führungskraft.

Adolf Lorenz

Die Führungsaufgabe
Ein Navigationskonzept für
Führungskräfte
2009. 192 S. Mit 6 Abb.
Zusatzprodukt: Mindmap.
Geb. EUR 39,90
ISBN 978-3-8349-1029-5

Alle Geschäftsabläufe systematisch im Griff - mit Checklisten und Fallbeispielen

Eva Best und Martin Weth zeigen wie eine kontinuierliche Leistungsmessung implementiert und innerbetrieblicher Widerstand konstruktiv genutzt werden kann. Zahlreiche Beispiele, quantitative Tools, Checklisten zur Reorganisation und viele Praxistipps machen das Buch zu einem einzigartigen Werkzeug für effektive Prozessoptimierung. Die 3., überarbeitete Auflage liefert neben aktuellen Beispielen praxiserprobte Methodenchecklisten am Ende jedes Kapitels.

Eva Best / Martin Weth

Geschäftsprozesse optimieren
Der Praxisleitfaden für erfolgreiche
Reorganisation
3., überarb. u. erw. Aufl. 2009.
236 S.
Geb. EUR 49,90
ISBN 978-3-8349-1384-5

Praxiserprobte Methoden und Beispiele für effiziente Wissensarbeit

Wertschöpfung durch Wissen wird die Hauptquelle unseres Wohlstands. Dieser Wohlstand lässt sich nur halten, wenn er auf produktiver und kreativer Wissensarbeit beruht. Dieses Buch stellt praxiserprobte Methoden und Beispiele für effiziente Wissensarbeit vor.

Klaus North / Stefan Güldenberg

Produktive Wissensarbeit(er)
Antworten auf die Management-
Herausforderung des 21. Jahrh. Mit
vielen Fallbeispielen
2008. 280 S.
Geb. EUR 44,90
ISBN 978-3-8349-0738-7

Änderungen vorbehalten. Stand: Juli 2009.
Erhältlich im Buchhandel oder beim Verlag

Gabler Verlag . Abraham-Lincoln-Str. 46 . 65189 Wiesbaden . www.gabler.de

GABLER